Postmodernism and Its Discontents

Postmodernism and Its Discontents

Theories, Practices

Edited by
E. ANN KAPLAN

VERSO
London · New York

This edition published by Verso 1988
Second impression 1989
Third impression 1990
© 1988 Verso
All rights reserved
Verso
UK: 6 Meard Street, London W1V 3HR
USA: 29 West 35th Street, New York, NY 10001 2291

Verso is the imprint of New Left Books

British Library Cataloguing in Publication Data
Postmodernism and its discontents: theories,
    practises.–(Haymarket).
    1. Culture. Postmodernism
    I. Kaplan, E. Ann
    306

ISBN 0–86091–211–6
ISBN 0–86091–925–0 Pbk

Typeset by Leaper & Gard Ltd, Bristol, England
Printed in Great Britain by Bookcraft (Bath) Ltd, Midsomer Norton, Avon.

In Memoriam
Allon White, 1951–1988

The Haymarket Series

Editors: Mike Davis and Michael Sprinker

The Haymarket Series is a new publishing initiative by Verso offering original studies of politics, history and culture focused on North America. The series presents innovative but representative views from across the American left on a wide range of topics of current and continuing interest to socialists in North America and throughout the world. A century after the first May Day, the American left remains in the shadow of those martyrs whom this series honors and commemorates. The studies in the Haymarket Series testify to the living legacy of activism and political commitment for which they gave up their lives.

Already Published

Forthcoming

OUR OWN TIME: A History of American Labor and the Working Day *by David Roediger and Philip Foner*

YOUTH, IDENTITY, POWER: The Chicano Generation *by Carlos Muñoz, Jr.*

THE 'FIFTH' CALIFORNIA: The Political Economy of a State-Nation *by Mike Davis*

RANK-AND-FILE REBELLION: Teamsters for a Democratic Union *by Dan Labotz*

THE MERCURY THEATER: Orson Welles and the Popular Front *by Michael Denning*

THE POLITICS OF SOLIDARITY: Central America and the US Left *by Van Gosse*

THE HISTORY OF BLACK POLITICAL THOUGHT *by Manning Marable*

Contents

Acknowledgements

This book is dedicated to Allon White whose recent work *The Politics and Poetics of Transgression* (written together with Peter Stallybrass) has provided inspiration for several authors in this volume. I also want to honor here Allon's bravery in fighting his illness over the past two years: this has been inspiring to me in another way.

I should like to thank *minnesota review* for permission to reprint David James's essay, 'Poetry/Punk/Production: Some Recent Writing in LA,' published in N.S. 23 (fall 1984).

Thanks also to the editors of *New Left Review* for permission to reprint Mike Davis's essay, 'Urban Renaissance and the Spirit of Postmodernism,' from *New Left Review* 151 (1985); and selections from Fredric Jameson's 'Postmodernism and the Cultural Logic of Late Capitalism' from *New Left Review* 146 (1984).

I want to thank The Bay Press, Port Townsend, WA for their permission to reprint selections from Fredric Jameson's essay 'Postmodernism and Consumer Society,' in Hal Foster, ed., *The Anti-Aesthetic: Essays in Postmodern Culture* (1983).

Finally, thanks to Michael Sprinker for his unflagging help with this volume.

E. Ann Kaplan
May 1988

Introduction

E. Ann Kaplan

With its reference to Freud's famous text, the title for this volume suggests a deliberate tension in relation to the discourse of postmodernism. On the one hand, I would argue for the postmodern as representing a cultural 'break' in the sense of Foucault's 'episteme', or Kuhn's paradigms: the postmodern moment is a break initiated by modernism, which is here viewed as a transitional period between nineteenth-century Romanticism and the current cultural scene. The word 'postmodern' is then useful in implying the links with modernism, while at the same time indicating a substantial move beyond/away from it. The break that modernism initiated is at once fulfilled with the development of recent sophisticated electronic technologies and, at the same time, drastically altered in the process so as to become 'postmodern'.

On the other hand, the 'discontents' of my title contests the very notion of such a cultural break. Some of the essays argue that it is the conception of the postmodern and the assertion of a break that is the problem. These essays question the metalanguage that has been used to describe our contemporary situation as postmodern and to claim a different 'reality'.

The idea for the book arose precisely out of this tension, which I believe is a useful and creative one. The essays by no means present a monolithic stance toward postmodernism as a stage of culture, as a critical concept or as an anti-aesthetic. Rather, the volume intends to raise questions about the usefulness and validity of the postmodern discourse, as well as clarifying the plethora of often contradictory definitions that have been advanced over the past ten years or so.

A great deal has been written about modernism and postmodernism –

too much for me to review here but enough to make essential some necessarily shorthand distinctions of my own. But before discussing what we can usefully call postmodernism, let me position my own discourse as one resistant to any theorizing about postmodernism that would invalidate the very possibility of the distinctions I am about to make – that would, indeed, question my presuming the possibility of a metadiscourse.

The theorizing I am referring to has been developed most fully by Jean Baudrillard, and Arthur Kroker and David Cook who follow him, and whom I discuss below. I then stand with Jameson and Habermas (different as those two thinkers may be from one another in several ways) in addressing the need for critical discourse, for seizing a position from which to speak. Habermas's well-known call for continuing the Enlightenment project and his appealing, if utopian, model for a democratic cultural community, may be read as a desperate reaction against postmodern culture.[1] Fredric Jameson's equally well-known discussions of postmodernism may come from a similar set of concerns, but he has engaged deeply with popular postmodern texts and cultural effects; writing within the American context, he has more understanding than Habermas about what is relevant to the American scene.[2] Andreas Huyssen's 'Mapping the Postmodern' is a useful historical account of the concept and aesthetic practices of postmodernism, but, like the two essays already mentioned, his does not address the important implications of postmodernism for gender issues, nor make the distinctions that I think must be made.[3]

In a different vein, Hal Foster's distinction between a postmodernism of resistance and a postmodernism of reaction takes a rather different direction from the categories required to think the concept adequately.[4] Foster distinguishes between a postmodernism that seeks to deconstruct modernism (seen as the status quo) from a deliberately critical perspective (the postmodernism of 'resistance'); and a postmodernism that, in the course of repudiating modernism and celebrating postmodernism, in fact returns 'to the verities of tradition' (the postmodernism of 'reaction'). Lacking here is any attention to differences in context of production and exhibition of works, to the commercial/non-commercial axis and to audience address (general or specialized). Foster appears to have in mind the world of the art museum and of alternative cultural production; within this framework, the distinction he makes is useful. But I am interested in definitions that apply broadly and that take into account the particular 'apparatus' being used, as well as how modes of production/exhibition govern aesthetic strategies and have gender implications.

Within this broader framework, let me distinguish two main meanings linked to the concept 'postmodernism', and bracket a third set of meanings that are often confusingly intermixed in theories of the postmodern. I am aware that these distinctions are difficult to maintain (and indeed I will shortly be looking at the parallels among the distinct usages of the term); but definitions are important in clarifying terminological confusion.

To begin with the bracket: postmodernism and the aesthetic practices we call postmodernist are sometimes labelled resisting and transgressive – a move that confuses postmodernism with modernism. For instance, what Foster says about his postmodernism of resistance – that it 'seeks to question rather than exploit cultural codes, to explore rather than conceal social and political affiliations' (p. xii) – seems to me a good description of some modernisms. Better to reserve the term 'transgression' for texts that function in the manner advocated by Brecht and Bakhtin, whose theories derived from such canonical modernist thinkers as Hegel, Nietzsche, Marx and Freud. These latter established paradigms that in one way or another depended on oppositions, although they each constructed different kinds of processes for dealing with (or in some cases working through) the oppositions. Thus, postmodernism and transgression can be seen to be incompatible theoretical concepts.

One can, however, differentiate what may be called a 'utopian' postmodernism (which moves in a Derridean direction) from a commercial or 'co-opted' one (which moves in a Baudrillardean direction); second, one can distinguish the contexts of production/exhibition/consumption of the respective texts; and finally, one should clarify the different levels of things that are involved in discussing the co-opted postmodernism that is the focus of several essays in the volume, and indicate the relevance of feminism to the postmodernist project.

We may begin with the second point about contexts in which various works called 'postmodern' are produced and exhibited, since it is differences in this area that make it necessary to define what postmodernism refers to in any particular instance. Confusion arises because the term 'postmodern' (or its attributes) are sometimes (as we have seen) applied to a broad range of works, regardless of their contexts of production, exhibition and consumption. Critics often range across a vast spectrum of texts, from community or street events to mass culture to the avantgarde, in developing a particular theory. This seems already part of the postmodern discourse mentioned above – it appears to have conceded that distinctions cannot be made, are undesirable, or no longer exist. One must question this assumption *ab initio.*

But perhaps the main confusion results from an unconscious slippage from what has been seen as one characteristic of postmodern *texts* (i.e. their effacement of the distinction between high culture and popular culture – their intermixing of elements of both) to an effacement of the institutional boundaries within which texts are produced, exhibited and consumed. While it may be true that in postmodernist culture, as never before, the museum has become part of commodity production and thus moved closer to commercial cultural institutions such as television, the museum nevertheless differs radically from the latter institutions in the sorts of product circulated and in the audiences addressed. We do not go to the Whitney Museum to see a soap opera, although we may go there to see Joan Braverman's deconstruction of a soap, as in her *Joan Does Dynasty.*

In addition, the term 'postmodern' has been used in different ways by literary and feminist scholars on the one hand, and by popular culture scholars on the other. The former group have tended to equate post-modernism (or in the case of Alice Jardine, 'modernity'),[5] with what I have called the 'utopian'. Indeed, in its 'utopian' form, postmodernism is partly a product of feminism (i.e. feminism, deconstruction and Lacanian psychoanalysis have together brought about a significant cultural break we could call postmodern). A 'utopian' postmodernism involves a movement of culture and texts beyond oppressive binary categories and could not be imagined without the work of, among others, Bakhtin, Derrida, Lacan, Cixous, Kristeva, and Roland Barthes. This sort of postmodernism has been central to some strands of femin-ism in its envisioning of texts that radically decenter the subject, its insistence on a series of different spectator positionalities, and its focus on texts where discourses are not hierarchically ordered. (Some Chantal Akerman and Straub-Huillet films exemplify this tendency, as does Mulvey and Wollen's *Crystal Gazing* or Duras's *India Song.*) The demand for an end to the 'death-dealing binary oppositions of mascu-linity and femininity'[6] would perhaps best summarize the utopian post-modern.

'Commercial' or co-opted postmodernism, on the other hand, has been theorized by Baudrillard (in the wake of McLuhan), and most recently by Arthur Kroker and David Cook. For these writers, post-modernism is linked to the new stage of multinational, multi-conglomerate consumer capitalism, and to all the new technologies this stage has spawned. This postmodernism is described as radically trans-forming the subject through its blanketing of culture. Inside is no longer separate from outside; private cannot be opposed to public space; high or avant-garde culture no longer stands in stark contrast to the all-consuming popular. Technologies, marketing and consumption have created a new, unidimensional universe from which there is no escape and inside which no critical position is possible. There is no 'outside', no space from which to mount a critical perspective. We inhabit, on this account, a world where the television screen has become the only reality, where the human body and the televisual machine are all but indistinguishable.[7]

How can two such vastly differing conceptions of postmodernism coexist in a single historical epoch and a single cultural space? How is it that each group developing a theory came to use the word/concept 'postmodernism' for what they wanted to say? Are there perhaps some ways in which the theories sharing the same word have underlying similarities?

Both usages of the postmodern involve a thinking that transcends the very binarisms of Western philosophical, metaphysical and literary traditions which have been put into question by poststructuralism and deconstruction. To this extent, the use of the term 'postmodernism' signals a moving beyond/away from the various positionings (not only aesthetic, but those dealing with class, race and gender) of previous totalizing theories. But this move away, interestingly enough, goes in diametrically opposite directions. The discourse of postmodernism in some literary and feminist circles involves a search for a liberatory new position that would free us from the constraints and confines of oppressive binary oppositions; the goal is nebulous and distant. The postmodern discourse in relation to popular culture, meanwhile, warns us about the end of binarisms that new technologies have produced, or is ambivalent about these changes. The impact on culture, on social organization and on the human body and psyche itself is described as already well underway. While the end of binarisms is emancipating in the first instance, in the second their demise is (usually) cast in negative terms.

The common term makes sense if we see the diverse theories as responding to a similar cultural situation: namely, the aftermath of the 1960s. Both concepts of postmodernism arise in the wake of theories and debates about race, class, sex and gender during the past twenty years. Significantly, however, in both cases the thinking has abandoned dialectics, as it had to if it was to embody the end of binarisms. But it is precisely here that the important question remains: if abandoning binarisms necessitates abandoning dialects, how can we envisage an intellectual, psychic, social or cultural life that moves forward, that renews itself, that is self-critical and purposive? The centrality of this question justifies the organization of the essays presented here.

Originally, five of the essays included (Galperin, Kaplan, Polan, Stam and Williams) were intended for *The Year Left* III an issue devoted to possibilities for politics and culture in the medium-term future. Postmodernism seemed a suitable topic for the section on culture that I was to edit: we wrote essays having in mind an audience sympathetic to

Marxism as a practice and a theory, but not necessarily familiar with recent work in literature, film and television. When we decided to create a companion volume to *The Year Left* III, instead of printing the essays as a culture section, we added the essays by James, Jameson, Montag and Pfeil, but left the original pieces as they were. This book, then, can be read in two ways: in connection with the political analyses that appear in *The Year Left* III; or as a free-standing collection that surveys the terrain of contemporary cultural practices in the US.

The essays in Part I take up the issue of postmodernism as a theory and an (anti-)aesthetic practice in differing ways. We have reprinted Fredric Jameson's seminal essay, 'Postmodernism and Consumer Society', for obvious reasons: the essay has to a large degree shaped the terms of debates about postmodernism in America in the years following publication of the original version in 1983. The density and complexity of Jameson's analysis make summary impossible, but let me note four points that have been contested: a) that postmodernism involves effacement of the old distinction between high culture and mass culture; b) that all theories of postmodernism entail a political stance on multinational capitalism; c) that postmodernism is best used as a periodizing concept, despite the theoretical problems of employing that sort of category (a move that permits Jameson to use the notion of a dominant cultural logic against which genuine difference might be explored); d) that the postmodern exhibits four basic features: i) the new depthlessness of both contemporary theory and the image or simulacrum; ii) a weakening historical sense – public and private, evident in the 'schizophrenic' structure of temporal arts; iii) a new emotional tone that Jameson calls 'intensities', which replace earlier (perhaps oedipal) ways of relating to objects; iv) the centrality of new technologies which are themselves linked to a new economic world system. Jameson provides numerous examples of these four main features, and ends by reflecting on 'the mission of political art in the bewildering new world space of late multinational capital'.

Jameson's essay has provoked debate both within Marxist circles and more broadly. Mike Davis's reply is reprinted here to give readers a sense of how a distinctive Marxist historical analysis responds to Jameson's more openly Hegelian theorizing. Part I concludes with Warren Montag's essay in a similar vein. The longer of the two, Montag's polemic takes on not only Jameson but two other theorists of postmodernism, Perry Anderson and Jean-François Lyotard. Having objected to Anderson's rejection *in toto* of Derrida, Foucault and Deleuze and Guattari, Montag also criticizes what he sees as a 'theoretical complicity between Jameson and Lyotard: their shared belief that Marxism is 'a metanarrative, a narrative of all narratives, that, by its very nature, requires a superior, transcendental space outside of the totality that it describes'. Montag focuses particularly on the way in which, in Jameson's account, 'the irreducible and overdetermined conflict is eclipsed by a pure systematicity'. He argues, following Marx and Trotsky, that 'a conjuncture is no more than an accumulation of contradictory and conflicting forces of different origins that produce different effects', concluding that we must be content to function within this set of contradictory forces, continually learning from our errors and correcting them.

The three essays between Jameson's opening one and the concluding critiques take up postmodernism as a theory and an (anti-)aesthetic practice in differing ways. All take their point of departure from Jameson, although they take the argument in new directions. My article uses the definitions outlined in this Introduction to illuminate the impact of postmodernism on feminism. I survey briefly the theories feminists first used in popular culture studies, situating strategies as broadly modernist, and then discuss the implications for feminist perspectives of the Baudrillard/ Kroker postmodernist discourse. The essay uses Music Television – as an institution and series of texts – as an example for exploring the relationship of feminism to postmodernism. The results are complex and contradictory, posing further questions, rather than presenting determinate solutions.

Dana Polan offers some definitions and clarifications – he is concerned about the way in which postmodernist theory has, while paying lip-service to them, generally neglected to give specific analyses of popular culture texts. He offers a gloss on Jameson's discussion of postmodern architecture, then turns to a close consideration of a single artifact, the film *Rocky IV*.

Fred Pfeil's analysis of the contradictions within what I have called the 'utopian' postmodern completes this group of three. Pfeil, rightly noting that novels are 'hardly the raw material from which the newest, sharpest, most cutting-edge analysis of the postmodern condition is likely to be worked up', explores fiction by Thomas Disch and Denis Johnson. These novels, he claims, 'may be understood as celebrations of the Kristevan semiotic, refusals of any steady border between the impure flux of abjection and the sanitized oedipal zone of ordered, isolated subjectivity, under the sign of the (male, white, bourgeois) Ego'. But Pfeil goes on to show the ambiguous and contradictory nature of this apparently paradisiac world – its potential horror, its tendency to slide over the 'asymptotic line towards which the magical mystery tour of consumer capitalism urges us ...'.

The essays in Part II offer analyses of fiction, film and popular culture that respond to current debates, albeit in some cases indirectly. Most of the authors are interested in what I have called the 'utopian' post-modern, even if they do not use that term. They engage in a search for spaces within hegemonic culture where something new can happen. The section opens with Linda Williams's contrast between Susan Keating Glaspell's 1917 short story, 'A Jury of Her Peers', and Marlene Gorris's recent film *A Question of Silence*. Using Elaine Showalter's concept of a non-dominant, 'muted' culture for women that includes a 'wild zone' off-limits to man, Williams shows how *A Question of Silence* negotiates the dilemma of woman's relationship to (male) language. Williams's positing of the need for the spectator of Gorris's film to identify with 'mute and wild zones of experience that are not yet known and that certainly may not help her beat the rap of male judgment' approximates that 'utopian' postmodern defined above.

Robert Stam's useful discussion of the 'real' Bakhtin seeks a way out of the postmodern impasse via a reworking of possibilities within Bakhtin's essentially modernist framework. Stam shows how Bakhtin's broad view, 'embracing many cultures and millennia of artistic produc-tion, has the potential of deprovincializing a critical course that remains too rigidly tied to nineteenth-century conventions of verisimilitude'. A Bakhtinian approach to mass culture, according to Stam, would cash in on the Frankfurt School notion that 'the consciousness industry cannot satisfy the real needs which it exploits'. Stam's reworking of Bakhtin's modernism comes close to the utopian postmodern invoked by Linda Williams: 'Aware of the double play of ideology and utopia (Jameson), a Bakhtinian approach proposes a dual movement of celebratory fabu-lation, and demystificatory critique. Aware of the inert weight of system and power, it also sees openings for their subversion.' Bakhtin thus points the way 'toward the transcendence of sterile dichotomies and exhausted paradigms'.

William Galperin theorizes recent changes in traditional television forms – soap operas and sports – that involve alterations in gender constructs. The blurring of previously rigidly controlled concepts of the 'masculine' and the 'feminine' is seen by Galperin as potentially opening up a new space that one might call postmodern. Galperin's complex analysis is at the same time fully aware of the way in which popular forms co-opt such moves back into the hegemonic system. Galperin, like Pfeil, studies the ambiguities and dangers thrown up by new spaces that at first seem to point in a utopian direction.

In his study of California punk culture, David James also looks at the near impossibility of any artistic practice avoiding being reinscribed in the very culture it seeks to escape. His hypothesis – that the destiny of all culture in capitalism is involved in 'the processes of consumption', whose 'return upon the activity of production, displace it from itself and its intrinsic pleasure and redefine its telos as something other' – is amply borne out by his detailed discussion of contradictions in Los Angeles punk subculture – a pattern of heterogeneity that again seems most aptly labelled postmodern. James deftly illustrates the intricate ways in which punk culture can never 'have access to an image of liberation outside the media' of the sort that Adorno and the Frankfurt School relied on; while at the same time, he shows how, in supplanting Hollywood as the dominant force in Southern California culture, punk 'not only provided space for a new and newly vigorous literary production but also caught other writing in its drift'.

In the fanzine *Lowest Common Denominator* James finds the potential for the utopian postmodern that could emerge fully only in a classless society. It is 'the reciprocation of the group's values in its modes of production and social insertion, both of which are entirely contingent upon its subcultural location' that represents the fanzine's value. However, as James wryly notes in conclusion, the fanzine's significance 'is inseparable from the fact that it is virtually unobtainable, that it hardly even exists'. This perhaps embodies the most ironic aspect of any 'utopian' postmodern while providing an apt end point for the present volume. If the gap between hegemonic modernism and emergent postmodernism is not to be reinscribed by capitalist culture as sheer commodity, postmodernism must remain only tenuously connected with the cultural systems to which it refers; it can, in that sense, barely *be* at all.

Notes

1. See Jürgen Habermas, 'Modernity Versus Postmodernity', in *New German Critique*, (winter 1981), pp. 3–14.

2. Fredric Jameson, 'Postmodernism, or The Cultural Logic of Late Capitalism', *New Left Review*, 146 (July–August 1984), pp. 53-92.

3. Andreas Huyssen, 'Mapping the Postmodern', in *After the Great Divide: Modernism, Mass Culture, Postmodernism* (Bloomington and Indianapolis: Indiana University Press, 1986), pp. 179–222.

4. Hal Foster, 'Postmodernism: A Preface', in Hal Foster, ed. *The Anti-Aesthetic: Essays on Postmodern Culture* (Port Townsend, WA: The Bay Press, 1983), pp. ix–xvi.

5. Alice Jardine, *Gynesis: Configurations of Woman and Modernity* (Cornell University Press: Ithaca and London, 1985).

6. Toril Moi, *Sexual/Textual Politics: Feminist Literary Theory* (London and New York: Methuen, Inc., 1985), p. 7.

7. See Jean Baudrillard, *In the Realm of the Silent Majorities ... Or The End of the Social*, trans. Paul Foss and Philip Beitchman (New York: Semiotext(e), 1983).

PART ONE

The Postmodernism Debate

1

Postmodernism and Consumer Society[1]

Fredric Jameson

The concept of postmodernism is not widely accepted or even understood today. Some of the resistance to it may come from the unfamiliarity of the works it covers, which can be found in all the arts: the poetry of John Ashbery, for instance, but also the much simpler talk poetry that came out of the reaction against complex, ironic, academic modernist poetry in the 1960s; the reaction against modern architecture and in particular against the monumental buildings of the International Style, the pop buildings and decorated sheds celebrated by Robert Venturi in his manifesto, *Learning from Las Vegas*; Andy Warhol and Pop art, but also the more recent Photorealism; in music, the moment of John Cage but also the later synthesis of classical and 'popular' styles found in composers like Philip Glass and Terry Riley, and also punk and new-wave rock with such groups as the Clash, Talking Heads and the Gang of Four; in film, everything that comes out of Godard – contemporary vanguard film and video – but also a whole new style of commercial or fiction films, which has its equivalent in contemporary novels as well, where the works of William Burroughs, Thomas Pynchon and Ishmael Reed on the one hand, and the French new novel on the other, are also to be numbered among the varieties of what can be called postmodernism.

This list would seem to make two things clear at once: first, most of the postmodernisms mentioned above emerge as specific reactions against the established forms of high modernism, against this or that dominant high modernism which conquered the university, the museum, the art gallery network, and the foundations. Those formerly subversive and embattled styles – Abstract Expressionism; the great modernist poetry of Pound, Eliot or Wallace Stevens; the International Style (Le Corbusier, Frank Lloyd Wright, Mies); Stravinsky; Joyce, Proust and Mann – felt to be scandalous or shocking by our grandparents are, for the generation which arrives at the gate in the 1960s, felt to be the establishment and the enemy – dead, stifling, canonical, the reified monuments one has to destroy to do anything new. This means that there will be as many different forms of postmodernism as there were high modernisms in place, since the former are at least initially specific and local reactions *against* those models. That obviously does not make the job of describing postmodernism as a coherent thing any easier, since the unity of this new impulse – if it has one – is given not in itself but in the very modernism it seeks to displace.

The second feature of this list of postmodernisms is the effacement in it of some key boundaries or separations, most notably the erosion of the older distinction between high culture and so-called mass or popular culture. This is perhaps the most distressing development of all from an academic standpoint, which has traditionally had a vested interest in preserving a realm of high or elite culture against the surrounding environment of philistinism, of schlock and kitsch, of TV series and *Reader's Digest* culture, and in transmitting difficult and complex skills of reading, listening and seeing to its initiates. But many of the newer postmodernisms have been fascinated precisely by that whole landscape of advertising and motels, of the Las Vegas strip, of the late show and Grade-B Hollywood film, of so-called paraliterature with its airport paperback categories of the gothic and the romance, the popular biography, the murder mystery and the science fiction or fantasy novel. They no longer 'quote' such 'texts' as a Joyce might have done, or a Mahler; they incorporate them, to the point where the line between high art and commercial forms seems increasingly difficult to draw.

A rather different indication of this effacement of the older categories of genre and discourse can be found in what is sometimes called contemporary theory. A generation ago there was still a technical discourse of professional philosophy – the great systems of Sartre or the phenomenologists, the work of Wittgenstein or analytical or common language philosophy – alongside which one could still distinguish that quite different discourse of the other academic disciplines – of political science, for example, or sociology or literary criticism. Today, increasingly, we have a kind of writing simply called 'theory' which is all or none of those things at once. This new kind of discourse, generally associated with France and so-called French theory, is becoming widespread and marks the end of philosophy as such. Is the work of Michel Foucault, for example, to be called philosophy, history, social theory or political science? It's undecidable, as they say nowadays; and I will suggest that such 'theoretical discourse' is also to be numbered among the manifestations of postmodernism.

Now I must say a word about the proper use of this concept: it is not just another word for the description of a particular style. It is also, at least in my use, a periodizing concept whose function is to correlate the emergence of new formal features in culture with the emergence of a new type of social life and a new economic order – what is often euphemistically called modernization, postindustrial or consumer society, the society of the media or the spectacle, or multinational capitalism. This new moment of capitalism can be dated from the post-war boom in the United States in the late 1940s and early 1950s or, in France, from the establishment of the Fifth Republic in 1958. The 1960s are in many ways the key transitional period, a period in which the new international order (neocolonialism, the Green Revolution, computer-ization and electronic information) is at one and the same time set in place and is swept and shaken by its own internal contradictions and by external resistance. I want here to sketch a few of the ways in which the new postmodernism expresses the inner truth of that newly emergent social order of late capitalism, but will have to limit the description to only two of its significant features, which I will call pastiche and schizophrenia; they will give us a chance to sense the specificity of the postmodernist experience of space and time respectively.

Pastiche Eclipses Parody

One of the most significant features or practices in postmodernism today is pastiche. I must first explain this term, which people generally tend to confuse with or assimilate to that related verbal phenomenon called parody. Both pastiche and parody involve the imitation or, better still, the mimicry of other styles and particularly of the mannerisms and stylistic twitches of other styles. It is obvious that modern literature in general offers a very rich field for parody, since the great modern writers have all been defined by the invention or production of rather unique styles: think of the Faulknerian long sentence or of D.H. Lawrence's characteristic nature imagery; think of Wallace Stevens's peculiar way of using abstractions; think also of the mannerisms of the philosophers, of Heidegger for example, or Sartre; think of the musical styles of Mahler or Prokofiev. All of these styles, however different from each other, are comparable in this: each is quite unmistakable; once one is learned, it is not likely to be confused with something else.

Now parody capitalizes on the uniqueness of these styles and seizes on their idiosyncrasies and eccentricities to produce an imitation which mocks the original. I won't say that the satiric impulse is conscious in all forms of parody. In any case, a good or great parodist has to have some secret sympathy for the original, just as a great mimic has to have the capacity to put himself/herself in the place of the person imitated. Still, the general effect of parody is – whether in sympathy or with malice – to cast ridicule on the private nature of these stylistic mannerisms and their excessiveness and eccentricity with respect to the way people normally speak or write. So there remains somewhere behind all parody the feeling that there is a linguistic norm in contrast to which the styles of the great modernists can be mocked.

But what would happen if one no longer believed in the existence of normal language, of ordinary speech, of the linguistic norm (the kind of clarity and communicative power celebrated by Orwell in his famous essay, say)? One could think of it in this way; perhaps the immense fragmentation and privatization of modern literature – its explosion into a host of distinct private styles and mannerisms – foreshadows deeper and more general tendencies in social life as a whole. Supposing that modern art and modernism – far from being a kind of specialized aesthetic curiosity – actually anticipated social developments along these lines; supposing that in the decades since the emergence of the great modern styles society has itself begun to fragment in this way, each group coming to speak a curious private language of its own, each profession developing its private code or idiolect, and finally each individual coming to be a kind of linguistic island, separated from everyone else? But then in that case, the very possibility of any linguistic norm in terms of which one could ridicule private languages and idiosyncratic styles would vanish, and we would have nothing but stylistic diversity and heterogeneity.

That is the moment at which pastiche appears and parody has become impossible. Pastiche is, like parody, the imitation of a peculiar or unique style, the wearing of a stylistic mask, speech in a dead language: but it is a neutral practice of such mimicry, without parody's ulterior motive, without the satirical impulse, without laughter, without that still latent feeling that there exists something *normal* compared to which what is being imitated is rather comic. Pastiche is blank parody, parody that has lost its sense of humor: pastiche is to parody what that curious thing, the modern practice of a kind of blank irony, is to what Wayne Booth calls the stable and comic ironies of, say, the eighteenth century.

The Death of the Subject

But now we need to introduce a new piece into this puzzle, which may help to explain why classical modernism is a thing of the past and why postmodernism should have taken its place. This new component is what is generally called the 'death of the subject' or, to say it in more conventional language, the end of individualism as such. The great modernisms were, as we have said, predicated on the invention of a personal, private style, as unmistakable as your fingerprint, as incomparable as your own body. But this means that the modernist aesthetic is in some way organically linked to the conception of a unique self and private identity, a unique personality and individuality, which can be expected to generate its own unique vision of the world and to forge its own unique, unmistakable style.

Yet today, from any number of distinct perspectives, the social theorists, the psychoanalysts, even the linguists, not to speak of those of us who work in the area of culture and cultural and formal change, are all exploring the notion that that kind of individualism and personal identity is a thing of the past; that the old individual or individualist subject is 'dead'; and that one might even describe the concept of the unique individual and the theoretical basis of individualism as ideological. There are in fact two positions on all this, one of which is more radical than the other. The first one is content to say: yes, once upon a time, in the classic age of competitive capitalism, in the heyday of the nuclear family and the emergence of the bourgeoisie as the hegemonic social class, there was such a thing as individualism, as individual subjects. But today, in the age of corporate capitalism, of the so-called organization man, of bureaucracies in business as well as in the state, of demographic explosion – today, that older bourgeois individual subject no longer exists.

Then there is a second position, the more radical of the two, what one might call the poststructuralist position. It adds: not only is the bourgeois individual subject a thing of the past, it is also a myth; it *never* really existed in the first place; there have never been autonomous subjects of that type. Rather, this construct is merely a philosophical and cultural mystification which sought to persuade people that they 'had' individual subjects and possessed this unique personal identity.

For our purposes, it is not particularly important to decide which of these positions is correct (or rather, which is more interesting and productive). What we have to retain from all this is rather an aesthetic dilemma: because if the experience and the ideology of the unique self, an experience and ideology which informed the stylistic practice of classical modernism, is over and done with, then it is no longer clear what the artists and writers of the present period are supposed to be doing. What is clear is merely that the older models – Picasso, Proust, T.S. Eliot – do not work any more (or are positively harmful), since nobody has that kind of unique private world and style to express any longer. And this is perhaps not merely a 'psychological' matter: we also have to take into account the immense weight of seventy or eighty years of classical modernism itself. There is another sense in which the writers and artists of the present day will no longer be able to invent new styles and worlds – they've already been invented; only a limited number of combinations are possible; the unique ones have been thought of already. So the weight of the whole modernist aesthetic tradition – now dead – also 'weighs like a nightmare on the brains of the living', as Marx said in another context.

Hence, once again, pastiche: in a world in which stylistic innovation is no longer possible, all that is left is to imitate dead styles, to speak through the masks and with the voices of the styles in the imaginary museum. But this means that contemporary or postmodernist art is going to be about art itself in a new kind of way; even more, it means that one of its essential messages will involve the necessary failure of art and the aesthetic, the failure of the new, the imprisonment in the past.

The Nostalgia Mode

As this may seem very abstract, I want to give a few examples, one of which is so omnipresent that we rarely link it with the kinds of developments in high art discussed here. This particular practice of pastiche is not high-cultural but very much within mass culture, and it is generally known as the 'nostalgia film' (what the French neatly call *la mode rétro* – retrospective styling). We must conceive of this category in the broadest way: narrowly, no doubt, it consists merely of films about the past and about specific generational moments of that past. Thus, one of the inaugural films in this new 'genre' (if that's what it is) was Lucas's *American Graffiti*, which in 1973 set out to recapture all the atmosphere and stylistic peculiarities of the 1950s United States, the United States of the Eisenhower era. Polanski's great film *Chinatown* does something similar for the 1930s, as does Bertolucci's *The Conformist* for the Italian and European context of the same period, the fascist era in Italy; and so forth. We could go on listing these films for some time: why call them pastiche? Are they not rather work in the more traditional genre known as the historical film – work which can more simply be theorized by extrapolating that other well-known form which is the historical novel?

I have my reasons for thinking that we need new categories for such films. But let me first add some anomalies: supposing I suggested that *Star Wars* is also a nostalgia film. What could that mean? I presume we can agree that this is not a historical film about our own intergalactic past. Let me put it somewhat differently: one of the most important cultural experiences of the generations that grew up from the 1930s to the 1950s was the Saturday afternoon serial of the Buck Rogers type – alien villains, true American heroes, heroines in distress, the death ray or the doomsday box, and the cliffhanger at the end whose miraculous resolution was to be witnessed next Saturday afternoon. *Star Wars* reinvents this experience in the form of a pastiche: that is, there is no longer any point to a parody of such serials since they are long extinct. *Star Wars*, far from being a pointless satire of such now dead forms, satisfies a deep (might I even say repressed?) longing to experience them again: it is a complex object in which on some first level children and adolescents can take the adventures straight, while the adult public is able to gratify a deeper and more properly nostalgic desire to return to that older period and to live its strange old aesthetic artifacts through once again. This film is thus *metonymically* a historical or nostalgia film: unlike *American Graffiti*, it does not reinvent a picture of the past in its lived totality; rather, by reinventing the feel and shape of characteristic art objects of an older period (the serials), it seeks to reawaken a sense of the past associated with those objects. *Raiders of the Lost Ark*, meanwhile, occupies an intermediary position here: on some level it is *about* the 1930s and 1940s, but in reality it too conveys that period metonymically through its own characteristic adventure stories (which are no longer ours).

Now let me discuss another interesting anomaly which may take us further towards understanding nostalgia film in particular and pastiche generally. This one involves a recent film called *Body Heat*, which, as has abundantly been pointed out by the critics, is a kind of distant remake of *The Postman Always Rings Twice* or *Double Indemnity*. (The allusive and elusive plagiarism of older plots is, of course, also a feature of pastiche.) Now *Body Heat* is technically not a nostalgia film, since it takes place in a contemporary setting, in a little Florida village near Miami. On the other hand, this technical contemporaneity is most ambiguous indeed: the credits – always our first cue – are lettered and scripted in a 1930s Art-Deco style which cannot but trigger nostalgic reactions (first to *Chinatown*, no doubt, and then beyond it to some more historical referent). Then the very style of the hero himself is ambiguous: William Hurt is a new star but has nothing of the distinctive style of the preceding generation of male superstars like Steve McQueen or even Jack Nicholson, or rather, his persona here is a kind of mix of their characteristics with an older role of the type generally associated with Clark Gable. So here too there is a faintly archaic feel to all this. The spectator begins to wonder why this story, which could have been situated anywhere, is set in a small Florida town, in spite of its contemporary reference. One begins to realize after a while that the small town setting has a crucial strategic function: it allows the film to do without most of the signals and references which we might associate with the contemporary world, with consumer society – the appliances and artifacts, the high rises, the object world of late capitalism. Technically, then, its objects (its cars, for instance) are 1980s products, but everything in the film conspires to blur that immediate contemporary reference and to make it possible to receive this too as nostalgia work – as a narrative set in some indefinable nostalgic past, an eternal 1930s, say, beyond history. It seems to me exceedingly symptomatic to find the very style of nostalgia films invading and colonizing even those movies today which have contemporary settings: as though, for some reason, we were unable today to focus our own present, as though we have become incapable of achieving aesthetic representations of our own current experience. But if that is so, then it is a terrible indictment of consumer capitalism itself – or, at the very least, an alarming and pathological symptom of a society that has become incapable of dealing with time and history.

So now we come back to the question of why nostalgia film or pastiche is to be considered different from the older historical novel or film. (I should also include in this discussion the major literary example of all this, to my mind: the novels of E.L. Doctorow – *Ragtime*, with its turn-of-the-century atmosphere, and *Loon Lake*, for the most part about our 1930s. But these are, in my opinion, historical novels in appearance only. Doctorow is a serious artist and one of the few genuinely left or radical novelists at work today. It is no disservice to him, however, to suggest that his narratives do not represent our historical past so much as they represent our ideas or cultural stereotypes about that past.) Cultural production has been driven back inside the mind, within the monadic subject: it can no longer look directly out of its eyes at the real world for the referent but must, as in Plato's cave, trace its mental images of the world on its confining walls. If there is any realism left here, it is a 'realism' which springs from the shock of grasping that confinement and of realizing that, for whatever peculiar reasons, we seem condemned to seek the historical past through our own pop images and stereotypes about that past, which itself remains forever out of reach.

Postmodernism and the City

Now, before I try to offer a somewhat more positive conclusion, I want to sketch the analysis of a full-blown postmodern building – a work which is in many ways uncharacteristic of that postmodern architecture whose principal names are Robert Venturi, Charles Moore, Michael Graves, and more recently Frank Gehry, but which to my mind offers some very striking lessons about the originality of postmodernist space. Let me amplify the figure which has run through the preceding remarks, and make it even more explicit: I am proposing the notion that we are here in the presence of something like a mutation in built space itself. My implication is that we ourselves, the human subjects who happen into this new space, have not kept pace with that evolution; there has been a mutation in the object, unaccompanied as yet by any equivalent mutation in the subject; we do not yet possess the perceptual equipment to match this new hyperspace, as I will call it, in part because our perceptual habits were formed in that older kind of space I have called the space of high modernism. The newer architecture therefore – like many of the other cultural products I have evoked in the preceding remarks – stands as something like an imperative to grow new organs to expand our sensorium and our body to some new, as yet unimaginable, perhaps ultimately impossible, dimensions.

The Bonaventure Hotel

The building whose features I will very rapidily enumerate in the next few moments is the Bonaventure Hotel, built in the new Los Angeles downtown by the architect and developer John Portman, whose other works include the various Hyatt Regencies, the Peachtree Center in Atlanta, and the Renaissance Center in Detroit. I have mentioned the populist aspect of the rhetorical defence of postmodernism against the elite (and utopian) austerities of the great architectural modernisms: it is generally affirmed, in other words, that these newer building are popular works on the one hand; and that they respect the vernacular of the American city fabric on the other, that is to say, that they no longer attempt, as did the masterworks and monuments of high modernism, to insert a different, a distinct, an elevated, a new utopian language into the tawdry and commercial sign-system of the surrounding city, but rather, on the contrary, seek to speak that very language, using its lexicon and syntax as that has been emblematically 'learned from Las Vegas'.

On the first of these counts, Portman's Bonaventure fully confirms the claim: it is a popular building, visited with enthusiasm by locals and tourists alike (although Portman's other buildings are even more successful in this respect). The populist insertion into the city fabric is, however, another matter, and it is with this that we will begin. There are three entrances to the Bonaventure, one from Figueroa, and the other two by way of elevated gardens on the other side of the hotel, which is built into the remaining slope of the former Beacon Hill. None of these is anything like the old hotel marquee, or the monumental *porte-cochère* with which the sumptuous buildings of yesteryear were wont to stage your passage from city street to the older interior. The entryways of the Bonaventure are as it were lateral and rather backdoor affairs: the gardens in the back admit you to the sixth floor of the towers, and even there you must walk down one flight to find the elevator by which you gain access to the lobby. Meanwhile, what one is still tempted to think of as the front entry, on Figueroa, admits you, baggage and all, onto the second-story balcony, from which you must take an escalator down to the main registration desk. More about these elevators and escalators in a moment. What I first want to suggest about these curiously unmarked ways-in is that they seem to have been imposed by some new category of closure governing the inner space of the hotel itself (and this over and above the material constraints under which Portman had to work). I believe that, with a certain number of other characteristic postmodern buildings, such as the Beaubourg in Paris, or the Eaton Centre in Toronto, the Bonaventure aspires to being a total space, a complete world, a kind of miniature city (and I would want to add that to this new total space corresponds a new collective practice, a new mode in which individuals move and congregate, something like the practice of a new and historically original kind of hyper-crowd). In this sense, then, ideally the mini-city of Portman's Bonaventure ought not to have entrances at all, since the entryway is always the seam that links the building to the rest of the city that surrounds it: for it does not wish to be a part of the city, but rather its equivalent and its replacement or substitute. That is, however, obviously not possible or practical, whence the deliberate downplaying and reduction of the entrance function to its bare minimum. But this disjunction from the surrounding city is very differ- ent from that of the great monuments of the International Style: there, the act of disjunction was violent, visible, and had a very real symbolic significance – as in Le Corbusier's great *pilotis* whose gesture radically separates the new utopian space of the modern from the degraded and fallen city fabric which it thereby explicitly repudiates (although the gamble of the modern was that this new utopian space, in the virulence of its Novum, would fan out and transform that eventually by the power of its new spatial language). The Bonaventure, however, is content to 'let the fallen city fabric continue to be in its being' (to parody Heideg- ger); no further effects, no larger protopolitical utopian transformation, is either expected or desired.

This diagnosis is to my mind confirmed by the great reflective glass skin of the Bonaventure, whose function I will now interpret rather differently that I did a moment ago when I saw the phenomenon of reflexion generally as developing a thematics of reproductive technology (the two readings are however not incompatible). Now one would want rather to stress the way in which the glass skin repels the city outside; a repulsion for which we have analogies in those reflector sunglasses which make it impossible for your interlocutor to see your own eyes and thereby achieve a certain aggressivity towards and power over the Other. In a similar way, the glass skin achieves a peculiar and placeless dissociation of the Bonaventure from its neighborhood: it is not even an exterior, inasmuch as when you seek to look at the hotel's outer walls you cannot see the hotel itself, but only the distorted images of everything that surrounds it.

Now I want to say a few words about escalators and elevators: given their very real pleasures in Portman, particularly these last, which the artist has termed 'gigantic kinetic sculptures' and which certainly account for much of the spectacle and the excitement of the hotel interior, particularly in the Hyatts, where like great Japanese lanterns or gondolas they ceaselessly rise and fall – given such a deliberate marking and foregrounding in their own right, I believe one has to see such 'people movers' (Portman's own term, adapted from Disney) as something a little more than mere functions and engineering components. We know in any case that recent architectural theory has begun to borrow from narrative analysis in other fields, and to attempt to see our physical trajectories through such buildings as virtual narratives or stories, as dynamic paths and narrative paradigms which we as visitors are asked to fulfil and to complete with our own bodies and movements. In the Bonaventure, however, we find a dialetical heightening of this process: it seems to me that the escalators and elevators here henceforth replace movement but also and above all designate themselves as new reflexive signs and emblems of movement proper (something which will become evident when we come to the whole question of what remains of older forms of movement in this building, most notably walking itself). Here the narrative stroll has been underscored, symbolized, reified and replaced by a transportation machine which becomes the allegorical signifier of that older promenade we are no longer allowed to conduct on our own: and this is a dialectical intensification of the autoreferentiality of all modern culture, which tends to turn upon itself and designate its own cultural production as its content.

I am more at a loss when it comes to conveying the thing itself, the experience of space you undergo when you step off such allegorical devices into the lobby or atrium, with its great central column, surrounded by a miniature lake, the whole positioned between the four symmetrical residential towers with their elevators, and surrounded by rising balconies capped by a kind of greenhouse roof at the sixth level. I am tempted to say that such space makes it impossible for us to use the language of volume or volumes any longer, since these last are impossible to seize. Hanging streamers indeed suffuse this empty space in such a way as to distract systematically and deliberately from whatever form it might be supposed to have; while a constant busyness gives the feeling that emptiness is here absolutely packed, that it is an element within which you yourself are immersed, without any of that distance that formerly enabled the perception of perspective or volume. You are in this hyperspace up to your eyes and your body; and if it seemed to you before that that suppression of depth I spoke of in postmodern painting or literature would necessarily be difficult to achieve in architecture itself, perhaps you may now be willing to see this bewildering immersion as the formal equivalent in the new medium.

Yet escalator and elevator are also in this context dialetical opposites; and we may suggest that the glorious movement of the elevator gondolas is also a dialectical compensation for this filled space of the atrium – it gives us the chance at a radically different, but complementary, spatial experience, that of rapidly shooting up through the ceiling and outside, along one of the four symmetrical towers, with the referent, Los Angeles itself, spread out breathtakingly and even alarmingly before us. But even this vertical movement is contained: the elevator lifts you to one of those revolving cocktail lounges, in which you, seated, are again passively rotated about and offered a contemplative spectacle of the city itself, now transformed into its own images by the glass windows through which you view it.

Let me quickly conclude all this by returning to the central space of the lobby itself (with the passing observation that the hotel rooms are visibly marginalized: the corridors in the residential sections are low-ceilinged and dark, most depressingly functional indeed: while one understands that the rooms are in the worst of taste). The descent is dramatic enough, plummeting back down through the roof to splash down in the lake; what happens when you get there is something else, which I can only try to characterize as milling confusion, something like the vengeance this space takes on those who still seek to walk through it. Given the absolute symmetry of the four towers, it is quite impossible to get your bearings in this lobby; recently, colour coding and directional signals have been added in a pitiful and revealing, rather desperate attempt to restore the coordinates of an older space. I will take as the most dramatic practical result of this spatial mutation the notorious dilemma of the shopkeepers on the various balconies: it has been obvious, since the very opening of the hotel in 1977, that nobody could ever find any of these stores, and even if you located the appropriate boutique, you would be most unlikely to be as fortunate a second time; as a consequence, the commercial tenants are in despair and all the merchandise is marked down to bargain prices. When you recall that Portman is a businessman as well as an architect, and a millionaire developer, an artist who is at one and the same time a capitalist in his own right, you cannot but feel that here too something of a 'return of the repressed' is involved.

So I come finally to my principal point here, that this latest mutation in space – postmodern hyperspace – has finally succeeded in transcending the capacities of the individual human body to locate itself, to organize its immediate surroundings perceptually, and cognitively to map its position in a mappable external world. And I have already suggested that this alarming disjunction point between the body and its built environment – which is to the initial bewilderment of the older modernism as the velocities of spacecraft are to those of the automobile – can itself stand as the symbol and analog of that even sharper dilemma which is the incapacity of our minds, at least at present, to map the great global multinational and decentered communicational network in which we find ourselves caught as individual subjects.

The New Machine

But as I am anxious that Portman's space not be perceived as something either exceptional or seemingly marginalized and leisure-specialized on the order of Disneyland, I would like in passing to juxtapose this complacent and entertaining (although bewildering) leisure-time space with its analog in a very different area, namely the space of postmodern warfare, in particular as Michael Herr evokes it in his great book on the experience of Vietnam, called *Dispatches*. The extraordinary linguistic innovations of this work may still be considered postmodern, in the eclectic way in which its language impersonally fuses a whole range of contemporary collective idiolects, most notably rock language and black language: but the fusion is dictated by problems of content. This first terrible postmodernist war cannot be told in any of the traditional paradigms of the war novel or movie – indeed that breakdown of all previous narrative paradigms is, along with the breakdown of any shared language through which a veteran might convey such experience, among the principal subjects of the book and may be said to open up the place of a whole new reflexivity. Benjamin's account of Baudelaire, and of the emergence of modernism from a new experience of city technology which transcends all the older habits of bodily perception, is both singularly relevant here, and singularly antiquated, in the light of this new and virtually unimaginable quantum leap in technological alienation:

He was a moving-target-survivor subscriber, a true child of the war, because except for the rare times when you were pinned or stranded the system was geared to keep you mobile, if that was what you thought you wanted. As a technique for staying alive it seemed to make as much sense as anything, given naturally that you were there to begin with and wanted to see it close; it started out sound and straight but it formed a cone as it progressed, because the more you moved the more you saw, the more you saw the more besides death and mutilation you risked, and the more you risked of that the more you would have to let go of one day as a 'survivor'. Some of us moved around the war like crazy people until we couldn't see which way the run was taking us anymore, only the war all over its surface with occasional, unexpected penetration. As long as we could have choppers like taxis it took real exhaustion or depression near shock or a dozen pipes of opium to keep us even apparently quiet, we'd still be running around inside our skins like something was after us, ha, ha, La Vida Loca. In the months after I got back the hundreds of helicopters I'd flown in begin to draw together until they'd formed a collective meta-chopper, and in my mind it was the sexiest thing going; saver-destroyer, provider-waster, right hand-left hand, nimble, fluent, canny and human; hot steel, grease, jungle-saturated canvas webbing, sweat cooling and warming up again, cassette rock and roll in one ear and door-gun fire in the other, fuel, heat, vitality and death, death itself, hardly an intruder.[2]

In this new machine, which does not, like the older modernist machinery of the locomotive or the airplane, represent motion, but which can only be represented *in motion*, something of the mystery of the new postmodernist space is concentrated.

The Aesthetic of Consumer Society

Now I must try very rapidly in conclusion to characterize the relationship of cultural production of this kind to social life in this country today. This will also be the moment to address the principal objection to concepts of postmodernism of the type I have sketched here: namely that all the features we have enumerated are not new at all but abundantly characterized modernism proper or what I call high modernism. Was not Thomas Mann, after all, interested in the idea of pastiche, and are not certain chapters of *Ulysses* its most obvious realization? Can Flaubert, Mallarmé and Gertrude Stein not be included in an account of postmodernist temporality? What is so new about all of this? Do we really need the concept of *post*modernism?

One kind of answer to this question would raise the whole issue of periodization and of how a historian (literary or other) posits a radical break between two henceforth distinct periods. I must limit myself to the suggestion that radical breaks between periods do not generally involve complete changes of content but rather the restructuring of a certain number of elements already given: features that in an earlier period or system were subordinate now become dominant, and features that had been dominant again become secondary. In this sense, everything we have described here can be found in earlier periods and most notably within modernism proper: my point is that until the present day those things have been secondary or minor features of modernist art, marginal rather than central, and that we have something new when they become the central features of cultural production.

But I can argue this more concretely by turning to the relationship between cultural production and social life generally. The older or classical modernism was an oppositional art; it emerged within the business society of the gilded age as scandalous and offensive to the middle-class public – ugly, dissonant, bohemian, sexually shocking. It was something to make fun of (when the police were not called in to seize the books or close the exhibitions): an offense to good taste and to common sense, or, as Freud and Marcuse would have put it, a provocative challenge to the reigning reality- and performance-principles of early twentieth-century middle-class society. Modernism in general did not go well with over-stuffed Victorian furniture, with Victorian moral taboos, or with the conventions of polite society. This is to say that whatever the explicit political content of the great high modernisms, the latter were always in some mostly implicit ways dangerous and explosive, subversive within the established order.

If then we suddenly return to the present day, we can measure the immensity of the cultural changes that have taken place. Not only are Joyce and Picasso no longer weird and repulsive, they have become classics and now look rather realistic to us. Meanwhile, there is very little in either the form or the content of contemporary art that contemporary society finds intolerable and scandalous. The most offensive forms of this art – punk rock, say, or what is called sexually explicit material – are all taken in stride by society, and they are commercially successful, unlike the productions of the older high modernism. But this means that even if contemporary art has all the same formal features as the older modernism, it has still shifted its position fundamentally within our culture. For one thing, commodity production and in particular our clothing, furniture, buildings and other artifacts are now intimately tied in with styling changes which derive from artistic experimentation; our advertising, for example, is fed by postmodernism in all the arts and inconceivable without it. For another, the classics of high modernism are now part of the so-called canon and are taught in schools and universities – which at once empties them of any of their older subversive power.

Indeed, one way of marking the break between the periods and of dating the emergence of postmodernism is precisely to be found there: in the moment (the early 1960s, one would think) in which the position of high modernism and its dominant aesthetics become established in the academy and are henceforth felt to be academic by a whole new generation of poets, painters and musicians.

But one can also come at the break from the other side, and describe it in terms of periods of recent social life. As I have suggested, non-Marxists and Marxists alike have come around to the general feeling that at some point following World War II a new kind of society began to emerge (variously described as postindustrial society, multinational capitalism, consumer society, media society and so forth). New types of consumption; planned obsolescence; an ever more rapid rhythm of fashion and styling changes; the penetration of advertising, television and the media generally to a hitherto unparalleled degree throughout society; the replacement of the old tension between city and country, center and province, by the suburb and by universal standardization; the growth of the great networks of superhighways and the arrival of automobile culture – these are some of the features which would seem to mark a radical break with that older prewar society in which high modernism was still an underground force.

I believe that the emergence of postmodernism is closely related to the emergence of this new moment of late, consumer or multinational capitalism. I believe also that its formal features in many ways express the deeper logic of that particular social system. I will only be able, however, to show this for one major theme: namely the disappearance of a sense of history, the way in which our entire contemporary social system has little by little begun to lose its capacity to retain its own past, has begun to live in a perpetual present and in a perpetual change that obliterates traditions of the kind which all earlier social formations have had in one way or another to preserve. Think only of the media exhaustion of news: of how Nixon and, even more so, Kennedy are figures from a now distant past. One is tempted to say that the very function of the news media is to relegate such recent historical experiences as rapidly as possible into the past. The informational function of the media would thus be to help us forget, to serve as the very agents and mechanisms for our historical amnesia.

But in that case the two features of postmodernism on which I have dwelt here – the transformation of reality into images, the fragmentation of time into a series of perpetual presents – are both extraordinarily consonant with this process. My own conclusion here must take the form of a question about the critical value of the newer art. There is some agreement that the older modernism functioned against its society in ways which are variously described as critical, negative, contestatory, subversive, oppositional and the like. Can anything of the sort be affirmed about postmodernism and its social moment? We have seen that there is a way in which postmodernism replicates or reproduces – reinforces – the logic of consumer capitalism; the more significant question is whether there is also a way in which it resists that logic. But that is a question we must leave open.

Notes

1. The present text combines elements of two previously published essays: 'Post-modernism and Consumer Society', in *The Anti-Aesthetic* (Port Townsend, WA: Bay Press, 1983), and 'Postmodernism: the Cultural Logic of Late Capitalism', *New Left Review* 146 (July–August 1984).

2. Michael Herr, *Dispatches* (New York: Knopf, 1977), pp. 8–9.

2

Feminism/Oedipus/ Postmodernism: The Case of MTV

E. Ann Kaplan

Feminist theorists have been preoccupied with the problem of Oedipus at least since Roland Barthes's convincing elaboration of Freud's 'discovery' of links between narrative and the oedipal complex. If classical narrative 'has the movement of a passage, an actively experienced transformation of the human being ... into man',[1] then it seemed essential, in a first move, for female artists to avoid the processes involved in classical narrative.[2] Correlatively the same theories provoked feminist critics into analyzing the passive position, subject to the Law of the Father, that women have occupied in traditional narratives.

Feminist films (produced as texts counter to dominant ones in the mid-1970s) of necessity used alternative aesthetic strategies in their attempt to avoid the oedipal paradigm centered around the phallus as signifier. Some of the feminist developments took as their starting point Kristeva's postulation of a pre-oedipal, pre-linguistic terrain which Kristeva found in the largely male artistic avant-garde (Joyce, John Cage). Others were attracted by her use of Bakhtin's carnivalesque and polyphony as ways to avoid the phallic, monologic text inevitably representing woman in oppressive ways. Still others, influenced by Brecht, Russian Formalism and Louis Althusser, constructed the well-known polarity whereby the classical realist text, seen as embodying dominant ideology, was pitted against the subversive, non-realist, non-narrative and avant-garde text. The binarisms in classical realist texts were said to function as what Althusser has called Ideological State Apparatuses – that is, as creating and positioning us as subjects who are then made to stand in a specific relation to each other and the State – which Althusser sees as primarily serving the ruling classes. The oedipal scenario (as revised by Lacan) is central for Althusser; it remains among the primary psychic mechanisms by which means we are 'hailed' as subjects.

Some feminists, following Kristeva, began to argue that modernism itself could be equated positively with a subversive 'feminine', since modernist literary techniques deliberately violated traditional forms that embodied (whether explicitly or implicitly) the oedipal scenario. Others saw modernism as misogynist and as problematic for feminist theory and practice because of its high culture, elitist discourse (epitomized by Ortega y Gasset).[3] From this point of view, the 'separateness of the aesthetic from the rest of human life'[4] is antithetical to feminism. Yet even the critics and artists making this objection wanted to retain modernism's transgressive stance.

In different ways, then, popular culture theorists in the 1970s and early 1980s took for granted that the concept of transgression as it had been developed by the great modernists was most useful in criticizing dominant narrative paradigms and in conceptualizing (and creating) counter-texts. Feminists, that is, adapted modernist strategies to their own distinctive ends: since women were writing and creating in an historical moment far different from that of the early decades of the century, modernist strategies functioned differently, taking on different meanings. But broadly speaking these strategies are still best categorized as modernist.

Two reactions to 1970s theories must be briefly mentioned here. First, the anti-narrative text was itself criticized in the mid-1980s as in its turn doing violence to women by denying the audience pleasure In 'Oedipus Interruptus', Teresa de Lauretis began to question the 'active-passive and gaze-image dichotomies in the theorization of spectator-ship'[5] that had led to concepts of the anti-narrative text; she began to rethink 'the possibilities of narrative identification as a subject-effect in female spectators'. She proposes a feminist cinema that would be 'narra-tive and oedipal with a vengeance', since it would aim to enact the contradiction of female desire in the terms of narrative (p. 40). In this way, feminist cinema could avoid 'the stoic, brutal prescription of self-discipline that seemed inevitable at the time [the early 1970s]' (p. 39).

In a second reaction against seventies theories, feminists analyzing popular culture began to move beyond showing merely that the oedipal scenario positions/limits/represses woman. Exploring the woman's melodrama in film and soap operas on television, they showed the ways in which some dominant texts are able to expose the constraints the oedipal scenario imposes and to reveal gaps where the female spectator is able to retrieve something for herself (for example, through the mothering relation or through female–female bonding). Some argued, in a manner similar to nineteenth-century feminists, that the patriarchally

defined feminine, which includes emotionalism, relatedness, connected-
ness, can be used to further women's own, human ends. The ensuing
debate, often articulated as being between so-called 'essentialist' and
'anti-essentialist' feminists (a debate I have analyzed elsewhere)[6]
reached its logical extreme in Toril Moi's recent *Sexual/Textual
Politics.*[7]

In both the first and second theoretical moves by feminist film and
television theorists, women were seen to 'need' narrative. In the first
case, feminist film-makers needed narrative as the system against which
to create counter-narratives questioning how women had been represented and throwing representation itself into crisis; in the second move,
feminists needed narrative as a form within which to position women
differently. In this latter, narrative's link to desire is seen as something
women have a stake in preserving: to refuse narrative is to refuse
pleasure.

But does the postmodern discourse that swept across the American
intellectual horizon in the mid-1980s on its way from France require
narrative equally? Is narrative a viable concept in the wake of Baudrillard and Lyotard (who represent opposing if complementary positions)?

I want to explore the implications of postmodernism as a putative
new cultural moment, as a theoretical and critical concept, and as a
variously valued (anti-)aesthetic for feminist theories of narrative as
sketched briefly above, particularly in the light of Craig Owens's observation that discussions of sexual difference have been signally absent
from writings about postmodernism.[8] How does postmodernism as a
theory and as deployed in popular culture affect feminist theory and
aesthetic practice?[9] Does postmodernism change female representation,
female spectatorship? Does it hinder or advance feminist cultural aims?
I will consider these questions through the optic of Music Television as a
postmodern cultural institution: specific rock videos exhibited on the
channel will help to clarify theoretical points.

The distinctions made in the Introduction to this volume will be
useful in answering the questions just posed. Music Television belongs in
the 'co-opted' category by virtue of its being a commercial station,
produced and exhibited within a profit-making institution. Its postmodern (anti-)aesthetic strategies need to be considered within that
larger context rather than in and for themselves. If some of the devices
approximate those used in the 'utopian' postmodern texts, we must
nevertheless ask if such a text can be produced within the commercial
framework.

Several critics who include popular texts in their discussion of the
'utopian' postmodern appear to accept that possibility. Some apply to
the latter area theories not originally developed with popular culture in

mind; or they use a theorist like Bakhtin, who wrote about a very different kind of popular culture preceding mechanization. Indeed, many such scholars look to Bakhtin as the one thinker who can provide a theoretical opening to a utopian text or to cultural alternatives.[10] Bakhtin's concept of dialogism, as rewritten by Kristeva, has seemed particularly useful in avoiding the traps and dead-ends of binarism. As is well known, the early Kristeva searches for a text where sex and other differences are transcended, where the metaphysical category of difference no longer exists: we see this in her concept of the 'semiotic' and in her reworking of Bakhtin's notion of the carnivalesque, 'where discourse attains its "potential infinity" ... where prohibitions (representation, "monologism") and their transgression (dream, body, "dialogism") coexist'.[11] It is what she finds in Sollers's *H* which 'is music that is inscribed in language, becoming the object of its own reasoning, ceaselessly, and until saturated, overflowing, and dazzling sense has been exhausted ... It whisks you from your comfortable position; it breaches a gust of dizziness into you, but lucidity returns at once, along with music ...'. (p. 7).

Similarly, the following theorists seem to be agreed in imagining a kind of art that does not take its shape from running counter to the dominant system, but is anti-essentialist, plural, where discourses are not hierarchically ordered, where sex and other differences are transcended, where the metaphysical category of difference no longer exists. This is what White and Stallybrass demand when they note the need for a concept of carnival to be linked to notions of transgression and symbolic inversion if it is to designate 'not just an infraction of binary structures, but movement into an absolutely negative space beyond the structure of significance itself'.[12]

This is what Lyotard is reaching for in his rejection of the master narratives of the past, and in his nostalgic attempt to return to something preceding modernism but nevertheless beyond it;[13] Robert Stam similarly envisions 'a fundamentally non-unitary, constantly shifting cultural field in which the most varied discourses exist in shifting multi-valenced oppositional relationships'.[14] And it seems to be what Fred Pfeil has in mind in his discussion of possibilities within what he calls 'the culture of the PMC' (i.e. the Professional–Managerial Class), when he hopes that 'much of what we now call postmodernism might be turned and engaged in more progressive political directions ....'. Pfeil is fully aware that the figurations he has in mind 'are at present no more than trace elements of a dream whose concrete realization would require on all sides enormous amounts of hard work and painful struggle'.[15]

Recently certain feminist film and literary theorists have begun to consider this same option. Teresa de Lauretis, for example speaks about the need for texts that construct a new aesthetic in a specific female and heterogeneous address – an address which insists on a series of different spectator positions through which one becomes involved in a process toward subjectivity, rather than being fixed.[16] And Alice Jardine has raised the possibilities for new ways of thinking woman in her exploration of 'gynesis' as this has been recently deployed in texts by French male theorists.[17]

This sort of utopian postmodernism builds on, and carries to its own subversive ends, certain strands of high modernism. Not all modernism was co-opted into mainstream culture; resistant trends (Eisenstein, Buñuel, Brecht – what Paul Willemen calls the 'true' avant-garde because it subverted art's autonomy in favor of a reintegration of art and life)[18] may be seen as precursors of the utopian postmodern briefly outlined above.

Let me now return to the question of whether this sort of art can ever be produced within dominant *commercial* culture: if not, how does the commercial institutional context constrain meanings and influence reception? The question is complicated because what is new about much recent popular culture – especially MTV – and what marks it as different from high modernism is the very intermingling of modernist/avant-garde and popular aesthetic modes that may also be characteristic of the 'utopian' postmodern. Some theorists (e.g. Stam and Pfeil) obviously believe that commercial culture provides at least limited space for a subversive postmodern, although they are scarcely clear about precisely what aesthetic terrain they have in mind when they speak about the utopian possibilities. We can imagine texts which transcend binary categories within an avant-garde context of production and exhibition (largely the terrain on which people like Kristeva, Cixous, de Lauretis think); but I am wary of such claims being made for the sphere of popular culture as it exists at present. Or at least, we need to address the contradictions and constraints of any 'spaces' we may find in mass texts. Do mixings of the popular and the avant-garde transcend binary oppositions or decenter the subject in a way that leads to something new? Or are they rather an example of Baudrillard's implosion or collapsing of meanings into something undesirable?

The answer to this question is intricately tied to one's theory about the TV apparatus. This phrase refers to the complex of elements including the machine itself and its various sites of reception from the living-room to the bathroom; its technological features (the way it produces and presents images); its mixture of texts, inclusion of ads, commentaries, displays; the central relationship of programming to the sponsors, whose own texts, the ads, are arguably the *real* TV texts;[19] the unbounded nature of the texts and reception; the range of potentialities one can produce through operating the machine.

Baudrillard's image is compelling: 'With the television image – television being the ultimate and perfect object for this era – our own body and the whole surrounding universe become a control screen.'[20] Situated in the illusory position of mastery and control, the spectator can play with various possibilities, none of which, however, makes the slightest difference to anything. Have we (as Baudrillard would argue) replaced Marx's 'drama of alienation' with the 'ecstasy of communication', and Freud's old 'hot sexual obscenity' with 'the contactual and motivational obscenity of today'?[21] Is TV, as Kroker and Cook argue, 'the real world of postmodern culture which has *entertainment* as its ideology, the *spectacle* as the emblematic sign of the commodity form, *lifestyle advertising* as its popular psychology, pure, empty *seriality* as the bond which unites the simulacrum of the audience, *electronic images* as its most dynamic, and only form of social cohesion … the diffusion of a *network of relational power* as its real product'?[22]

I am persuaded by much of Baudrillard's and Kroker's and Cook's scenario for where high culture is headed, and the role the TV and the computer screens play in it. The somewhat complicit vision in texts like *Blade Runner*, *Videodrome* and *Max Headroom* on the one hand, or the more subversive one in those like *The Man Who Fell to Earth* or *Brazil*, no longer seem impossible. I agree with Kroker that the enemy is partly liberal humanist philosophy with its easy compromises and denials; but I have trouble with Baudrillard's notion that the resistance of the object (i.e. 'infantilism, hyper-conformism, total dependence, passivity, idiocy') is the proper response to the dangerous 'hegemony of meaning'.[23] In either case, however, once the signifiers have been freed from their signifieds, once the fixed frameworks and constraints of traditional gender-based genres have been relinquished, we have no way of controlling what comes into the space. Both positive and negative things may happen, particularly for women.

MTV is a useful area within which to debate competing claims about postmodernism, and by which to distinguish the postmodern from the transgressive text. It also provides an occasion to ask how we can create a popular culture that will move beyond dominant binary oppositions (and the classical realism within which such binarisms are encased), without the collapse of oppositions being recuperated through their reduction to empty surfaces.

Many rock videos have been seen as postmodern insofar as they abandon the usual binary oppositions on which dominant culture depends.[24] That is, videos are said to forsake the usual oppositions between high and low culture; between masculine and feminine; between established literary and filmic genres; between past, present and future; between the private and the public sphere; between verbal and visual hierarchies; between realism and anti-realism, etc. This has important implications for the question of narrative as feminists have been theorizing it, in that these strategies violate the paradigm pitting a classical narrative against an avant-garde anti-narrative, the one supposedly embodying complicit, the other subversive, ideologies. The rock video reveals the error in trying to align an aesthetic strategy with any particular ideology, since all kinds of positions emerge from an astounding mixture of narrative/anti-narrative/non-narrative devices. The five video types I have outlined elsewhere in an effort to organize the multitude of rock videos on the channel are only broad categories that by no means cover all the various possible combinations of narrational strategies.[25]

Narrative/non-narrative is no longer a useful category within which to discuss videos. What is important is, first, whether or not any position manifests itself across the hectic, often incoherent flow of signifiers which are not necessarily organized into a chain that produces a signified, and, second, what are the implications of the twenty-four-hour flow of short (four-minute or less) texts that all more or less function as ads.

In line with Baudrillard's theory, MTV partly exploits the imaginary desires allowed free play though the various sixties liberation movements, divesting them, for commercial reasons, of their originally revolutionary implications.[26] The apparatus itself, in its construction of a decentered, fragmented spectator through the rapid flow of short segments, easily reduces politics to the 'radical chic' (USA For Africa) or the pornographic (Rolling Stones' 'She Was Hot').

Yet, paradoxically, MTV's chosen format of short texts enables exhibition of thematic and aesthetic positions that criticize the status quo. That is, MTV's twenty-four-hour rapid flow of short segments on the one hand renders all of its texts 'postmodern' because of the manner of their exhibition (i.e., a stream of jumbled, hectic signifiers for which no signified was intended or has time to be communicated; the reduction of all to surfaces/textures/sounds/the visceral and kinaesthetic: the hypnotizing of the spectator into an exitless, schizophrenic stance by the unceasing image series); yet, on the other hand, if we rather artificially 'stop the flow', we can find individual texts that in their four-minute airplay do offer subversive subject positions.

Since the subject positions the channel offers are important for the female spectator, let me 'stop the flow' for the purposes of analysis, fully aware that what one finds in this process differs from what one experiences as a 'normal' spectator. The existence of alternative subject positions is theoretically important, even if such positions are normally swept up in the plethora of more oppressive ones. Hence, I will look briefly at strategies in a typical 'postmodern' video having negative results for women, and then at videos leaning in the avant-garde, transgressive direction descending from high modernism and opening up useful space for the female spectator.

Take for instance Tom Petty and the Heartbreakers' 'Don't Come Around Here No More'. This video, like many others, stands in a strange intertextual relationship to a well-known original – here Lewis Carroll's *Alice In Wonderland*. The text cannot be labelled 'parody' in the modernist sense that Jameson has outlined; and yet it is clearly playing off the original. It thus falls between parody and actually moving beyond the binarisms of conventional narrative. The issue of the gaze becomes confused: we have a sense of the text playing with oedipal positionings in the apparent sadism enacted on Alice's body, in the monstrous father torturing the child; but it deflects this reading by the semi-comic, self-conscious stance it takes toward what it is doing, and by the brilliance of its visual strategies. One becomes entranced by the visual and aural dimensions, which overwhelm all others. One holds in abeyance the reaching for a signified and is absorbed in the surfaces/textures/shapes/sounds which dominate reception channels.

The pastiche mode makes it difficult to say that the text is taking a sado-masochistic pleasure in violence against women, so that while the imagery offends the female spectator she fears she is being trapped into taking it too seriously. The video just might be intending reference to the sadism in the original *Alice*; it might even be 'exposing' male abuse of the female body through the grotesque image of Alice's body being eaten as cake. But one cannot be sure. The spectator is made to doubt through this sort of play, which characterizes the co-opted postmodern.

Madonna's successful 'Material Girl' positions the spectator equally uncomfortably, while not addressing or moving beyond established polarities in the manner of the utopian text. 'Material Girl' stands in a strange intertextual relationship to Howard Hawks's film, *Gentlemen Prefer Blondes*. It offers a pastiche of Monroe's 'Diamonds Are a Girl's Best Friend' number, while declining any critical comment upon that text. In this video, Madonna may be said to represent a postmodern feminist stance by combining seductiveness with a gutsy kind of independence. She incorporates the qualities of both Jane Russell and Monroe in Hawks's film, creating a self-confident, unabashedly sexual image that is far more aggressive than those of the Hollywood stars.

It is perhaps Madonna's success in articulating and parading a desire to be desired – the opposite of the self-abnegating urge to lose oneself in the male evident in many classical Hollywood films – that attracts the hordes of twelve-year-old fans to her performances and videos. A cross between a bag-lady and a bordello queen, Madonna's image is a far cry from the 'patriarchal feminine' of women's magazines; yet it remains within those constraints in still focusing on the 'look' as crucial to identity. Madonna's narcissism and self-indulgences co-opt her texts back into a consumerist postmodernism, as do also the seductive participatory rhythms of this and other pop rock melodies. Such melodies bind the female spectator to the images so that the repressive aspects slip by unnoticed because of the comforting, appealing beat.

Some videos on the channel do use the new form in ways reminiscent of a transgressive/modernist mode. They use narrative in differing degrees and in various ways, much as did the great modernists, and they employ realist or non-realist strategies as befits a particular moment in a text. There is no set form for videos offering a critique of dominant female representations or of woman's position in male culture as signs for something in the male unconscious. The videos range from the black-comedy parody in Julie Brown's 'The Home Coming Queen's Got A Gun', to a sophisticated feminist critique of female representations and of woman's construction as passive sexual object in Annie Lennox's and Aretha Franklin's 'Sisters Are Doin' It for Themselves' and Tina Turner's 'Private Dancer'; to Laurie Anderson's anti-narrative, deconstructive video 'Language is a Virus', which attacks dominant bourgeois culture generally and commercial TV in particular.

We can thus see how difficult it is to make a case for MTV as progressive or retrogressive in its narrative modes. In a sense, those categories do not apply. MTV is something else – or it is elsewhere. It defies our usual critical categories while not setting up something we can recognize as liberating in new ways such as those Derrida and Kristeva search for.

Let me conclude by summarizing the contradictory aspects of postmodernism for feminist cultural concerns. Contemporary feminism, as a political and cultural discourse, has assumed a set of strategic subjectivities in order to attack the old patriarchal theorists. Feminists have both made use of and criticized the powerful, often subversive discourses of both Marx and Freud in creating the feminist stance against dominant gender constructs. If those discourses are seen as no longer relevant, on what ground can any strategic feminism stand? We might hope that we no longer needed such feminism, that we could work toward transcending 'death-dealing binary oppositions of masculinity and femininity', but events like the recent 'Baby M' case show how distant is American culture from any such stage. Does postmodernism make feminism archaic as a theory, while refusing to address the remaining oppressive discourses that perpetuate woman's subordination? For Kroker and Cook, technology is the only remaining ideology; feminists, however, can see in the Baby M case how various gender ideologies interact with new technologies in a complex, often contradictory manner.

The postmodernism that is produced by the collapse of the enlightenment project and of the belief in the transcendental (male) subject benefits women when it leads to the utopian postmodern text discussed earlier. And even in the commercial postmodernism exemplified in MTV, we saw that there are benefits for the female spectator: the breaking up of traditional realist forms sometimes entails a deconstruction of conventional sex-role representations that opens up new possibilities for female imagining. The four-minute span does not permit regression to the oedipal conflicts of the classical Hollywood film that oppresses women. Meanwhile, the fragmentation of the viewing subject perhaps deconstructs woman's conventional other-centered reception functions – woman positioned as nurturer, care-giver – releasing new ways for the female spectator to relate to texts. Postmodernism offers the female spectator pleasure in sensations – color, sound, visual patterns – and in energy, body movement. Madonna represents new possibilities for female desire and for the empowered woman, even if we would want these forms of desire and empowerment to be only a transitional phase.

On the other hand, we could argue that commercial postmodern culture builds on and satisfies already dominant masculine qualities such as violence, destruction, consumption, phallic sexuality, and appropriation of the female in the non-male image. In much postmodernism, the domestic and the familial – modes that in the past offered some satisfaction to women – no longer function. It is possible that the new 'universe of communication' is attractive to some male theorists seeking relief from Baudrillard's old 'Faustian, Promethean (perhaps Oedipal) period of production and consumption', just because women have begun, through feminist discourse, to make and win demands within that system and to challenge male dominance there.

But the postmodern discourse theorized by Kroker and Cook is not anti-feminist; rather, it envisions a world beyond feminism as we have known it in the past twenty-five years. In the postmodern world, both men and women are victims; all bodies are 'invaded' and exploited because they are no longer adequate to the advanced technologies. Marilouise and Arthur Kroker are concerned about the (ab)use of women's bodies in fashion and about the reduction of woman to a baby-making 'machine' through new reproductive technologies. These devices alienate woman from her body and disconnect her from the baby she produces. But the Krokers also point out the new 'fallen' image of the penis in the age of AIDS and other sexual viruses, and many other ways in which humans, as we have conceived of them for centuries, are being drastically altered by electronic implants and additions.

Indeed, a movie like *Videodrome* is surprising more for its representation of the male than of the female body. Female figures in the film
interestingly fall back into traditional stereotypes (the masculinized
'bitch' woman, the oversexed, masochistic woman), but we see the male
body invaded and made monstrous in the hero's machine-produced
hallucinations. It is true that the horrific deformation of the body
involves its turning into a kind of vagina-like, bloody opening,[27] but this
is a reference to the horror of technology that deforms all bodies and
blurs their gender distinction. There are as many images of castration
(the deformed arm, the powerless gun) as of female orifices. The point is
that the hero's body turns into a playback machine; the body is
controlled by electronic frequencies that prevent the owner from
controlling himself. We have entered a Baudrillardean world (Brian
Oblivion being a thinly disguised Baudrillard) in which there is no
'reality' other than video; the human body is reduced to the video
machine – it and the TV set are one and the same.

As feminists we need to listen to the discourse for what it can tell us
about the possible future: as an ethics of description, the postmodern
discourse of this kind may warn against the devastating results of the
abuse of science and technology by capital. Popular culture theory needs
to attend to the Baudrillard/Kroker accounts, while avoiding their more
seductive but improbable extremism. In what is hopefully only a
transitional phase, we need more than ever to construct critical analyses
of the new cultural scene, and the shift in consciousness wrought by
science and technology; we need to engage in work that will redress
dangerous directions, or prevent what is envisaged from coming to be.
As humans implicated against our wills in the effects of new technologies, we also still exist as historical subjects in specific political contexts:
we must continue feminist struggles wherever we live and work, at the
same time being aware of the larger cultural constructions that implicate
us and for which feminist ideologies may no longer be adequate.

In terms of cultural studies, the first two of my trilogy of male theorists (i.e. Barthes and Bakhtin) are useful particularly as they have been
theorized by French feminists (Kristeva, Cixous, Montrelay); Lacan,
Althusser and Foucault are equally important, again in connection with
French feminists (Cixous, Irigaray). Let me conclude by listing the
different kinds of cultural work that feminists need to be doing: I will
discuss this work in terms of the three main categories discussed above,
namely: a) the modernist/transgressive text; b) the 'utopian' postmodern text; and c) the 'popular/commercial' postmodern text.

First, feminists must continue to make use of transgressive strategies,
as some feminist film-makers have been doing (e.g., Mulvey and
Wollen's *Riddles of the Sphinx*, Sally Potter's *Thriller* or her *Gold-*

diggers, Sigmund Freud's 'Dora'; Trinh T. Minh-ha's *Naked Spaces - Living Is Round,* among others). In this way, feminists can continue to question and undo the patriarchal construction of femininity, to pose the problem of representation, to demonstrate the social constructions of gender. Unlike the high modernists (most of whom were male, many misogynist), such feminists have the benefit of recent work on deconstruction, and can employ sophisticated theories of representation and gender that have also recently been developed through semiotics and psychoanalysis. Inevitably, such texts will be produced and exhibited mainly in alternate spaces, given the demands they make on the viewer through their counter-text strategies. However, we should not underestimate the impact of such texts, now that they are making their way into the academy.

Such texts vary in their strategies, particularly in relation to the use or non-use of narrative. Some feminists, like Teresa de Lauretis, keenly aware that narrative movement is that of masculine desire, 'the movement of a passage, an actively experienced transformation of the human being into ... man', nevertheless are wary of the automatic adoption of anti-narrative devices. De Lauretis argues that we must create a new kind of narrative, based not on male desire but rather on a different kind of desiring. Other feminists believe that all narrative involves essentializing (i.e., positing some 'female' desire in place of the prior 'male' desire) and that, therefore, we can offer a truly transgressive position only through anti-narrative techniques.

This work needs to be differentiated from a second feminist concern, which we could position within the 'utopian' postmodernism discussed above. Here, feminists theorize and try to construct texts that radically decenter, disrupt and refuse all categories hitherto central in Western thought, much in the manner of Derrida. The efforts in the transgressive sort of text should provide the groundwork for the utopian postmodernist text in leading us through the problems and tangles of binary oppositions toward a glimpse of how the beyond might appear.

An important third area of work needs to address the possibilities within what I have called the dominant 'co-opted' postmodernism of our time. Here it seems to me that we can bring to bear tools developed just prior to the postmodern moment in analyzing women in popular culture (the classical Hollywood melodrama, 1950s television, the soaps). An important issue here is the degree to which the new co-opted postmodernism is an aggressive attempt to recover popular culture, traditionally linked to a scorned 'feminine', for males. We can begin to analyze the implications of the changes in films and in television shows that earlier addressed a specifically female audience – and that therefore spoke to women's special needs, fantasies and desires within partriarchy.

If postmodernism takes away such gaps, perhaps it offers other possibilities. We need to explore fully the contradictions involved in 'co-opted' postmodernism, for once the fixed frameworks and traditional gender-oriented genres are relinquished, once signifiers are freed from the constraints such frameworks and genres impose, then both negative and positive outcomes for women may occur. Since co-opted post-modernism addresses a mass female audience, it is perhaps the most important terrain for feminist cultural studies. We need actively to resist and challenge the male qualities of violence, aggression and misogyny that mark much co-opted postmodernism and toward which women are being drawn in the mistaken belief, perhaps, that this offers liberation from earlier 'feminine' constraints. We also need to recognize the genuine places where new possibilities are offered to the female spectator by virtue of prior genre constraints being lifted.

We cannot expect a commercial medium like MTV to resist the pressures of what may indeed be a deep cultural change. And we need to see postmodernism of both kinds in the context of the great modernist movement, of the search for an alternative consciousness, cultural practice and representation to the dominant. Unfortunately, we cannot actually produce the positive or utopian postmodernism until we have managed to challenge the symbolic order sufficiently to permit its articulation. That is, we have to work through the binary oppositions by constantly challenging them before we can be beyond them. Much utopian postmodernism does just that: it stands on the shoulders of modernism and the great modernist thinkers, while struggling to move beyond their critical categories and aesthetic strategies. It moves through them by meditating upon the possibility of transcending them.

But much of what people celebrate as liberating in what I call 'co-opted' postmodernism is an avoidance of the struggle, an attempt to sidestep the task of working through the constraining binary oppositions, including sexual difference. The liberating elements in some popular culture like rock videos are important, but often superficial. Women are invested in culture's move beyond dysfunctional gender polarities, but a superficial collapsing of previously distinct female representations, for instance, gets us nowhere. This sort of strategy, as many others evident in rock videos, is preferable to the old 'realist-talking-heads', essentializing and monolithic (male) discourse of the past. But we must still be wary of making too extreme claims for what is going on. We must also be wary of assuming the acceptance by historical female subjects of the co-opted postmodernist world. Work needs to be done on the various kinds of resistances these subjects devise in the face of the commercial and technological onslaughts.

As cultural workers, we do not want to return to the error of insisting upon fixed points of enunciation, labelled 'truth'; rather, as Tony Bennett and Ernesto Laclau have both pointed out,[28] we must continue to articulate oppositional discourses – recognizing them as discourses rather than an ontological truth that theory has cast doubt on – if we are to construct new subjects capable of working toward the utopian post-modernism we all hope will be possible. This means not validating or celebrating the erosion of all categories and differences and boundaries – as Baudrillard and his followers sometimes appear to do. Feminists in particular need to continue to construct strategic subjectivities, and to use the category 'woman' as a tool to prevent the too easy and too early collapsing of a difference that continues to organize culture. As long as that difference operates, we need to counter it with the only tools we have, while simultaneously working toward a much more difficult trans-cendence – or, in Craig Owens's words,[29] toward a concept of difference without opposition.

Notes

1. Stephen Heath, quoted by Teresa de Lauretis, 'Oedipus Interruptus', in *Wide Angle*, 7, 1 & 2 (1985), pp. 34–40.
2. Marthe Robert, *The Origin of the Novel*, trans. Sacha Rabinovitch (Bloomington: Indiana University Press, 1980), which discusses and further develops Freud's early essays on 'Creative Writing and Day Dreaming', and on 'The Family Romance'. See also Roland Barthes, *The Pleasure of the Text* (New York: Hill and Wang, 1975). For excerpts from theoretical texts by French feminists dealing with alternative textual strategies, see Elaine Marks and Isabelle de Courtivron, *New French Feminisms* (Amherst, Mass: University of Massachusetts Press, 1980).
3. See Jose Ortega y Gasset, *The Dehumanization of Art* (1925) (Princeton, NJ: Princeton University Press, 1948).
4. Martha Rosler, 'Notes on Quotes', *Wedge*, 2 (fall 1982), p. 69.
5. De Lauretis, 'Oedipus Interruptus', p. 38. Page numbers refer to this version.
6. E. Ann Kaplan, 'Feminist Film Criticism: Current Issues and Problems', in *Studies in the Literary Imagination*, XIX, 1 (spring 1986), pp. 7–20.
7. Toril Moi, *Sexual/Textual Politics: Feminist Literary Theory* (London: Methuen, Inc., 1985).
8. See Craig Owens, 'The Discourse of Others: Feminists and Postmodernism', in Hal Foster, ed. *The Anti-Aesthetic: Essays on Postmodern Culture* (Port Townsend, WA: The Bay Press, 1983), p. 61.
9. Given the focus of this article, it will not be possible to deal with how postmodern-ism affects all the different kinds of feminisms; hence, I shall beg the reader's indulgence for an analysis positing a generalized 'feminism' that necessarily embodies my own biases.
10. The reasons for this are fascinating, and perhaps have to do with Bakhtin's links to both Freud and semiotics, while not adhering to either theory fully. See Robert Stam's essay in this volume.
11. See Julia Kristeva, 'Word, Dialogue, and Novel', in *Desire in Language: A Semiotic Approach to Literature and Art*, ed. Leon S. Roudiez; trans. Thomas Gora, Alice Jardine and Leon S. Roudiez (New York: Columbia University Press, 1980), p. 79. Subse-quent page references appear parenthetically.
12. See Allon White and Peter Stallybrass, *The Politics and Poetics of Trangression* (London: Methuen, Inc., 1986), p. 18.

44

13. Jean-François Lyotard, *The Postmodern Condition: A Report on Knowledge*, trans. Geoff Bennington and Brian Massumi (Minneapolis: University of Minnesota Press, 1984).

14. Robert Stam, 'Mikhail Bakhtin and Left Cultural Critique', in this volume.

15. Fred Pfeil, 'Makin' Flippy-Floppy: Postmodernism and the Baby-Boom PMC', in *The Year Left: An American Socialist Yearbook*, I, ed. Mike Davis, Fred Pfeil and Michael Sprinker (London: Verso, 1985), pp. 272, 292.

16. See Teresa de Lauretis, 'Aesthetic and Feminist Theory: Rethinking Women's Cinema', *New German Critique* 34 (winter 1985), pp. 154–75.

17. Alice A. Jardine, *Gynesis: Configurations of Woman and Modernity* (Ithaca and London: Cornell University Press, 1985).

18. See Paul Willemen, 'An Avant Garde for the Eighties', *Framework* 24 (spring 1984), pp. 53–73. One of the issues complicating the debates about postmodernism has of course been the different theories of modernism from which critics start. Willemen's article is a useful clarification of some of the confusions around modernism.

19. See Sandy Flitterman, 'The *Real* Soap Operas: TV Commercials', in E. Ann Kaplan, ed., *Regarding Television: Critical Approaches–An Anthology* (Los Angeles: The American Film Institute, 1983), pp. 84–97.

20. Jean Baudrillard, 'The Ecstasy of Communication', in Hal Foster, ed., p. 127.

21. Ibid., pp. 130–31.

22. Arthur Kroker and David Cook, *The Postmodern Scene: Excremental Culture and Hyper-Aesthetics* (New York: St Martin's Press, 1986), p. 279.

23. Jean Baudrillard, 'The Implosion of Meaning in the Media and the Implosion of the Social in the Masses', in K. Woodward, ed., *The Myths of Information: Technology and Postindustrial Culture* (Madison: Coda Press, 1980), pp. 138–48.

24. For example, see the issue of the *Journal of Communication Inquiry*, 10, 1 (winter 1986), devoted to Music Television.

25. See my *Rocking Around the Clock: Music Television, Postmodernism and Consumer Culture* (London and New York: Methuen, Inc., 1987), Chapter 3.

26. Let me note here to avoid confusion that in the following comments I am talking about the 'model' spectator the apparatus constructs, rather than about the possible modes of specific reception–including resistance–individual historical spectators may engage in. In interviews with teenagers, it became clear that historical subjects are not necessarily *tabulae rasae*, soaking up spectator positions, but employ a number of strategies to subvert or alter what they are given. Some teenagers turn off the sound and put on their own, preferred music to accompany images; others talk and comment about the images, ridiculing and spoofing the stars. Female spectators apparently manifest less of this behaviour, but a complexly organized reception study would be necessary to establish the validity of generalization.

27. See Tania Modleski, 'The Terror of Pleasure: The Contemporary Horror Film and Postmodern Theory', in Tania Modleski, ed., *Studies in Mass Entertainment: Critical Approaches to Mass Culture* (Madison, WI: University of Wisconsin Press, 1986), p. 163.

28. See Tony Bennett, 'Texts in History: The Determinations of Readings and Their Texts', in D. Attridge, G. Bennington and R Young, eds, *Post-Structuralism and the Question of History* (Cambridge: Cambridge University Press, 1987); and Ernesto Laclau, 'Populist Rupture and Discourse', *Screen Education*, 34 (spring 1980).

29. See Craig Owens, 'The Discourse of Others: Feminists and Postmodernism', in Hal Foster, ed., *The Anti-Aesthetic*, pp. 57–82.

3

Postmodernism and Cultural Analysis Today

Dana Polan

An anecdote. I was in the audience at the Modern Language Association Convention where Fred Pfeil gave a paper on the professional–managerial class that would eventually end up as his contribution to the first volume of *The Year Left.* As Fred pointedly discussed the work of Laurie Anderson to suggest how a certain new American postmodern art operated to meet the interests of an upwardly mobile sector of America concerned and fascinated with the breakup of subjectivity and the breakdown of the nuclear family, an older, left-wing professor in the process of putting together an anthology of essays on left approaches to contemporary culture, leaned over to me and asked, 'Who is Laurie Anderson?' Since he at least had the curiosity to know, his question was pleasing, but it also seemed to me symptomatic of an all too frequent divorce between the work of cultural analysts and the very cultural references that seem so much a part of American everyday life today.

More than ever, the realm of everyday consciousness becomes one whose significations are indistinguishable from the images, spectacles and messages that circulate through mass media and mass culture. We can evolve a theory and practice of the materiality of our world only if we look in detail at the ways that cultural capital becomes a central part of that materiality. In saying this, I don't mean to fall into the position of those critics who simply dismiss mass culture as a tool of domination, a force of pure regression. Quite the contrary, my own position understands culture to be a complicated blend of progressive and regressive elements. But whether we understand everyday culture as progressive or regressive or as a blend of the two, we will never be able to understand the desires that move people in our world, that bind them to certain powers and make them resist others, until we understand the role(s) of culture in relation to desire. I intend the following comments as one step in this direction.

I want specifically to concentrate on a growing interest in characterizing culture today as *postmodernist*. The postmodernist characterization suggests that we have moved from modernism's optimistic faith in technology, vision, endeavor (all reflected in the soaring lines and gleaming steel of the high modern architecture of the corporate buildings of the late 1950s and early 1960s) to a lack of interest in all expressiveness – a spectacle of superficiality which intends no celebration of myths, no superior meanings. Increasingly and significantly, cultural theorists on the left have begun to pick up the terms of postmodernist criticism. In a series of important essays, for example, Fredric Jameson has suggested that many of the qualities of life in late capitalism – in particular, the downgrading of the bourgeois individual by a vast monopolistic system of production that no longer needs, and often intentionally dismisses, him/her – has its echo in the cultural realm in a new fascination for confusion, breakdown of subjectivity, what Jameson sums up as a style of schizophrenia.

This sort of analysis is highly insightful and has already led to much productive work, but two questions should be addressed to this description of our contemporary condition as *postmodern*. First, to what extent can a description of a postmodernism *in* our culture be extended into a description of our culture *as a whole*? Already, a number of analysts of the American scene, like Mike Davis in the *New Left Review*, have suggested that 'postmodern' best applies only to certain aspects – sectors, groups, individual practices – of the cultural sphere; as Davis suggests, Jameson's invocation of LA's Bonaventure Hotel as a place that gives utopian glimpses of new forms of social interaction may miss the extent to which the Bonaventure bases its practice, however interactive, on a necessary exclusion and class division. (Built up out of the LA barrio, the hotel is divided between the very different worlds of inside and outside.)

Significantly, despite the declaration of critics like Jameson that there is *a* postmodern practice of architecture, the discourse of the architects themselves offers an agonistic field where each figure judges his postmodernism against the others: Charles Jencks criticizes Jameson's prize postmodernist, John Portman, as the last of the high modernists; Robert Venturi rejects Jencks's duck-architecture for the decorated shed architecture that Jencks abhors; Kenneth Frampton attacks Paolo Portoghese's Biennale for a notion of site-specific regionalisms, and Portoghese accuses Jencks of bourgeois subjectivity.

Of course, it is all too possible that there is a 'political unconscious', as we might call it, underlying all of this difference, but we also need to recognize the ideological irreducibility of much of that difference as it is embodied in the theory and worked out in practice. For example, Jencks's particular form of postmodernism increasingly comes to present itself in sacred terms as a new redemptive art for a fallen, agnostic age. Jencks may well reject modernism's rendition of spirituality in pure, sweeping lines of transcendental strength, but he still adheres to a notion of art as specially endowed revelation – in this case, the revelations produced by the impurities of heterogeneous ornament. Not for nothing does his postmodernism reject the Venturi position which learns from Las Vegas not that mass culture is the new religion of our age but, quite differently, that mass culture is a fully secular, non-symbolic form, which self-referentially signs nothing but its own mass-culturedness. If Jencks's references are to Milton and Blake, Venturi's are to Caesar's Palace and hot dog stands, and these differences of preference derive from a full difference in their conception of art and society, and relations between them. Not that we would want to value Venturi over Jencks: if Jencks concentrates in *Towards a Symbolic Architecture* on a whole archi-tecture of literal escapism – Cape Cod retreats, Irish vacation homes, ultra-luxurious Los Angeles and London mansions – an escapism that leaves most of the powerful operations of everyday life intact (so that one of Jencks's commissions involves designing a room for a young boy who 'might some day go into public life as a businessman or a states-man'), Venturi's theory and practice seem all the more subservient to the status quo as in his (in)famous declaration of uninterest in the open space of the piazza: '[T]he open piazza is seldom appropriate for an American city today.... The piazza, in fact, is "un-American". Ameri-cans feel uncomfortable sitting in a square: they should be working at the office or home with the family looking at television.' Significantly, Jencks's aestheticism has an ironic or parodic echo in Venturi, for whom the needs of artistic self-referentiality sometimes overcome interest in the function of architecture for its users. Hence, Venturi leaves out balconies from his version of a nursing home because ugly, flat windows signify the situation of the aged.

This last example of a postmodern practice that appears to pit the needs of art against the needs of everyday life leads to the second question we need to raise if we are to take an interest in postmodernist analysis. Even if accurate as a description, what are the implications of naming (in however totalizing a way) this or that aspect of American culture as postmodern? To what extent does an adherence to the concept of postmodernism get mapped onto a theory of cultural value, of this or that practice as more 'progressive' than some other? As we increasingly turn to postmodernity as an explanatory model, we have to examine the extent to which we assume an equivalence of postmodernity and the liberatory, of postmodern culture as inherently a revolutionary culture. Our goal, then, in looking at postmodernism has simultaneously to be theoretical – to what extent can we use 'postmodernism' as a concept in culture study? – *and* practical – to what extent would such a use help us understand the complexity of cultural politics in modern America? And to the extent that an analysis of the operations of the academy is of interest, an analysis of the increasing concern with post-modernism in humanistic and social science endeavor can also teach us about the practice of university scholarship, of the ways it functions as a source of theoretical insight (or containment of insight).

Drawn from the heart of the modernism moment, a famous letter from D.H. Lawrence to Edward Garnett can offer some early glimmer-ings of the emergence of a postmodern aesthetic:

> [W]hat is interesting in the laugh of the woman is the same as the binding of the molecules of steel or their action in heat: it is the inhuman will, call it physiology, or like Marinetti – physiology of matter, that fascinates me. I don't care so much about what the woman *feels*.... That presumes an *ego* to feel with. I only care about what the woman *is* – what she *is* – inhumanly, physio-logically, materially.... You mustn't look in my novel for the old stable ego of the character. There is another ego, according to whose action the individual is unrecognisable, and passes through, as it were, allotropic states which it needs a deeper sense to discover are states of the same single radically-unchanged element.

While this statement may seem not fully postmodern – for example, it does not specifically encourage that blend of high and popular that has come to characterize the postmodern for so many recent critics; further-more, it still partakes too much of that notion of deeper states, of richer intensities of meaning, that is indicative of modernism – none the less, we might read in Lawrence's letter a number of the familiar tactics of post-modernism. Some of these – like the way Lawrence *centers* his call for *decentering* on a discussion of *woman*, of what she is, of what she feels – I'll return to later. For the moment, I want to emphasize something else, less a theme of Lawrence's letter than part of its very practice. In this respect, we might note how the postmodern, although a concept not yet available to Lawrence, serves an enabling function in his writing: it func-tions precisely to permit that writing, to put it into play. Rethinking the ego as material, reframing the will as physiology, enables an unblocking of writing possibilities, an overcoming perhaps of the very block Raymond Williams suggests in *The English Novel* is summed up at the turn of the century by that composite novelist whose single name is Wells–Bennett–Galsworthy, and who stands so much as a pressuring force for new novelists like Lawrence.

'Postmodernism,' then, offers the new writer all the possibilities of a generative apparatus, a machine of writing, a machinal mechanism that encourages a recoding of previous forms and a proliferation of new ones. The power of the concept of postmodernism serves as a machine for generating discourse, and this is the phenomenon most in need of analysis. It is all too obvious that recent years have seen a ferocious emergence of a discourse of the postmodern, an inescapable emergence that demands reaction, the taking up of a stance or position. And yet it is all too easy to feel a certain trepidation in offering new thoughts on postmodernism. If postmodernism is indeed a machine that encourages an outpouring of critical discourse, one necessarily wonders if this machine doesn't try to limit the range of possible outcomes through such mechanisms as negative feedback and the binding of output to input that Jean-François Lyotard suggests in *The Postmodern Condition* characterizes the very performativity of machines. In other words, we might wonder if in this case, the object of discourse – postmodernism as condition of contemporary culture or politics – doesn't work to control its discourse, rather than the other way around. Can one speak of postmodernism, take a perspective on it, without being part of the postmodern effect?

It might well seem that the postmodern condition would challenge any discourse attempting to make this condition a fixed object of reference or critical analysis. Reading through some of the recent collections of writings on postmodernism – for example, in *New German Critique* or *Theory, Culture, and Society*, or *Telos* – it is easy to feel that for all their interest, their ability to provide new angles, these writings cannot say anything non-repetitive. It is as if the current forms of the postmodernist discussion simultaneously establish a certain number of terms or basic elements and set the procedures by which one can operate with these terms. One is constrained in advance to refer to certain figures, certain key texts – for example, Lyotard versus Habermas; Horkheimer and Adorno on the administered society of modern rationality – and constrained to do no more than take up any one of a number of pre-set positions on them. For example, one believes in the autonomy of the aesthetic realm or one does not; or, to take another recurrent *topos*, one believes in the Habermasian possibility of a realm of rational communication or doubts it. The postmodernist effect intensely frames critical discourse as a kind of mechanistic *combinatoire* in which everything is given in advance, in which there can be no practice but the endless recombination of fixed pieces from the generative machine.

Is there a way to take up a different or differential position in relation to the postmodern effect in contemporary critical discourse? I want to suggest that there are several strategies we can adopt to reconstellate the terms of postmodernism to increase their historical yield. At the very least, we might begin in a position of what Jameson calls 'meta-commentary', even if Jameson himself seems caught by the postmodern effect when he comes to write about it. In a metacommentary, we don't theorize postmodernism so much as we map the necessary conditions for the standard thought on postmodernism: why has it become so necessary to talk about *a* postmodern condition, what needs does that talking fulfill? The question then is not so much about the referents of post-modern discourse – what the postmodern condition is, and whether the discourse has described that condition correctly – but about what that discourse enables, and how it functions.

At its worst, postmodernist discourse frequently functions to allow entrenched academics a new way of doing the same old work. It is rare to find critics using the terms of postmodernism to look at everyday popular culture and its complexities (counter-examples that come to mind are Ann Kaplan and John Fiske on music video or Tania Modleski on the horror film). Instead, postmodernism becomes a way for the academic to insist again on the rich difficulty of difficult art. Negatively, a genealogy of high criticism in the capitalist age might suggest that this criticism preserves a realm of both freedom and responsibility for itself vis-à-vis the rest of society by repeatedly invoking a notion of an increasing heterogeneity within the purities of aesthetic form. By recognizing the intrusion of popular culture into the ostensible spirituality of high culture, heterogeneity allows the writer to claim an everyday relevance for critical work (as, for example, in Wordsworth's preface to *The Prelude*), while the very fact of heterogeneity as a complexity (as in Venturi's title, *Complexity and Contradiction in Architecture*) reserves a privilege for the critic as someone who has the superiority over mass taste by being able to cognize and render explicit what that taste can only miss or, at most, uncritically intuit. From Keatsian negative capability to the Baudelairean blend of the permanent and the transient in the heroism of an art of everyday life, to New Critical tension and ambiguity, to de Manian rhetoric and allegory, to the progressive, against-the-grain Hollywood text, to postmodernism, criticism has looked to constitute a realm of practice that might preserve plurality against logic, aesthetic richness against quotidian function.

As I hinted at the beginning of this paper, every postmodern discourse on difference involves a discourse on *sexual* difference, no matter how allegorical, no matter how much this discourse remains below the surface as part of the discourse's 'political unconscious'. All too frequently, postmodernist hierarchies of difference versus reference are mapped onto hierachies of an adventurous masculine privilege as against a dangerously debasing, earthy world of a feminine in-itself; note, for example, how one of the most significant tropes in Paul de Man's *Allegories of Reading* turns out to be 'seduction', seen as a grounding force that works against free-floating allegory and reading and is embedded in the figure of the servant girl, Marie, read by de Man as nothing more than a mere after-effect of the play of language. Increasingly, as a number of analysts of arts and the criticism of experimentation, like Tania Modleski, Andreas Huyssen and Alice Jardine, have suggested in their analyses of postmodernism, much of the postmodernist adventure seems to require the positing of a debasing stability, usually associated with the feminine, against which the heroic endeavors of postmodernism can be judged and valued. In Linda Williams's words, '[T]he myth of the individualist hero endowed with mature human dignity may in fact be the flip side to the unchanging stereotype, one subject, the other object.' In Lawrence, to go back to my earlier citation, the postmodernist example centers on the woman as repository of naive feeling, the limitations of a territorialized ego. Similarly, for all his emphasis on a generalized spirituality born from the powers of the vernacular, Charles Jencks's symbolic architecture figures the return of a fairly systematic arrangement of sexual difference. If Jencks's book, *Symbolic Architecture,* begins with a frontispiece portraying the architect as a 'strong woman', the course of the book proceeds to restore architecture to its 'proper' place by evoking the spirituality of the pyramids (with the women buried alive with their husbands) and their pharaonic cult then portraying Jencks's own adventurous work as one in which women participate only by adding ornamental flourishes or providing advice (usually about the kitchen or garden) when asked.

A second tendency of postmodernist discourse can show up in its attitude toward the popular. Increasingly, a central theme of postmodernist discourse has been a new culture's breakdown of auratic art for a hybridization wherein high and popular mutually inform each other. It seems that this thematization issues from critics who were formerly analysts of high culture alone and who now, with breathless excitement, inform us of the fascinating complexity of a new mass culture. While it is no doubt good that critics attend to popular culture, all too often this newfound interest enacts traditional evaluative classifications. In some cases, the complicated popular culture that the critics vibrantly announce is a popular culture for intellectuals, for what Fred Pfeil calls the baby-boomer 'professional–managerial class'. Not surprisingly, the popular culture that the postmodernist extolls is frequently a museum culture or a culture for a monied group (as in Fred Jameson's invocations of the public-sphere culture of the Bonaventure Hotel which, as Mike Davis points out, stands out against the LA barrio as a mark of class exclusion and fragmenting isolation). To take only one example, when Walter Benjamin-scholar Richard Wolin writes in *Telos* of postmodern popular culture, he can offer little more than a replay of that sort of upper-West-Side-New-York-culture that is a source of clichéd parody in the films of Woody Allen:

> [T]here exist significant moments of alterity amid the vast desert of cultural conformism, in the fields of film (Woody Allen), literature (the South American novel), and even popular music (Talking Heads, Brian Eno), which point beyond the usual repetition–compulsion and standardization inherent in culture industry products.

My own conviction is that the best work in cultural analysis today comes from those persons who grew up in popular culture and have long been sensitive to its complications – its restrictions of experience but also its effective and potentially expansive plays on pleasure; its realisms but also its heterogeneous blending of probable and improbable, of referentiality and self-reflexivity; its reifications of convention but also its discoveries of innovation and alterity. This complication of popular cultural form is something I have tried to analyze elsewhere. This is not to suggest that the freeing of popular culture from the constraints of a narrative logic necessarily means its freedom from the constraints of an inscription, no matter how contradictory, in ideology. Quite the contrary, contemporary cultural analysis has tended to be limited by two related premises: that mass and popular cultural practice is primarily narrative in form, *and* that ideology also necessarily exists in stories. Not until we evolve a cultural analysis that moves beyond the pressures of narrative theory will we be able to argue the functions of culture in our informational society, our society of the spectacle. We need, precisely, to theorize the function of spectacle, the powers of performance, the distribution and movement of non-narrativized signs and images in everyday life.

To take just one example, for Stuart Kaminsky in *American Film Genres* the kung fu film becomes ideological in its offering of mythic narratives of individualist male triumph over large corporate systems of control and exploitation. The seemingly different interpretation of kung fu by Derridean Claudine Eizykman in *La jouissance-cinéma* may not really be so different after all. Eizykman's view that kung fu is an experimental form which escapes from representation by offering a purely kinetic ballet of sights and sounds may well describe how kung fu is outside representation, but it doesn't necessarily lead to a notion of kung fu as outside of ideology. There might well be an ideological practice of the spectacular, a politics of the kinetic, in which one's role as spectator is not to take up myths but to avoid all myths, to fall for a pure looking that offers no critical representation of social relations, that works precisely to trade analysis of the world for a kinetic experience of it. Indeed, the very concentration on distribution of these films to inner-city minorities may well encourage an ideology of spectacle: for capitalism's reserve army of labor, it is perhaps most functional not to interpellate these groups into representation, as Althusser's theory of ideology would have it, but to offer them no representation, no narrative position.

The definition of ideology in Althusser (interpellation as the means to reproduction of productive relations) gives ideology a coherence and affirmative character that may over-generalize the diversity of particular ideological practices. The Althusserian notion of ideology seems best for that expansive capitalism geared to productivity and needing endlessly to make workers disposed toward the world of production. But today's capitalism may be as much a matter of *de*industrialization as of industralization, and here ideology may have as a function less to reproduce productive relations than to disenfranchise workers by offering no interpellative space. If an Althusserian theory of ideology had its effect in film study's concern with spectator positioning – how patterns of looking and enunciating interpellate spectators – we might also look at ways spectators are de-positioned, cut off from transcendental control, given no sense of power, no logic.

Against a notion of ideology as offering inspiring myths (e.g. Robert Ray's *A Certain Tendency of Hollywood Cinema*, which maps Althusser onto myth criticism with basic archetypes treated as ideology-ridden representations), we might consider an operation of ideology that refuses myth, cultivating incoherence. It seems to me that this is much of the function of mass culture today, with its increasing incorporation of those elements that characterize postmodernism: superficiality, pastiche, bricolage, and so on. These qualities may evidence a rejection of the narrative logic of myth, but they can still work in support of dominant power by encouraging a serialized sense of the social totality as something one can never understand and that always eludes one's grasp.

Take the case of *Rocky IV*. On one level, it seems nothing so much as the promotion of a rigorous us–them myth: the film seems intensely obvious, opening with gloves bearing American and Soviet flags flying toward each other and exploding upon contact. This mythic simplicity is echoed by stylistic naivety – the univocal voice of propaganda deploying contrastive montage (alternating shots of Rocky and Drago training), and a full-face close-up at the end when Rocky speaks about world peace.

But even more striking in the film is incoherence, the inability of all its elements to have anything to do with this dominant myth. If, as Susan Suleiman suggests in *Authoritarian Fictions*, one of propaganda's strategies is emphatic repetition of a theme, *Rocky IV* seems an emphatic breakdown of repetition, as vague motifs are suggested without crystallizing into anything meaningful. Across the film, elements reflect on each other, but the logic of this reflection is denied. For example, it would appear to be important that the wife of Rocky's opponent is played by Sylvester Stallone's bride-to-be; given the power of mass media, this bit of knowledge moves from the background to the foreground in our viewing. But it is hard to say just *how* this knowledge occupies the foreground. It hints at a meaning that never adds up. To take another example, the central theme of the inefficiency of technology against human spirit – encapsulated in the montage of Drago's training with computers and Rocky's training out in the wilderness – seems to pick up on the running joke that commences when Rocky's low-life brother-in-law is given a robot he must eventually bend to his will. But this linking of scenes can only turn the film into a parody of its myth: to compare Rocky with Pauley is to make of Rocky a joke. The film even plays on this joke when Pauley declares that he wishes he were like Rocky and then withdraws this wish when he sees how hard Drago can punch. Part of the difficulty of new postmodern mass culture is knowing how much it believes in its own myths. In the case of *Rocky IV*, the seriousness of myth is indistinguishable from a pastiche of seriousness and a deliberate cultivation of cliché (Rocky says at one point that a man's got to do what a man's got to do). Similarly, the film criticizes Apollo Creed for mistaking Drago's strength and turning their bout into Las Vegas spectacle; yet the film also presents this in vibrant detail in a number that becomes a hit-single and video. If boxing offered Sartre a figure for historical totalization, in *Rocky IV* it offers the totalization of postmodern incoherence, a complete explanation of life as beyond all explanation.

This implies, though, that a theory of postmodernity also requires historical analysis, investigation of the specific sites in which spectacles, roles and meanings circulate. This doesn't mean, however, that such history is to be thought of as a totalizing discourse, a full positivity that restores the meaning of the postmodernist venture by providing its necessary context. Instead, we would want to see history writing as an ever-moving reconfiguration or, in Walter Benjamin's terms, reconstellation that incorporates simultaneously a theory and analysis of social production *and* a theory and analysis of cultural production.

Here, I want to sketch out the beginnings of such reconstellating by engaging in, and moving out from, a preliminary critique of Lyotard's *Postmodern Condition.* On the surface, Lyotard's analysis does seem right for certain aspects of our contemporaneity, but what may finally emerge is the selectivity of the analysis. Obviously inspired by Adorno and, in a different way, by Daniel Bell, Lyotard presents the essential condition of postmodernity as the increasing scientization of the social realm – the loss of explanatory great myths and their replacement by paradigms of technicist performativity. Like Adorno, Lyotard still believes in essential realms of freedom within all this massive unfreedom – for example, the realm of the proliferation of incompatible language games that in their incompatibility maintain an integrity in relation to each other.

In its abstractness, Lyotard's scheme has its attractions, but this very abstraction makes it inadequate to deal with the complexities of culture in a particular historical moment. Against Lyotard's invocation of *a* postmodern condition, we might suggest the non-synchronous existence of a number of conditions, all of which necessitate specific analyses. For example, at the level of cultural representation, the Reagan moment can seem as characterized by a reinvestment in great myths as much as in a proliferation of tactical games: even the assassination attempt becomes a mythic narrative moment complete with its epic hero (a president who jokes on the way to the hospital and soon is playing out cowboy mythologies – chopping wood, riding a horse). Indeed, if Lyotard can argue that 'The Trilateral Commission is not a popular pole of attraction' – in other words, that the new sources of authority are not sites of mythic investment – we might note how the 1980s lead to certain attempts to make the large corporation mythic and inspiring: if the soaring lines of high modern architecture failed to provide nurturing myths of the company and suggested instead cold glass-and-steel alienations of corporate practice, the new populist strategy is to present the corporate president as a home-spun, rugged man of the people. Remington's T-shirted president speaking from his bathroom provides a beefy, tough-guy praise of electric shavers; eyepatched cable magnate Ted Turner takes breaks from boating races to do battle against bigger companies; Chrysler's Lee Iaccoca presents the everyman savior of his company and then publishes an autobiography that stays for weeks on the *New York Times* best seller list.

Yet it would be reductive to see the present moment as nothing more than the return of strong narrative. Quite the contrary, it exhibits an array of cultural practices with different forms, different functions, different subcultural audiences, and different relations to the confirmations of ideology. Narrative logic and postmodern paralogic can even coexist in the same work: it seems only appropriate that the mythic import of the assassination attempt is accompanied by a weird emphasis on the attempt as a riveting show (pre-empting the Academy Award presentations scheduled for that evening), a great spectacle in which, for example, the trajectory of the bullets is endlessly replayed in slow motion. The appropriate conclusion or punchline is that this was all done for the love of Jody Foster as she appeared in the film *Taxi Driver.*

In some cases, myth and spectacle enter into conflict. In *Speaking of Soap Operas,* Bobby Allen has analyzed this mass cultural form as a plural text that allows each subculture its own potentially incompatible reading. In other cases, we can see a mutual ideological reinforcement of myth and post-mythic postmodernism: in the American eighties, a whole slew of narratives suggest that one should run wild, be excessive, get crazy (as the title of one film has it), but only as long as the best way to do so remains within the constraints of an American productivity. Films like *Porky's, Police Academy* and especially *Stripes* reproduce the message that zaniness, disobedience, and egoism all can find their greatest welcome in the new space of the modern army. In a different register and for a distinct clientele, films like *Something Wild, Blue Velvet,* or *Desperately Seeking Susan* reinforce the same point.

At the same time, we need to move from an analysis of postmodern *culture* to *political structure,* suggesting that Lyotard's understanding of modern economics as increasing rationality is also a partial analysis. Just as the level of culture shows a range of practices from myth to spectacle to combined forms, so is there no one economic practice that characterizes the whole of late capitalism. Indeed, the theorization of late capitalism has become a target of intense debate in which different conceptual and historical models battle for privilege as the ultimate explanatory code: dependency theory, accumulation theory and commodification, capitalogic, disaccumulation theory and deindustrialization all offer competing accounts of late capitalist economic structures. It may well be that each of these approaches has its validity in specific realms of late capitalism. To take only one example, the US sunbelt economy, which extends from the deep south through the west to the computer industry world of Northern California's Silicon valley, may be the site of an intense Lyotardian performativity – no great myths here, just a world of technicians controlling input and output – and a world of increasing information and commodification. But it is also a world undergoing increasing disinvestment, periodic crisis, ecological backfire, a decline of basic services. No notion of input/output alone could account for the complicated interplay of culture and politics in such a space. As I write, the San Francisco Opera has announced that it is cancelling its entire season – the increasing non-performativity of the Silicon Valley scene where the boom of computerization seems definitively over has a rebound effect on the cultural sphere: declining salaries and spiralling inflation mean low subscriptions for cultural services.

Significantly, one of the most northern points of this complicated system is LA's Bonaventure Hotel, designed by John Portman and seen by Jameson as a supreme example of postmodernism. But what becomes apparent in Jameson's analysis, which speaks of *a* postmodernism, is the limitation of any one notion of what such a hotel implies: the Bonaventure is both functional (it was one of the hotels for the 1983 Modern Language Association) and dysfunctional (its stores go out of business); it is a utopian realm of public interaction *and* a paradigm of all the divisions that destroy the possibility for such a public to exist and sustain itself.

The contradictions within the texts of postmodernism must also be understood in terms of the contradictions of social production and economy: what does it mean, for example, that I write this essay in a deindustrialized city where performativity of the machine no longer seems to matter (some former steel towns surrounding Pittsburgh have unemployment as high as 90 per cent), where the corporations do little to foster grand myths (for example, US Steel, which has its corporate headquarters in the city where it has shut down most of its steel production, recently changed its name to the more technicist 'USX'). But Pittsburgh is also a city in which everyday life demonstrates an amazing proliferation of mythic narratives. For example, it sustains an intense interest in public figures, a fanatical devotion to sports, and an extreme investment in holidays and rituals (Oktoberfests, church bazaars and so on). Not surprisingly, perhaps, these contradictions have their correspondence in the cultural realm: Pittsburgh has become a city of administered entertainment (it is defined as a market for action films) and simultaneously a site of commercial experiment (Pittsburgh is the city where the most advanced cable system, with the most numerous offerings, was test-marketed).

All this is to say that our goal in relation to this cultural moment may be less to focus on one form – narrative, for example – or to encourage a proliferation of non-communicating, incompatible forms, but to work to conjoin seemingly isolated forms in newly expansive critical frameworks. It also matters that this critical montage juxtaposes not any elements whatsoever, but blends a theory of culture with a theory of social production and a theory of desire. Let me end with an example that may move toward this conjunction: significantly, it is an example whose status – is it a primary work of postmodern culture, is it a work of critical analysis? – is undecidable. Always engaging in a cut-up procedure, an inventive bricolage, the punk rock magazine *Maximum Rocknroll* suddenly shifted to a new practice in its October 1986 issue. While the bottom of the cover promised the usual pieces on 'Maimed for life', 'Butcher', 'Deformed', most of the front cover was given over to an emphatic announcement:

If you

don't wonder why the United States feels so threatened by small, insignificant countries and finds it necessary to control them or smash them into oblivion . . .

aren't frustrated by continued American economic support for the racist regime in South Africa . . .

aren't puzzled by continued US testing of nuclear weapons while the USSR has unilaterally ceased doing so . . .

could care less why so many immigrants are forced to leave their homelands to 'steal' your jobs in the US . . .

are never going to read a lengthy article in this magazine cuz you're lazy or think we're a bunch of self-righteous commies . . .

Then if you read the transcription of a speech by Noam Chomsky in this issue, do it with anything approaching an open mind, and do the least amount of follow-up investigation of the information presented, we feel that the time spent may change your entire way of thinking. This especially applies to those of you who feel 'pride' for your country, for those who wear an American flag on their jackets, and for those thinking about enlisting in the military.

Inside, for eight tight, double-columned, single-spaced pages, was printed a speech by Chomsky on 'The Global Drift Towards Nuclear War'.

It is all too easy for this article to become part of a generalized post-modern effect, one more disconnected sign that floats within the hetero-geneity of proliferating spectacles; indeed, a first reaction to the whole phenomenon might be to register the weirdness of this act, the sublime surreality by which this speech can show up there (and be made known to me by the owner of a comic book store). And yet, certain aspects of this conjoining resist the pure reduction of text to interactive elements whose content becomes a matter of indifference. Not that the discourse of rock or the discourse on nuclear war have fully positive real referents; in our immediate context, however – a context in which rock all too often weaves its postmodern effect by a spectacle of meaningless juxta-position – this conjunction might have a new productive effect, a new way of configuring culture and society. In this example, no doubt a minor one, I wonder if we might not see one case of a postmodernist practice that goes beyond certain effects of postmodernism, that turns those effects into an object for its own intense and critical meta-commentary.

4

Potholders and Subincisions: On *The Businessman, Fiskadoro,* and Postmodern Paradise

Fred Pfeil

There is a well-known drawing – it often shows up in books on visual perception in the fine arts or in cinema – which, depending on how it strikes you, looks either like a properly fitted-out young Gibson girl, the ideal type of young womanhood in early twentieth-century America, or like an ugly old street hag: the point, of course, is simply that it is impossible to see the drawing simultaneously as both. Yet that point, so quickly noted and passed over in the textbooks, hardly exhausts the picture's meanings; it is not just any interchangeable *trompe l'oeil* we are staring at, after all, but one whose power to startle, shock, and amuse even now is imbricated in and complicit with a whole repertoire of classist and sexist themes through which a past generation's sense of beauty/ propriety/value and ugliness/degradation/horror was constructed and maintained.

I think of that drawing now, of the way it works and the ideologies on which it draws, because *The Businessman* and *Fiskadoro,* the two books I want to describe and discuss here, offer us a similarly ambiguous, complicated pleasure. A doubly ambiguous pleasure, more specifically: first, insofar as the power of both derives from their distinct but related strategies for effacing the boundaries between order and nightmare, laughter and horror; second, insofar as those effacements, and the vertiginous slides they effect in us, from delight to dread in turn, are symptomatic of our own entanglement in an ideological web of themes and discourse we have come to describe as the postmodern. This essay began with the curious powerful mixture of delight and discomfort, *jouissance* and revulsion, which both these books touched off in me; then it took on a more decided shape as I came to see how readily and appropriately the strange representations and deranged plottings they offer us may be understood as celebrations of the Kristevan semiotic, refusals of any steady border between the impure flux of abjection and the sanitized oedipal zone of ordered, isolate subjectivity, under the sign of the (male, white, bourgeois) ego. My claim for these texts, in short, is that they offer us something like the taste of a certain poststructuralist, feminist utopia: or, if you like, they provide us with an embodiment of some of postmodernism's most fundamental utopian themes.[1] (And if, as I strongly suspect, Thomas Disch and Denis Johnson, our two novelists, are unaware of the theoretical discourses in which this utopianism has been expressed by Barthes, Kristeva, Cixous, etc., then so much the better!) But having set forth and, I hope, persuaded you of that claim in the descriptions that follow, it is my first reaction to these depictions, that initial queasiness, to which I shall return, and from which I hope to pry some theoretical and political conclusions at last.

Before we enter into the descriptions that follow, though, a word of defense and apology is in order. Novels are, after all, hardly the dominant form of cultural expression and representation in our time, and, accordingly, unlikely to be the raw material from which the newest, sharpest, most cutting-edge analysis of the postmodern condition is to be worked up. Indeed, what follows assumes that most readers of this and other essays on postmodern culture and politics are as ignorant of Disch's and Johnson's fiction as those authors are of poststructuralist theory; it will therefore be necessary to quote from and describe each of these books at some length, merely to get their particular, peculiar flavors across to you. To justify such retrograde choices, I offer two lines of defense: first, the slightly perverse argument that the very marginality of the novel within the ensemble of contemporary cultural forms and practices *enhances* the salience and symptomacity of the representations of postmodern structures of feeling as we find them here – even, as it were, in these two *books*, of all things; second, that the disadvantage of necessarily extensive quotation is at least to some extent offset by the fact that books are directly quotable in print, in a way that films, video, and the Westin Bonaventure quite obviously are not.

And yet it may be that the best introductory terms of comparison for Thomas Disch's *The Businessman: A Tale of Terror* come from film, after all; certainly it has less in common with other books I've read (except for others by Disch himself) than with movies like *Ghostbusters* or *An American Werewolf in London*, which offer something like the same dialectically subversive mixture of comedy and horror it provides. The basic joke, you will recall – and source of horror as well – in those films is precisely the grotesque coincidence of the terrifying and the banal: as in *Werewolf*, for example, whenever Jonathan's undead friend shows up in a new stage of putrefaction to find out how things are going, what's happening in his friend's sex life, and when he's going to kill himself or get himself killed so that his rotting pal can fully die and depart in peace; or in *Ghostbusters*, most notably when the fiendish arch-devil nemesis finally arrives on the scene, stumping gigantically up Central Park West in the guise of the Sta-Puff Marshmallow man. So. too, it is in Disch's 'tale of terror', in which a demon halfling assumes the guise of a cocker spaniel, a robin, and an all-American boy named Jack, one way into paradise leads up through the main escalator of the Sears Building on Lake Street in downtown Minneapolis, and, as we shall shortly see in more detail, personal dissolution and heavenly bliss are attainable through a kind of ecstatic fusion with a red-and-white potholder held magnetically to the front of the fridge.

Yet such playfully random minglings of the banal with the horrific and sublime do not begin to suggest the full extent of Disch's blithe transgressiveness, which also shows up in both *The Businessman*'s pointedly unconventional plotting and in the smooth irreverent shifts in voice and diction from high formality to dumbbell chattiness. These features have always characterized Disch's style, but here are taken to new extremes. One has, in fact, only to read the jacket copy (written by Disch himself) for the hardcover American edition to see both features abundantly in evidence, together with the minglings of terror, wonder, and the most banal, commodified quotidian life just described:

> Murdering your wife might not sound all that difficult, and in the case of Bob Glandier it was dead simple. Agenda: fly to Las Vegas, enter the Lady Luck Motor Lodge, strangle, get back on the plane to Minnesota, and resume life as an upper-echelon executive. What came afterward was not so simple.
>
> Still in the grave when the novel opens, and none too pleased, Bob's wife Giselle can foresee that she will be obliged to haunt him. There isn't much else to think about in her situation. Quite inadvertently, Giselle's mother, Joy-Ann, releases her daughter's spirit one day, the only casualty being that she loses her own life in the process.
>
> While Giselle is out discovering how unpleasant it is to haunt her husband, Joy-Ann arrives in Paradise (not to be confused with 'Heaven', which is the next stage along and designed along less mortal, more 'Looking-into-the-face-of-God' lines). Joy-Ann meets Paradise's coordinator, the famous nineteenth-century actress Adah Menken, who explains the use of 'Home Box Office', where events of your own and your relatives' lives can be played in any order. Adah and Joy-Ann can see that they have a lot of intervening to do to sort out the evil that began at the Lady Luck Motor Lodge.
>
> The ghost of poet John Berryman plays a major – often heroic – role in this drama, which is just as well because at the time he meets Giselle he has become thoroughly bored with suburban séances (his dyslexia making him particularly hopeless at Ouija boards). Elaborate hauntings lie ahead for

Berryman and Giselle, transmogrifications and, above all, a battle against the force which will turn a white Scottish terrier and a heron into killers – not to mention a rather engaging little boy who will soon be known as 'Charlie Manson writ small'.

How a novel can at once be so lighthearted and so utterly terrifying is something only Thomas M. Disch can answer. *The Businessman* is like *The Exorcist* in a playful mood. The living, the dead and the indeterminate form a cast of characters who interact in a fashion that is disarmingly logical. 'Who would have thought that the afterlife had so many rules?' asks Berryman. Many murders and unspeakable horrors later, it seems oddly clear that terms could never have been struck with the businessman any other way.[2]

Except perhaps for the patently mendacious claim that the actions depicted in the course of the novel are 'disarmingly logical' – so much so that by the novel's end it is 'oddly clear' why things had to happen the way they did — all this is perfectly true to the way *The Businessman* actually sounds and works. Unlike other postmodern authors, who have sought to loose narrative from the double-hinged grip of the proairetic ('what happens next?') and hermeneutic ('what's the point?'), as Disch himself has done in earlier work (his *334*, just reissued in paperback, is nothing less than a structuralist masterpiece, the novel of late-capitalist urban life as *combinatoire*), here Disch destroys the plot from within, as it were, by so multiplying its codes and proliferating and entangling its narrative lines and characters as to render plot a diffuse, zany blur. His heroine, Giselle, dead and rotting as the novel begins, becomes a barely sentient tree three-quarters of the way through the book, and effectively disappears, as indeed does the businessman of the book's title, fat murderous Bob Glandier, for much of the time. Meanwhile, the play of codes around what the jacket copy calls 'the living, the dead and the indeterminate' – all the random rules of the afterlife for communication between, possession of, and even sexual relations with the still living – proliferates and mutates so constantly and arbitrarily, in the midst of so much frenzied action, that as Adah Menken at one point tells Giselle's dead mother Joy-Ann, 'There's no time to get into the theory of what's real and what isn't' (p. 110). No more time than there is, in effect, to think about the codes and discourse at work on the billboards flashing by on the beltway into the city, or on the torrent of thirty-second spots that rush past during station breaks on the tube.

And this comparison with the rapid, fluid discourse of the TV commercial, simultaneously sophisticated in technique and allusiveness, and crude or even infantile in its basic appeal, fits as a way into the workings of Disch's style as well. As he himself has described it elsewhere, it is 'a prose that slides by quarter-notes and leaps by octaves; lyric outbursts leading to deadly banalities; details dwelt upon at inexplicable length and whole masses of exposition disposed of at a shrug; and always the feeling of the whole not quite balancing, of the narrator being quite mad and at the same time completely ordinary.'³

Is the jacket copy I have quoted above sufficient evidence of the accuracy of this self-description? Perhaps not: so here are three passages, each concerned with one or another of the manifold climactic actions or outcomes of *The Businessman*'s woolly plot. In the first, a passage to which we will later have occasion to return, the dead Giselle, released now from the task of haunting her husband Bob Glandier, is able at last to enter into the rapture of the red potholder for which she has yearned so long:

> When she touched it, the barking or crying grew louder. The tip of her finger tingled. The sensation spread through her body in waves, and then her body altogether disappeared, and she had entered the space she had so many times before sought to enter and failed: a pattern of crossed lines, an immense red-checked veil that parted now to reveal another veil, identical to itself, towards which she fell as towards a net. But the net parted, or she passed through its interstices, and the pattern was repeated, mindlessly, meaninglessly, again and again, until the white spaces within the red lines gradually darkened, like a twilight that slowly deepens to night. From time to time she would hear the barking of the dog, and then there was a larger darkness and a deeper silence and sleep closed around her like a blanket being tucked into place by a gigantic hand. (pp. 196–7).

Note the smooth slack languor of the additive sentences depicting this ecstasy; the faded, *recherché* quality of the twilight–darkness imagery, which begins as a simile and then, in the next sentence, slides over into a truth ('a larger darkness'), which itself provides the occasion for an even more wholeheartedly clichéd and bathetic figure of speech ('like a blanket being tucked into place ...'); the curious hush, simultaneously reverential and insipid, that hangs over the passage as a whole.

Now watch the equivalent play, though differently staged, between the elevated and the banal in this description of Bob Glandier's grisly end, as the demon halfling and spawn that has dogged his trail throughout the second half of the novel now leaps into his dead wife's rotting corpse at the funeral home and tricks Glandier onto the moving belt leading into the crematorium:

> Glandier's screams, as he was pulled by his necktie down the metal-rollered incline beyond the double doors (in much the same way a carton of canned goods enters the basement of a supermarket), could not be heard above the hymn's joyous conclusion. The doors closed behind him, and for a moment all was blackness. Then through the grating of the grille on which he lay he saw

the hundred blue flames of the crematorium winking on, row upon row, as his wife's grinning, fleshless mouth rose towards his to seal their union with a final kiss. (p. 276).

Here, of course, the joke is the apparently tossed-off comparison lying embedded in parentheses at the heart of the otherwise elegantly periodic sentence that opens the paragraph and establishes its official high-toned horror: a kind of casual aside which nonetheless lingers through the faintly stale, elevated syntax ('for a moment all was blackness') and diction ('to seal their union with a final kiss') that follow, blunting the conventional intentions and effects of such high style with its low-life presence, idly planting a trace-image of the half-dead life of commodified production and consumption at the heart of the horror. But this element or register of the numb, the stale, the commodified, is capable at other moments of all but completely overwhelming the elevated and/ or sacred altogether. Consider the following, when Adah Menken and John Berryman (or their souls, anyhow) are found in the middle of an otherworldly landscape called the Spiritual Mississippi, and are picked up by Jesus himself in a dirigible

at least as large as the mother ship that lands on Satan's Bluff at the end of *Close Encounters*. Its vast bulk was given over to a complicated array of blinking lights that alternated the single, cheery exclamation
SAVED!!
with explosions and geysers and pinwheels of shimmery color, each of them an advertisement and a promise of heavenly bliss. (p. 281).

Traditionally, as Rosemary Jackson has argued, the literature of the gothic and fantastic works by recontaining the defiled and/or demonic psychosocial elements it first released: the ghosts are exorcized, the transgressors punished or destroyed, the endless maze or heap of evil circumstances replaced by the orderly rule of the rational, the forces of darkness by the forces of light.[4] For Jackson, and even more decisively for Julia Kristeva in her *Powers of Horror*, those defiled, demonic elements at the core of the text of horror have their source in the oedipal drama at precisely that moment when the oedipal subject is fully separated and distinguished from a mother-figure who must henceforward be feared and despised as the *abject*: the dangerous mire in which the order of the oedipal symbolic collapses and sinks, where the monstrous, perverse, polluted and abominable reign; the place, within patriarchy, of despised femininity itself, conjured up in the horror text only so that it may be all the more decisively mastered and forcibly expelled by its close.[5] One definition of the *feminist* text of horror would then be a text which refuses such closure, which valorizes and leaves unrestrained the free-floating play of the abject elements released from the Ego's grip; but another, arguably just as valid, might be the text which simultaneously observes and subverts conventional resolution, and in so doing erodes the demarcation between abject and subject, the pre-oedipal and oedipal, feminine and masculine itself, so intrinsic to patriarchal order and rule. And if the latter, is not *The Businessman* itself as I have been describing it above, with all its randomly proliferating rules and codes, its sliding, deco-pastiche style, parodic resolutions, and diffuse, floating excess of character and plot, precisely an example of such a text – the text as 'that uninhibited person who shows his behind to the Political Father', in effect?[6]

Many readers whose data banks are sufficiently well stocked with key lines from the canonical texts of poststructuralist critical theory will realize without checking the last footnote that I have shifted over from *Powers of Horror* to *The Pleasure of the Text*, from Kristeva to Barthes. And when we do, we find *The Businessman* waiting to greet us as well, this time as *le texte de jouissance*, the 'text of bliss: the text that imposes a state of loss ... that unsettles the reader's historical, cultural, psychological assumptions, the consistency of his tastes, values, memory, brings to crisis his relations with language'; the text 'we read ... the way a fly buzzes around a room: with sudden, deceptively decisive turns, fervent and futile'; the text in which 'the opposing forces are no longer repressed in a state of becoming: nothing is really antagonistic, everything is plural', and in which 'I [the blissful reader] pass lightly through the reactionary darkness'.[7]

Or, while we're at this marshalling of banners, why not note as well the degree to which *The Businessman* enlists as well and as gleefully in Hélène Cixous's campaign against the repressive hegemony of the unitary (i.e., male, oedipal) subject and the 'fetishization of "character"' which is the chief expression of that hegemony within literary–aesthetic ideology? ' "I", ' ... Cixous writes, 'must become a "fabulous opera" and not the area of the known. Understand it the way it is: always more than one, diverse, capable of being all those it will at one time be, a group acting together, a collection of singular beings that produce the enunciation. Being several and insubordinable, the subject can resist subjugation.'[8] We will have occasion in the closing section of this essay to return to that last sentence and consider more closely its adequacy as a prescription for a radical politics. For now, I merely want to suggest that in *The Businessman*'s swirl of metamorphosing characters, including the dead, the sort-of-dead, and the sort-of-alive, we have a quintessentially postmodern text which meets these feminist–poststructuralist demands as well; what more could Cixous wish for than a text in which the ostensibly principal characters (one of whom, as I have already mentioned, becomes the spirit of a tree) are displaced from any central hold or stable position in the book's actions by a welter of other entities, several of whom are capable, under the capricious, volatile "rules" of the after-life, of assuming the shape of a frog or a dog or a statue of a black jockey or of the Virgin Mary, to name only a few of the changes *The Businessman* puts its 'characters' through? Indeed, given these qualities, plus its curious style and wandering, loopy plot, could we not nominate Disch's novel for consideration as a 'woman-text' in Cixous's terms: one, that is, 'which gets across a detachment, a kind of disengagement, not the detachment that is immediately taken back but a real capacity to lose hold and let go [which] takes the metaphorical form of wandering, excess, risk of the unreckonable'?[9]

I have introduced these quintessentially poststructuralist definitions, assumptions and problematics just now, and quoted from them at length, not merely because of their uncanny relevance to *The Businessman*, but because of the equivalent but quite different ways in which many of them seem to apply to Denis Johnson's *Fiskadoro* as well, yet another contemporary American novel written by a man who probably knows nothing about poststructuralist critical theory. With this novel, however, rather than beginning with promotional copy[10] let us start with the opening paragraph, which introduces the strange, dis-embodied, unplaceable narrative voice that floats in and out of the rest of the book.

> Here, and also south of us, the beaches have a yellow tint, but along the Keys of Florida the sand is like shattered ivory. In the shallows the white of it turns the water such an ideal sea-blue that looking at it you think you must be dead, and the rice paddies, in some seasons, are profoundly emerald. The people who inhabit these colors, thanked be the compassion and mercy of Allah, have nothing much to trouble them. It's true that starting a little ways north of them the bodies still go on and on, and the Lord, as foretold, has crushed the mountains; but it's hard to imagine that such things ever went on in the same universe that holds up the Keys of Florida. It strains all belief to think that these are the places the god Quetzalcoatl, the god Bob Marley, the god Jesus, promised to come back to and build their kingdoms. On island after island, except for the fields of cane popping in the wind, everything seems to be asleep. (p. 3).

Here is an opening in which the conventional introductory tasks of spatial and temporal placement are as much flouted as observed. We are referred to the Florida Keys, all right, whose landscape and atmosphere are described at some length; but where is the 'Here, and also south of us' from which this narration is launched? Similarly, though we might correctly suspect from the reference to Bob Marley and to massive destruction that the events to be depicted in the course of the novel are set in a post-apocalyptic future, the opening paragraph suggests the narrative which follows will be a retrospective one, or that, in other words, the narration is moving between two indeterminable planes of futurity: an earlier, originary time from the unnamed narrator's point of view, from which the actions to be recuperated and recounted come; and a second future, the future-present of the narration itself, set within the context of a new, polyglot civilization (as evidenced by the apparently equally weighted references to an Aztec god, a Rastafarian reggae superstar, and the son of God in the Christian faith) whose dimensions and character remain as unknowably mysterious to us as they are taken for granted by the narrator him(?)self.

The equivalent of the dissolute forces of the swirling spirit-world in *The Businessman* as assault forces on the settled order of conventional space-time in classical narrative is thus in *Fiskadoro* post-apocalyptic futurity itself; the splintered, fragmentary story it has to tell, we are informed by the narrator, is set 'in a time between civilizations and a place ignored by authority' (p. 12), in a spatio-temporal suspension between nuclear holocaust behind (and north) of the Florida Keys, and the emergence of a new religious kingdom and order sometime later, somewhere else. And throughout the rest of the book the narration's sudden, inexplicable point-of-view shifts from character to character and slack, oblique plotting work together to maintain that sense of suspension and drift. The boy Fiskadoro, title character and, according to the narrator in his/her indeterminate future, something of a hero-to-be as well ('Fiskadoro, the one known to us best of all, the only one who was ready when we came', p. 12) is, like Glandier and Giselle of *The Businessman*, absent from the book much of the time, as attention and point of view shift over to a number of other characters, chief among whom are Mr Cheung, manager of the Miami Symphony Orchestra, such as it is, resident of and one-time mayoral candidate in Twicetown (a.k.a. Key West in pre-apocalytic nomenclature), and his grandmother, half-British, half-Chinese survivor of both the fall of Saigon and the holocaust, now over a hundred years old, 'the oldest person on earth' (p. 12).

Each of these characters lives an almost totally anomalous, non-synchronous relationship to the present world of part-objects, fragments, and squashed language which they all tangentially inhabit. Fiskadoro, when we first encounter him, is awash in adolescent transition to adulthood, uncertainly situated in an oedipal sexual constellation of the primitive fishing village of Army (once, in our time, a military base, presumably) where his mother and family live, the sketchy boro of Twicetown where Mr Cheung lives, and the night beaches, where

Fiskadoro dances around fires set in radioactive oil drums together with the tribal people who come out of the swamps after dark. Mr Cheung, in turn, is devoted to conserving the few ill-matched scraps of history and knowledge – the names of the states, a demotic version of the Declaration of Independence, the classical music he refers to as 'the blues', his grandmother herself – he has been able to shore up and stash away: 'History,' he thinks, 'the force of time – he was aware he was obsessed in an unhealthy way with these thoughts – are washing over us like this rocknroll. Some of us are aligned with a slight force, a frail resistance that shapes things for the better – I really believe this: I stand against the forces of destruction, against the forces that took the machines away' (p. 122–3). But for the old woman, Grandmother Wright, who behaves 'as if she forgot everything as soon as it happened' (p. 32), the end of the world began 'on the day when her father took his life' (p. 72) and has not ceased happening – not with her flight from Vietnam, nor with the nuclear holocaust, nor any other event – ever since: 'Whatever it was, it was happening now, today, all of it, this very moment. This very moment – *now*, changing and staying the same – was the fire' (p. 125).

In addition to being centered around a protagonist rendered as a unitary subject, a relatively unproblematic and evolving Ego-Ideal in effect, the traditional novel opposed by Barthes and Cixous to the 'text of bliss' or 'woman-text' offers us a coherent accumulation of represented experience, tagged and ordered for ready consumption. In the decentered, gelatinous universe of *Fiskadoro*, however, aside from the tenuous circumstances tying the characters together (through Mr Cheung, significantly enough, as both the old woman's grandson and Fiskadoro's sometime music teacher and would-be mentor), any sense of narrative development is undercut and diffused by the constant, oblique shifts in chronology and point of view, into a complex and covert thematic music of memory leading up to and washed away by the undertow of loss, forgetfulness, and oblivion. In fact, the two main events of the novel both begin with the death of a father – Grandmother Wright's father's suicide when she was still a girl in Saigon; Fiskadoro's father's drowning at sea. Both are recounted only retrospectively, and both end in a loss of memory and identity so complete as to constitute simultaneously a life lived absolutely in a pure present tense and a death of the self. Fiskadoro flees from 'the border of this black country [the ocean] where his father lived' (p. 112) into the swamps, in pursuit of a young black swamp-woman – into what seems at first, in other words, a quintessential landscape of the unknown, the feminine, the Kristevan abject:

She was gone into nothing, but he knew how to follow her steps as certainly as

if he carried a map – there wasn't any way to go but down. Below the level of
the dune the wind was stuck. It was like being swallowed alive. The air choked
him; and he recognized the odor – it was hers; she smelled like the swamps,
like her birthplace and her home. To follow her over the dunes and out of
earshot and eyesight of his people, his head spinning and his throat blocked
with the honey of tears, was not to know whether he would live or die. Don't
look what I'm doing! he begged the dark sea. (p. 114).

Yet, if there is already something not quite sufficiently stable or
conventional about this ocean/swamp opposition as a figure for the
oedipal split between phallic Father and feminine Abject – the sea is,
after all, the element in which Fiskadoro's father Jimmy has drowned,
and is also, in conventional poetic and psychoanalytic imagery, precisely
an image for pre-oedipal immersion in the omnipresent Mother – what
follows Fiskadoro's flight complicates and muddles this psychic landscape even more. For the swamp itself, we will learn retrospectively,
many pages later, becomes the site of a male initiation ritual which fails
– and is, perhaps, intended to fail – to deliver Fiskadoro to the order of
the Symbolic as much as it succeeds. Mistaken by the people of the
swamp for a young man of their tribe who in reality has drowned in the
surf – mistaken as a new body carrying the same soul, that is – he is
swept along into a complex initiation rite in which the drugs he is given
first endow him with total recall of his entire life, and then – at somewhere near the same moment that he subincises his own penis with a
sharp rock – obliterate his memory completely: 'His head was a blank,
he felt no pain. Now he was like other men' (p. 185).

If this is Fiskadoro's induction into masculinity, then, it is a perversely
non- or even anti-oedipal one: as one of the novel's minor characters, a
drifting smuggler, trader, and con-man named Martin puts it later, '"I
think ... all what they have to remember back for the ceremony, es a
lotta trash. Not important. The old fathers just only want the boys to
forget. When es all done finish, the boys don't even know they name"'
(p. 163). So Fiskadoro is, by this abjection–subjection, plunged into a
non-linguistic perpetual present in which 'Every time he looked at
something, it came up before his eyes for the first time, unexplained and
impossible to understand' (p. 185) and in which, once he is back home
in Army again, even his mother, Belinda, is only a body discovered lying
nearby at night, something to feel for, touch, and probe until she
smacks him away. Eventually, thanks in part to Mr Cheung's minis-
trations, Fiskadoro's short-term memory will return to some extent; but
even then, in the closing pages of the book, 'Fiskadoro didn't know what
his teacher was talking about, as he hardly ever knew what anybody was
talking about' (p. 217). Still, as even Mr Cheung realizes and admits in
the same scene, that very incomprehension and oblivion are also a

source of strength. '"You'll be a great leader,"' Cheung prophesies; '"You've been to their world and now you're in this world, but you don't have the memories to make you crazy"' (p. 217).

Such oblivion, moreover, is the same endpoint Grandma Wright reaches in her perpetual replay of her nightmarish flight from Saigon and the helicopter crash that follows it, as a result of which the young girl Marie Wright must float in the sea for something over two days and nights, long after almost everyone else around her has drowned:

> By sunset she was only a baby, thinking nothing, absolutely adrift, waking to cough and begin crying, drifting and weeping, sleeping and sinking, waking up to choke the water from her mouth and whimper, indistinguishable from what she saw, which was the gray sky that had no identity, interest, or thought. This was the point when she reached the bottom of everything, when she had no idea what she'd reached or who had reached it, or even that it had been reached. (p. 220).

Only in such a state of perfect oblivion can she be saved; just as only now that he has been disburdened of his history, his language, and his past, is Fiskadoro capable of leading the way into the new future that, at the novel's close, might just be coming towards all three of them through the haze over the sea – 'a white boat, or was it a cloud' (p. 220). Characteristically, we never find out which; instead, in the novel's closing paragraph, the line between what lies behind and what looms ahead, between memory and oblivion, life and death, is further blurred as the point of view shifts to Grandmother Wright, who is either still remembering, or seeing what is there in the actual present, or perhaps dying at last 'Nodding down into a nap beneath the canopy of her memories, she jerked awake and saw the form again in the early mist of the second morning and the third day – a rock, a whale, some white place to cling to, sleep, and breathe. And in her state of waking, she jerked awake. And from that waking, she woke up' (p. 221).

This descriptive analysis of Fiskadoro's themes and workings thus leads towards a conclusion similar to the one we have already reached apropos of *The Businessman*. Here is a novel, after all, which not only subverts the fixed categories and conventions of classical narrative – stability of narration, specificity and rationality of space-time, unitary characterization, and the developmental linear trajectory of plot – but which takes up the problematization and dismantling of bourgeois-oedipal constructs of identity, continuity, and eventfulness as its very subject matter. A novel, moreover, in which even the one character who still stands up for those retrograde notions admits the appeal of (as Deleuze and Guattari might put it, to invoke yet two more French poststructuralist theorists[11]) the new, unrestricted schizoid self, awash in its desiring flows, freely floating in the warm, amniotic currents of the Kristevan or Barthesian semiotic, untethered by memory to any fixed sense of the self: 'There was something to be envied in that,' thinks Mr Cheung, oblivion's ineffectual antagonist, in the presence of Fiskadoro's new non-self. 'In a world where nothing was familiar, everything was new. And if you can't recall the previous steps in your journey, won't you assume you've just been standing still? If you can't remember living yesterday, then isn't your life only one day long?' (p. 192).

The question is for Mr Cheung a more or less rhetorical one; it expresses a fantasy of what seems to him at the moment a kind of blissful state he can imagine yet, given his attachment to continuity, culture and history, cannot share. It is at just this point that I want to urge the same question as well, together with a set of crude questions of my own. How does it sound, this blissful state of being, this perpetual schizoid present, this rapture Fiskadoro enters on the other side of his subincision, and *The Businessman*'s Giselle finds passing in and through the potholder towards her final incarnation as the spirit of a tree?

> Thinking was no more than a kind of tune she could hum or not hum as she chose. ... There was something so pleasing about having no thoughts at all. Rather like swimming under water, but without the need to hold her breath. Yet in a way she *was* thinking. Even this slow, subaqueous drift of dim pleasure was a *kind* of thought, a tree's thoughts, a way of swaying in the breeze and going nowhere. (*The Businessman*, p. 211).

If those postmodern texts do, as I have argued so far, offer us an incarnation, an embodiment, a *taste* of something like the radical utopia an ostensibly feminist and anti-capitalist poststructuralism has marked out theoretically for us, does our readerly experience of such moments unambiguously tempt us to deconstruct and disseminate ourselves (if we have not yet already done so), to pass through the potholder, take the swamp-people's drug, become tree spirits ourselves?

These are rhetorical questions of course, rude provocations against which, unless I tread with care, rather more substantive objections than merely those against my lack of tact might be raised. So let me hasten to say that I do not consider any of the representations afforded us by these novels, or, for that matter, any of our reactions to those representations, however clear, ambiguous, or complex they might be, to originate in some never-never land out beyond ideology, in untrammeled, unmediated Experience itself, on the firm solid earth of the Real. Nor, as is perhaps already clear, do I believe that poststructuralist theory emanates from any such transcendental zone. Yet to admit the inherently ideological nature of all such representations, reactions, and arguments, including my own here, need not and should not lead to any glib dismissal of them as *mere* ideology: not if the ideological (and discursive) arises only in conjunction with active social practice, specific collectivities and institutions; not insofar as given ideological discourses do irrefutably have their effects, make their marks quite literally upon the world.

It is in this sense, then, and with these caveats in mind, that even in this post-Althusserian age we can still follow up Frank Kermode's dictum that 'Fictions are for finding things out; and they change as the needs of sense-making change.'[12] What does it mean, then, that we have on the one hand what is by now a veritable legacy of theoretical texts, concepts, and arguments which criticize classical narrative and the unitary bourgeois self in the name of heteroglossia, dissemination, decentering, the flux of the semiotic, and a new, post-oedipal, non-unitary subjectivity which 'Being several and insubordinable ... can resist subjugation' (Cixous); and on the other, these two postmodern novels, with their representations and embodiments, their *trying-ons*, I want to say, of just such radical states of being-in-flux – trying-ons which, in turn, excite in us an ambivalent, fearful delight, a blend of *jouissance* and revulsion at best? With what social practices, institutions, collectivities are these various inherently ideological discourses and reactions aligned; what kinds of social practice, institutions, collectivities do they reflect, prophesy, reinforce?

A full genealogical working out of these questions would obviously require an argument many times the length of the present essay. Rather than attempt it, then, I shall instead try to formulate some necessarily tentative and, I hope, provocative propositions and overlapping suggestions, as a starting-point for theoretical and political work which lies before us to be done. One central aspect of that work, as I imagine it, would involve taking up the question of the socio-historical field in which our current structuralist and poststructuralist ideologies *of* the relations between ideology and subject-formation first appeared and took their present shape; first in the work of Althusser, and subsequently in that of Barthes, Kristeva, Cixous, and, in Britain, their squads of *epigoni* in and around the film journal *Screen*. I do not mean to denigrate or besmirch the value of much of that work; indeed, it seems to me that Althusser's conception of the subject as the site of intersection of a whole overdetermined welter of ideological discourses and appeals which keep it pinned, as it were, in place, has produced a large and important space for new political strategies and theoretical work. But what strikes me now, almost twenty years after the famous essay on Ideological State Apparatuses,[13] as the most historically symptomatic feature of that influential work, is the emphasis Althusser lays within it on the spurious *unity* of the effectively interpellated subject. This emphasis, combined with his quite exclusive concern with Ideological *State* Apparatuses – with interpellation exclusively as *subjection*, in other words, into docile worker, happy consumer, obedient citizen – helped to open the way to a virtual equation between unified subjectivity and subjugation, and a corresponding valorization of the decentered or disseminated subject, in the erstwhile radical work that followed that essay through the 1970s and well into the present decade.

I call it historically symptomatic because this emphasis and the equation that was subsequently piled on its back are most suspect as founding assumptions of an understanding of the nature of the subject, and of ideological subjection, within the First World metropoles of late capitalism. Here it seems, at least for us (an *us* I mean to specify further shortly), that the problem to be worked through and, ultimately, politically strategized is precisely that of the *dis*unified and *de*centered subject, of a vast array of ideological apparatuses, from advertising to education, politics to MTV, which work as much to *dis*articulate the subject as to interpellate it, which offer not the old pleasures of 'self-understanding', of knowing and accepting our place, but the new delights of ever-shifting bricolage and blur. 'This,' writes John Brenkman, 'is the double tendency of late capitalism and its culture – to make the subject's separation in the object consumed the core of social experience, and to destroy the space in which proletarian counter-ideologies can form.... Capital cannot speak, but it can accumulate and concentrate itself in communications media, events, and objects which are imbued with this power to turn the discourses of collective experience into a discourse that resembles intersubjectivity as seriality.'[14]

There appears, then, to be something almost nostalgic about the Althusserian emphasis on the spurious unity of the ideologically interpellated subject, a nostalgic or regressive component in its opposition to a mode of subjection whose time is passing or past. In this respect, Althusser's work on ideology in the ISA essay shares with the events of May 1968 (to which it is said to constitute a sympathetic response) a curious, ironic complicity with the disarticulating forces of consumer capitalism's perpetual present. As Regis Debray himself has said in retrospect of the May 1968 events: 'We set our sails for Mao's China, and ended up in Southern California.' This complicity then deepens in much of the poststructuralist work that follows in the wake of that originary moment, and becomes a significant element in the utopian forms and projects that work attempts to describe. The point remains always 'to *uncouple* and *disrupt* the prevailing array of discourses through which subject identities are formed'[15]; the goal is the uncoupled, disrupted self, the 'woman-text' or 'fabulous opera' described by Cixous, melting in a broth of Barthesian *jouissance*. Or perhaps, as at least one post-Marxist, poststructuralist critic seems to suggest, that goal has already been reached, that world is ours right now.

> So we discover that we live in a world where, by choice or circumstance [?!], we have all become experts. We confront and use signs – clothes and hair-styles, radio and tv programmes, newspapers, cinema, magazines, records – that, circulating in the profane languages of habitual sights and sounds, have no obvious author. And in the end, it is not individual signs, demanding isolated attention, but the resulting connections or 'bricolage' – the style, the fashion, the image – that count.[16]

It is the horror of such a heaven, within such a bliss, that the post-modern novels of Johnson and Disch touch off in us, by allowing us to try on such a paradisiac state of being somewhere near, or beyond, the asymptotic line towards which the magical mystery tour consumer capitalism urges us: towards Fiskadoro's passage through a post-nuclear, post-oedipal bricolage landscape to a state of pure presentness and receptivity, a life that is 'always one day long'; towards Giselle's passage through the potholder, its pattern repeating 'mindless, meaninglessly, again and again', towards a 'slow, subaqueous drift of dim pleasure ... a tree's thoughts, a way of swaying in the breeze and going nowhere'. Or, less ambiguously still, towards Mrs Hanson's perception of her own life within the post modern metropole of Disch's *334* as a pure 'pastime':

> Not a game, for that would have implied that some won and others lost, and she was seldom conscious of any sensations so vivid or threatening. It was like the afternoons of Monopoly with her brothers when she was a girl: long after her hotels, her houses, her deeds, and her cash were gone, they would let her keep moving her little lead battleships around the board, collecting her $200, falling on Chance and Community Chest, going to jail and shaking her way out. She never won but she couldn't lose. She just went round and round. Life.[17]

Yet the negative assessment of the poststructuralist project and its postmodern utopia I have delivered so far is too harsh, too global, and too simple as it stands; accordingly, it needs to be qualified and compli-cated in at least two directions, albeit ones I can only very briefly indicate here. First of all, I want to insist again on a point I have argued more extensively elsewhere: that postmodernism (and, *a fortiori*, post-structuralism, its foremost philosophico-theoretical expression) is not most valuably or accurately understood as some essential secretion of late capitalism *tout court*, and still less as a set of discourses and prac-tices without its own social subject or home base.[18] That home base or epicenter still seems to me to be what has been called the professional–managerial class of the developed West, situated as it is in contradictory relation to both Capital above and Labor below (and, increasingly, beyond) its own ever-enlarging realm, ranks, and ken, and both author and primary target audience for most postmodernist work, mainstream (i.e., including even more TV commercials, at least by now in the US) and avant-garde.[19] Extrapolating from that structure of feeling we call postmodernism beyond the boundaries of this admittedly large, heterogeneous, unevenly developing, and ambiguously placed class, as if everyone in the West were uniformly subject to its rhythms, raptures, and horrors, seems a neat way of sidestepping or foreclosing all the important political questions about how both postmodernism and the PMC can be mobilized and radicalized: that is, with what other discourses, practices, and social subjects they may be linked up, in what ways, and towards what ends. Either postmodernism is everywhere, saturating the universe of white corporation lawyers, single mothers on welfare, and black (ex)factory workers alike, like the residues of car exhaust that can now be found even on the nether slopes of Everest, in which case we can at best only wait for the revolutionary trumpet to sound somewhere in the Third World at some unknowable future date; or, if postmodernism is simply a new kit of discourses and practices, we are free to incorporate them too now into our own endless, jaded bricolage games as the skilled, hip consumers we are. Either way, the truly political difficulties and possibilities that arise from postmodernism and our own position within the present mode of production are quite successfully evaded and obscured – and will, accordingly, be picked up and worked through politically by other powers from 'the reactionary darkness' Barthes invites us to 'pass lightly through'.[20]

My second qualification comes from a quite different direction: from feminism. Or, more specifically, from a position within feminism from which the poststructuralist attack on the bourgeois oedipal subject, and hostility towards any normative concept of the unified self, make a great deal more political sense than I have so far been willing to grant them here. It is not merely that the grand unity (or myth thereof) of the oedipal is, notoriously, constructed against and through the counter-construction of a dominated and abject Feminine non-self as its assymmetrical Other; it is, as Denise Riley has recently argued, that the category 'women' itself has throughout history been put to work by both men and women in conjunction with a bewildering array of other categories (especially, she suggests, those of 'the social' and 'the body') to forward an equally wide variety and spectrum of agendas. '"Women,"' she writes, 'is a simultaneous foundation of and irritant to feminism, and this is constitutionally so':

Indeed the trade-off for the myriad namings of 'women' by psychologies, politics and sociologies is that at this cost 'women' do become a force to be reckoned with. But the caveat is that none the less the risky elements to the processes of consolidation in sexed ranks are never very far away; the collectivity which distinguishes you may also be wielded, if often unintentionally, against you. . . . The dangerous intimacy between subjectification and subjection needs careful calibration.[21]

Against the background of such historically justified suspicion, the hostility of poststructural feminists like Cixous towards any stable identity or name for 'woman', and advocacy of a resistant, mercurial subjectivity-in-slippage, become, to a great extent, *strategically* comprehensible. Yet it still bears noting that the efficacy of such strategic refusals to name, identify, consolidate, is strictly limited to resistance. Radical *transformation*, by contrast, whether towards feminism or socialism, requires more than disruption, uncoupling, slipping away; it requires precisely the construction of new *collective* subjectivities and communities capable of purposive action towards shared ends and goals. As Terry Eagleton puts it, at the close of his largely sympathetic exposition of Kristeva's work:

Nor is the dismantling of the unified subject a revolutionary gesture in itself. Kristeva rightly perceives that bourgeois individualism thrives on such a fetish, but her work tends to halt at the point where the subject has been fractured and thrown into contradiction. For Brecht, by contrast, the dismantling of our given identities through art is inseparable from the practice of producing a new kind of human subject altogether which would need to know not only internal fragmentation but social solidarity, which would experience not only the gratifications of libidinal language but the fulfillments of fighting political injustice.[22]

My concluding intention here, though, is not to back a Marxist modernism against a postmodern feminism, and issue a rousing, nostalgic, and ultimately futile endorsement of Brecht over Kristeva. It is rather to call for a recognition of precisely the separation that *does* exist for us – as socialists, as feminists, as members of the PMC – between 'dismantling' and 'producing' – a recognition that should not only be accompanied by a discontent with the inadequacy of the former strategy alone, as I have been using the powerful, delightful and disturbing embodiments of postmodern bliss provided us by Disch and Johnson to argue here, but followed up by a project of historical self-understanding as well. With a properly historical and materialist understanding of the social origins of postmodernism and poststructuralism within late capitalism and consumer society, and of our own specific place within,

and equivocal, complicitous fascination/revulsion with both this structure of feeling and the particular social universe which is our own, we
might be able to move on to the real strategic task of constructing new
political subjectivities and wills, among ourselves and together with
others. Without that understanding, though – and this is my final vulgar
provocation – we will be condemned to recycle our fascination/
revulsion in essay after essay, conference after conference, anthology
after anthology on postmodernist culture and the delirious, horrifying
decentered subjectivity we live with, love, and revile: to stage and re-
stage, as left intellectuals, our own version of the passage through the
potholder to our own earned oblivion in a doubtful paradise, a heaven
where, as Talking Heads' David Byrne sings, 'nothing ever happens',
and in which we will deserve no better than what we – eventually, incessantly, *ad nauseam* – get.

Notes

1. See E. Ann Kaplan's discussion of feminist possibilities for a utopian postmodernism
in 'Feminism/Oedipus/Postmodernism: The Case of MTV', included in this volume.
2. Jacket copy for the first hardcover edition of *The Businessman* (New York: Harper
& Row, 1984). Subsequent page references are to this edition.
3. *Fundamental Disch* (New York: Bantam Books, 1981), p. 379.
4. *Fantasy: The Literature of Subversion* (New York: Methuen, 1981), p. 3.
5. See Julia Kristeva, *Powers of Horror*, trans. Leon S. Roudiez (New York: Columbia University Press, 1982), passim; and also Barbara Creed's insightful discussion, 'Horror
and the Monstrous-Feminine: An Imaginary Abjection', in *Screen*, 26, 2 (spring 1987), pp.
47–68.
6. Roland Barthes, *The Pleasure of the Text*, trans. Richard Miller (New York: Hill
and Wang, 1975), p. 53.
7. Barthes, pp. 14, 31.
8. 'The Character of "Character"' trans. Keith Cohen, in *New Literary History*, 5
(1974), p. 387.
9. 'Castration or Decapitation?', trans. Annette Kuhn, in *Signs*, 7, 1, p. 53.
10. Though the copy on my paperback edition of *Fiskadoro*, significantly enough, also
shuffles through both 'high' and 'low' culture to come up with its comparative terms.
Note, for example, the blended references to canonical literature and contemporary popular culture in these excerpts from (respectively) *The New York Times* and *Washington Post*
puffs quoted on the paperback's cover:

> Wildly ambitious ... the sort of book that a young Melville might have written had he
> lived today and studied such disparate works as the Bible, 'The Waste Land', *Fahren-
> heit 451* and *Dog Soldiers*, screened *Star Wars* and *Apocalypse Now* several times,
> dropped a lot of acid and listened to hours of Jimi Hendrix and the Rolling Stones.

> He [Johnson] is a wonderful storyteller, and if at times *Fiskadoro* seems a mixture of
> Samuel Beckett, Philip K. Dick, and *Road Warrior*, that is only to his credit.

All subsequent page references are to this edition (New York: Vintage Contemporaries,
1986).
11. See, for example, *Anti-Oedipus: Capitalism and Schizophrenia*, trans. Robert

Hurley, Mark Seem, and Helen R. Lane (New York: Viking, 1977).

12. *The Sense of an Ending: Studies in the Theory of Fiction* (New York: Oxford University Press, 1966), p. 39.

13. 'Ideology and Ideological State Apparatuses', in *Lenin and Philosophy*, trans. Ben Brewster (New York: Monthly Review Press, 1971), pp. 127–86.

14. 'Mass Media: From Collective Experience to the Culture of Privatization', in *Social Text* 1 (spring 1979), pp. 100–101, 105.

15. Tony Bennett, 'Text and history', in Peter Widdowson, ed., *Re-reading English* (New York: Methuen, 1982); emphasis mine.

16. Ian Chambers, *Popular Culture: The Metropolitan Experience* (New York: Methuen, 1986), p. 12.

17. *334* (New York: Carroll and Graff, 1987), pp. 169–70.

18. Most extensively, in '"Makin' Flippy-Floppy": Postmodernism and the Baby-Boom PMC', in *The Year Left*, ed. Mike Davis, Michael Sprinker, and Fred Pfeil (London: Verso, 1985), pp. 263–95. But interested readers should also check out Richard Ohmann's descriptive analysis of the cultural hegemony of this class with regard to literature and literary studies in the second half of *English in America* (New York: Oxford University Press, 1973) – an analysis which can and should now be extended to other cultural fields and media as well.

19. The term originates in Barbara and John Ehrenreich's classic essay of the same name, which can be found most readily in Pat Walker, ed., *Between Labor and Capital*, (Boston: South End Press, 1979), pp. 5–45. The other essays in the collection, responses to the Ehrenreichs' piece, are also worth noting insofar as they are indicative of the debate which has followed, in which there has been little outright disagreement with the Ehrenreichs' basic contentions, nor much of any real engagement with them, either. Instead, the attempt has been to bury the analysis and the pressing political problems it sets before the American left in a thicket of cranky terminological squabbles and arcane, academicized split hairs.

20. *The Pleasure of the Text*, p. 31. But another word or two is due, if only in this footnote, on the nature and social origins of some of the elements of that 'reactionary darkness' in these two books. I owe to my friend Sohnya Sayres the observation that *Fiskadoro* and *The Businessman* both admit and fend off the ideological challenge of resurgent religious discourse – *Fiskadoro* through the aestheticized detachment of its high poetic style, *The Businessman* through its elaborate undermining of any conventional boundary between the sacred and secular and/or banal, its intransigent, blithe wackiness. In *Fiskadoro*, moreover, this operation is specifically tied to the promise and anxiety of the rise of another, presumably non-white and non-Western, civilization following the self-destructive collapse of this one. Is it not possible, then, to understand both these books as homoeopathic medicine for the PMC, introducing and defusing potentially threatening discourses arising from other races, classes, and quarters outside our own compound? Or, to put the same point slightly differently: from whose point of view do such discourses appear as 'reactionary darkness' more or less by definition, a darkness which must one way or another be sufficiently diluted so that *we* can 'pass lightly through' it without undue discomfort or sense of threat?

21. 'Does sex have a history? "Women" and feminism', *New Formations*, 1 (spring 1987), p. 44.

22. *Literary theory: An Introduction* (Minneapolis: University of Minnesota Press, 1983), p. 191.

5

Urban Renaissance and the Spirit of Postmodernism

Mike Davis

It has been customary for historians to speak about the death of the Victorian Age in 1914, or the reign of a politico-monetary Long Sixteenth Century persisting well into the middle of the calendrical seventeenth century. By the same token, there are innumerable incitements in contemporary cultural, if not political, analysis to regard the Old Twentieth Century – defined, pre-eminently, by the two Great Wars and their attendant revolutions – as having drawn to a close sometime between the Beats and the Punks, Sartre and Foucault. Fredric Jameson's essay, 'The Cultural Logic of Late Capital' (*New Left Review* 146), is an audacious attempt to argue the case for such an epochal transition. Indeed, Jameson, charting a caesura from the beginning of the 'long Sixties', goes as far as to suggest the ascendancy of a new, 'postmodernist' sensibility or cultural attitude, overwhelmed in a delusionary, depthless Present, and deprived of historical coordinates, imaginative empathy, or even existential *angst*. With extraordinary facility for unexpected connections and contrasts (as between architecture and war reporting), he stalks the logic of the new cultural order – based on the manic reprocessing and 'cannibalizing' of its own images – through various manifestations in current writing, poetry, music and film. It is, however, architecture, 'the privileged aesthetic language', that reveals the most systematic, virtually 'unmediated' relationship between postmodern experience and the structures of late capitalism. Thus, according to Jameson, the 'new world space of multinational capital' finds it 'impossible' representation in the mirror-glass and steel 'hyperspaces' of the Los Angeles Bonaventure Hotel and other contemporary urban megastructures.

This vision of the end of the twentieth century as the triumph of post-modernism – and, correlatively, the conception of postmodernism as the cultural 'dominant' corresponding to the highest, 'purest' stage of capitalism – has an exhilarating allure. It regiments sundry partial, discrepant observations into a coherent focus, while providing some sure footing on that most slippery of terrains for Marxists: the theorization of contemporaneity. The ability to summarize vast tracts of modern and postmodern history, to focus their respective vectors in exemplary instances or moments, and to provide a synoptic overview of how the pieces in this complex puzzle fit together – this is an achievement to which few can lay claim, and for which contemporary workers in the fields of culture, politics and history must be continually grateful. But like all imposing totalizations (modes of thought that Althusser, among others, has taught us to be wary of), Jameson's postmodernism tends to homogenize the details of the contemporary landscape, to subsume under a master concept too many contradictory phenomena which, though undoubtedly visible in the same chronological moment, are none the less separated in their true temporalities.

To begin with a merely formal complaint. The category 'cultural dominant', which occupies such a crucial epistemological position in Jameson's argument, seems as if it might be just another name for that elusive Great White Whale of cultural criticism – the specific *object* thereof – which so many have pursued, struggled with for a while (some drowning in due course) and, then, invariably lost hold of. Described in Jameson as a 'force field', 'systematic cultural norm', or 'cultural language', postmodermism in its dominative or hegemonic position seems variously to assume the status of 'sensibility', 'aesthetic', 'cultural apparatus', even 'episteme'. A continuous slippage between subjective and objective moments, spectator and spectacle, begs the introduction of that necessary though not sufficient clarification which Perry Anderson (in debate over the meaning of modernism with Marshall Berman in NLR 144) makes between the *experience* of (post)modernity and the *vision* of (post)modernism.

Even more problematic is the assertion that postmodernism is the cultural logic of late capitalism, successor to modernism and realism as the respective cultures of the monopoly and competitive stages of capitalism. This concept of three stages of capital and the three stages of bourgeois culture may strike some as the return of essentialism and reductionism with a vengeance. Certainly there is a superificial similarity, at least, with that neatly ordered, old-fashioned world of conveniently correspondent superstructures that we associate with Comintern Marxism after Lenin. But even if we set aside the question of whether Jameson is operating as a kind of Lukács manqué, there are intractable difficulties in establishing a first 'fit' between postmodernism and Mandel's concept of the late capitalist stage.

For Jameson it is crucial to demonstrate that the sixties are a point of rupture in the history of capitalism and culture, and to establish a 'constitutive' relationship between postmodernism, new technology (of *reproduction* rather than production) and multinational capitalism. Mandel's *Late Capitalism* (first published in 1972), however, declares in its opening sentence that its central purpose is to understand 'the long *postwar* wave of rapid growth'. All of his subsequent writings make clear that Mandel regards the real break, the definite ending of the long wave, to be the 'second slump' of 1974–75, and that exacerbated inter-imperialist rivalry to have been one of its primary features (he has criticized emphasis on 'multinationalization' as the principal characteristic of contemporary capitalism). The difference between Jameson's and Mandel's scheme is crucial: was late capitalism born circa 1945 or 1960? Are the sixties the opening of a new epoch, or merely the super-heated summit of the postwar boom? Where does the slump fit into an accounting of contemporary cultural trends?

If American architecture is taken as an example, it is clear that Mandel's is a better grid to plot the relationship between cultural forms and economic phases. As every reader of Tom Wolfe knows, the corporate 'workers' housing' of the High Modern (or International) Style totally dominated postwar urban renewal, reaching an apotheosis of sorts during the late 1960s in the construction of super-skyscrapers like the World Trade Center, the John Hancock and Sears buildings. 'Modernism', at least in architecture, remained the functional aesthetic of Late Capitalism, and the sixties must be seen as a predominantly *fin-de-siècle* decade, more a culmination than a beginning.

If Jameson's equation between postmodernism and late capitalism *tout court* gives way, then to what politico-economic trends can we correlate the change in sensibility represented by postmodernism? Preserving the hypothesis that the American Downtown Renaissance, and its futuristically built environments, are keys to deciphering a larger cultural and experiential pattern, I would suggest the reinterpretation of postmodernism in terms of two alternative coordinates: first, the rise of new international rentier circuits in the current crisis phase of capitalism; secondly, the definitive abandonment of the ideal of urban reform as part of the new class polarization taking place in the United States.

The Spirit of Postmodernism

In a typically Schopenhauerian flourish, Mies van der Rohe once declared that the destiny of modern architecture was to translate 'the will of the epoch into space'; indeed the 1960s skyline bore the signature of the epoch of Fordism and the power of the Fortune 500 industrial corporations. The postmodern trend in architecture, however, has little organic or expressive relationship to industrial production or emerging technology; it is not raising 'cathedrals of the microchip' or even, primarily, singing the hymns of IBM. Instead it has given freer exhibition than ever before to the spirit of fictional capital. Revolting against the austerity of Miesian functionalism, it has broken any allusion to the production process and loosened the commodity-form of the building from its use-value supports. In doing so, it has achieved a jocular inversion of the previous relationship between monumentality and the individual commodity: Philip Johnson's Chippendale ATT Building (or the 'pink pay phone' as it sometimes called) is one of the most popularly notorious examples of the comedic or bathetic triumph of the familar object over abstract, functionalized structure. In the hands of post-modernist architecture the skyscraper passes from monumental machine to massive collectible. (Thus Johnson has proposed, with his partner John Burgees, to replace the famous New York landmark of the 1 Times Square Building with a giant apple!)

How can we read this Warholesque transformation except as a complete usurpation by the logic of speculation and merchandizing over residual principles of capitalist productivism? Where the 'classical' skyscraper romanticized the hegemony of corporate bureaucracy and mass production, the postmodern tower is merely 'a package of stan-dardized space to be gift-wrapped to the clients' taste'.[1] Indeed, the postmodernist phenomenon seems irreducibly specific to the reckless overbuilding of commercial space that has taken place since 1974, continuing frenetically even through the trough of the severe 1981–82 recession. As everyone knows, this great construction bubble has been inflated, not by expanding civilian industrial production, but by oil rents, Third World debts, military outlays, and the global flight of capital to the safe harbor of Reagan's America. This hypertrophic expansion of the financial service sector is not a new, higher stage of capitalism – even in America speculators cannot go on endlessly building postmodernist skyscrapers for other speculators to buy – but a morbid symptom of the financial overaccumulation prolonged by the weakness of the US labor movement and productive capital's fears of a general collapse. Thus, while Jameson's account of the phenomenal reality of postmodernism is acute and penetrating, his theorization of this moment as the surface meaning of a deeper structure of multinational integration in the capital-ist world system (Jameson significantly, and incorrectly, conflates the quite different accounts of capitalism given by Wallerstein and Mandel) misses the crucial point about contemporary capitalist structures of accumulation: that they are symptoms of global crisis, not signs of the triumph of capitalism's irresistible drive to expand.

The history of downtown redevelopment in Los Angeles is a particularly vivid example of how the new urban 'renaissance' has increasingly become a function of international financial speculation on an unprecedented scale. In the first, immediate postwar phase, the seedy Bunker Hill area adjacent to the LA civic centre was slated for large-scale public housing. However, the traditional downtown interests, orchestrated by the *Los Angeles Times* chief political operator Asa Call, sabotaged this plan, redbaiting public housing advocates and ousting progressive Mayor Fletcher Bowron. There followed a second phase, marked by the wholesale eviction of poor working-class neighborhoods (like the famous Chavez Ravine barrio, razed to make way for Dodger Stadium) and the repeal of earthquake height-limitations to make way for LA's first skyscrapers. Under the aegis of Call's 'Committee of Twenty-Five', a number of major corporations were persuaded to construct new headquarters in the downtown area during the 1960s. (From this period date typical modernist statements like the twin black monoliths of the ARCO Towers and the stainless steel Wells Fargo Building.) In the 1970s, however, the accelerating pace of redevelopment came under the control of offshore managers of truly vast pools of mobile capital, and individual buildings gave way to multiblock developments like the Westin Bonaventure (financed by the Japanese) and the California Plaza (3,200,000 square feet of office space, 220,000 of retail, 750 residential units, a 100,000 square foot museum, and a five-acre park – being built by $1.5 billion of expatriate Canadian funds). Overall, foreign investors now totally dominate downtown construction, financing 32 of the 38 major skyscapers built in the last decade.[2]

This transformation of a decayed precinct of downtown LA into a major financial and corporate control node of the Pacific Rim economy (battening also on Southern California's runaway real-estate inflation and its booming defence industries)[3] has gone hand-in-hand with a precipitous deterioration of the general urban infrastructure and a new-wave immigration that has brought an estimated one million undocumented Asians, Mexicans and Central Americans into the inner city. The capitalism of postmodernism, far from eliminating the last enclaves of pre-capitalist production as Jameson suggests, has brazenly recalled the most primitive forms of urban exploitation. At least 100,000 apparel homeworkers toil within a few miles' radius of the Bonaventure and child labor is again a shocking problem. This restructuring of the relations of production and the productive process is, to be sure, thoroughly capitalist, but it represents, not some higher stage in capitalist production, but a return to a sort of primitive accumulation with the valorization of capital occurring, in part, through the production of absolute surplus value by means of the super-exploitation of the urban proletariat.

Baron Haussmann in Los Angeles

It is only within the context of this larger 'redevelopment' – the burgeoning city of Third World immigrants that totally surrounds and lays siege to the sumptuary towers of the speculators – that it is possible to grasp the real meaning of the architectural language used by John Portman and other leading downtown developers. To do so, it will be useful to distinguish between the last great Marxist theorization of the capitalist city and the quite different schema that Jameson proposes. Jameson evokes the Bonaventure as a contemporary counterpart to the role of the Parisian Arcades in Walter Benjamin's analysis of modernism: an exemplary prism that refracts and clarifies the constituent tonalities of a particular 'urbanity'. But, where Jameson is primarily concerned to focus on the thing itself, Benjamin, in his search for the 'cultural logic' of Baudelaire's era, reconstructed the specific political and economic conditions that brought the world of the *flâneur* into being. In particular, he linked the phantasmagoria of the boulevards, crowds and arcades to the famous precursor of modern urban renewal: Baron Haussmann's counter-revolutionary restructuring of Paris in the 1850s.

Before considering the specific 'counter-revolutionary' context of today's downtown revival, however, it may be helpful briefly to consider the genealogy of modern megastructures like the Bonaventure. It is fair to say that all current multi-block, multi-purpose developments descend from the example of Rockefeller Center, built between 1931 and 1940. The Italian Marxist, Manfredo Tafuri,[4] in his brilliant account of the Center's architectural history, has emphasized how a generation of designers' and planners' hopes for architectural reform were focused on the Rockefellers' great project, with its proposed centralization of work, residence and recreation in coordinated structures. In the end, however, 'all concepts accepted were stripped of any utopian character', the final plan for the development was 'a contained and rational concentration, an oasis of order – a closed and circumscribed intervention'. Built at the height of the New Deal, Rockefeller Center clearly showed the limits of capitalist urban design – indeed, the impossibility of planning the American city on any large or comprehensive scale.

Still, compared with today's downtown megastructures, Rockefeller Center interacted vitally with La Guardia's New York: its famous Plaza (originally intended to be a latter-day Garden of Babylon) and mass amusements became a magnetic attraction for a varied and represent-ative Manhattan public. In the early postwar period its scheme was copied in a number of Northern urban redevelopment plans (notably, in Philadelphia's Penn Center, Chicago's Civic Centre, and Pittsburgh's Golden Triangle). But increasingly the Rockefeller strategy of using vitalized public spaces to valorize private speculation was undermined by the crisis of the inner city, as industry fled to the suburbs, followed by the white working class, and the downtown residential districts filled up with the displaced Southern poor. The wave of ghetto insurrections between 1964 and 1969 powerfully concentrated the attention of urban developers and corporate architects on the problem of cordoning off the downtown financial districts, and other zones of high property values, from inner-city residential neighborhoods. Genuine public spaces, whether as parks, streets, places of entertainment, or in urban transport, were devalued as amenities and redefined as planning problems to be eliminated or privatized.[5]

Although in a few American cities (usually with dominant university–hospital–office economies, as in Boston and San Francisco) the new rich and middle classes are gentrifying the entire urban core, in most large city centers redevelopment has produced only skyscraper-fortress enclaves. For the wealthy, token few of the downtown salariat and managerial workforce who actually choose to live within the skyscraper, two different architectural solutions have arisen to the problem of guar-anteeing their segregation and security. One has been the erection of new super-skyscrapers, integrating residential space, what Tafuri correctly calls 'gigantic antiurban machines'. The other strategy, pioneered by hotel architect John Portman, and designed to mollify the skyscraper's inhumanity, was to incorporate pseudo-natural, pseudo-public spaces within the building itself. Drawing on Frank Lloyd Wright's many experiments in search of an aesthetic of open space and endless movement, essays which include the 'lost' Larkin Building, the Johnson Wax Building and the Guggenheim Museum, Portman changed the theory and economics of hotel design by showing that sizeable interior space could be a practical investment. The prototype of Portmanesque space – spaceship elevators, multi-storey atrium lobby, and so on – was the Hyatt–Regency built in 1967 in Atlanta's Peachtree Center. It is import-ant to provide a concise image of the setting and external function of this 'mother of Bonaventure': 'Downtown Atlanta rises above its surround-ing city like a walled fortress from another age. The citadel is anchored to the south by the international trade center and buttressed by the municipal stadium. To the north, the walls and walkways of John Port-man's Peachtree Center stand watch over the acres of automobiles that pack both flanks of the city's long ridge. The sunken moat of 1–85, with its flowing lanes of traffic, reaches around the eastern base of the hill from south to north, protecting lawyers, bankers, consultants and regional executives from the intrusion of low-income neighborhoods.'[6]

It is not surprising that Los Angeles's Portman-built new downtown (like that of Detroit, or Houston) reproduces more or less exactly the besieged landscape of Peachtree Center: the new Figueroa and Bunker Hill complexes are formed in the same protective maze of freeways, moats, concrete parapets, and asphalt no-man's lands. What is missing from Jameson's otherwise vivid description of the Bonaventure is the savagery of its insertion into the surrounding city. To say that a structure of this type 'turns its back away' is surely an understatement, while to speak of its 'popular' character is to miss the point of its systematic segregation from the great Hispanic–Asian city outside (whose crowds prefer the open space of the old Plaza). Indeed, it is virtually to endorse the master illusion that Portman seeks to convey: that he has recreated within the precious spaces of his super-lobbies the genuine popular texture of city life.

In fact, Portman has only built large vivariums for the upper middle classes, protected by astonishingly complex security systems. Most of the new downtown centres might as well have been built on the third moon of Jupiter. Their fundamental logic is that of a claustrophobic space colony attempting to miniaturize nature within itself. Thus the Bonaventure reconstructs a nostalgic Southern California in aspic: orange trees, fountains, flowering vines, and clean air. Outside, in a smog-poisoned reality, vast mirrored surfaces reflect away not only the misery of the larger city, but also its irrepressible vibrancy and quest for authenticity (including the most exciting neighborhood mural movement in North America).

Finally, it should be noted that where the aim of Portman is to dissimulate and 'humanize' the fortress function of his buildings, another postmodernist vanguard is increasingly iconizing that function in its designs. Recently opened off Wall Street, 33 Maiden Lane by Philip Johnson is a 26-story imitation of the Tower of London, advertised as the 'state of the art in luxury accommodation ... with emphasis on security'. Meanwhile Johnson and his partner, John Burgees, are working on the prospective 'Trump Castle' for Gotham City's own JR, 37-year-old billionaire developer, Donald Trump.[7] According to its advance publicity, Trump Castle will be a medievalized Bonaventure, with six coned and crenellated cylinders, plated in gold leaf, and surrounded by a real moat with drawbridges. These current designs for fortified skyscrapers indicate a vogue for battlements not seen since the great armory boom that followed the Labour Rebellion of 1877. In so doing, they also signal the coercive intent of postmodernist architecture in its ambition, not to hegemonize the city in the fashion of the great modernist buildings, but rather to polarize it into radically antagonistic spaces.

This profoundly antiurban impulse, inspired by unfettered financial forces and a Haussmannian logic of social control, seems to me to constitute the real *Zeitgeist* of postmodernism. At the same time, however, it reveals 'postmodernism' – at least in its architectual incarnations and sensibilities – as little more than a decadent trope of a massified modernism, a sympathetic correlate to Reaganism and the end of urban reform. As such it hardly seems a possible entryway to the new forms of collective social practice towards which Jameson's essay ultimately beckons us.

Notes

This essay was originally published in *New Left Review* 151 (May–June 1985).

1. Ada Louise Huxtable, 'The Tall Building Artistically Reconsidered: The Search for a Skyscraper Style', *Architectural Record*, (January 1984), p. 64.

2. *Business Week*, (23 April 1984), p. 17

3. For a provocative analysis of contemporary Los Angeles as a hybrid 'Singapore–Houston–New York', see Edward Soja, Rebecca Morales and Goetz Wolff, 'Urban Restructuring: An Analysis of Social and Spatial Change in Los Angeles', *Economic Geography*, 59, 2 (April 1983).

4.Giorgio Ciucci et al., eds, *The American City: From the Civil War to the New Deal.* Trans. Barbara Luigia La Penta (Cambridge, Mass: MIT Press, 1979).

5. In his discussion of architectural modernism's propensity to an elite, urban 'pastoralism', Marshall Berman quotes Le Corbusier's 1929 slogan, 'we must kill the street!' According to Berman, the inner logic of the new urban environment, 'from Atlanta's Peachtree Plaza to Detroit's Renaissance Center', has been the functional segmentation and class segregation of the 'old modern street, with its volatile mixture of people and traffic, businesses and homes, rich and poor'. (*All That Is Solid Melts Into Air*, London: Verso 1983, p. 168). Unfortunately, Berman's otherwise splendid evocation of modernist New York pays no more attention than Jameson's portrait of postmodernist Los Angeles to the decisive role of urban counter-insurgency in defining the essential terms of the contemporary built environment. Since the ghetto rebellions of the late 1960s a racist, as well as class, imperative of spatial separation has been paramount in urban development. No wonder, then, that the contemporary American inner city resembles nothing so much as the classical colonial city, with the towers of the white rulers and colons militarily set off from the casbah or indigenous city.

6. Carl Abbott, *The New Urban America*, (Chapel Hill: University of North Carolina Press, 1983), p. 143.

7. Trump Castle will complement previously built Trump Plaza and Trump Tower. The latter boasts of being the most exclusive address in the world, with condominia so expensive, at up to $10 million each, that 'only the likes of Johnny Carson and Steven Spielberg can afford them' (*New York Times Magazine*, 8 April 1983).

6

What is at Stake in the Debate on Postmodernism?

Warren Montag

To read Lyotard's *The Postmodern Condition,* Baudrillard's *Simulations* and *In the Shadow of the Silent Majorities,* various texts by Jameson, Eagleton and Habermas, and Perry Anderson's *In the Tracks of Histori- cal Materialism* is to see irreducibly divergent forces objectively united to force knowledge back to the domain deemed proper to it by the established theoretical order.[1] For Marxists, the task is not only to strike out at this counter-offensive against the principles of historical material- ism, but equally to understand why it now occupies a privileged position in theoretical debate.

Notice the terms of the debate on postmodernism and the disjunctive dilemmas that it imposes: (1) Marxism will be transcendental or it will not be (Jameson asserts and Lyotard is only too happy to agree); (2) works of art either represent something more real than themselves which is therefore the depth beneath their surface (making them susceptible to a hermeneutic reading) or they are absolutely autonomous, indeter- minate and therefore "unanalyzable"; (3) either the subject is master of itself, its own thoughts and actions or it has simply vanished into the pure systematicity of the historical present. In addition, the first set of alternatives (transcendentality, art as representation, the subject as origin–center) is often placed in historical opposition to the second set (the absence of transcendentality, the indeterminacy of art, the death of the subject) as a once existing past that has given way to the present as one historical totality to another. So, for example, the classically conceived subject once existed but no longer does, just as art once repre- sented reality but has somehow ceased to do so.

These of course are the very dilemmas that have ordered political, philosophical and aesthetic speculations for centuries. Even so, who would have imagined that it would one day be argued that philosophy only became a struggle between antagonistic tendencies *after* Lenin (or even Althusser) described it as such? Or that works of art once truly reflected a reality external to them but were then suddenly cast adrift without cause or meaning? Those who took a position within the space opened up by the break witnessed a reorganization or recasting of the entire field organized around the concept of representation which transformed its very origins. Suddenly, Plato's anxiety before the work of art became much more clear. His hostility to the Sophists (as champions of non-being) was a displacement. For it was not the falsity or immateriality of the work of art that he feared but its materiality, not its indeterminacy but its overdetermination (and the complexity of its effects).[2]

The irreversibility of any theoretical break is necessarily linked to its unevenness and incompleteness, to the obstacles that it inevitably throws up to its own development. Philosophy, in turn, is never simply the guardian of a theoretical truth; it is the space in which the meaning of developments in knowledge is constantly determined and fought over. It is a conflict between tendencies that seek to annul a given break or mutation (or, failing that, to exploit this 'event' to their ends, to minimize its effects) and tendencies that seek to clear the way to its further development. Therefore in no sense is there any irreversibility in philosophy. On the contrary, it is constantly subject to 'retreats and reverses, and even to the risk of counter-revolution'.[3] As Althusser said repeatedly after 1967, philosophy is a perpetual war between antagonistic tendencies, a war in which there are no rules, in which anything goes, no holds are barred and for which there is no out of bounds, no neutral territory. In *Philosophie et la philosophie spontanée des savants*, Althusser wrote: 'From the very beginning we have been able to speak of philosophy only by occupying a definite position in philosophy. For in philosophy, we cannot, like Rousseau's Noble Savage, occupy an empty corner of the forest. In philosophy every space is always already occupied. Within it, we can only occupy a position against the adversary who already occupies that position.'[4] This side of the work of Althusser and his disciples has attracted little attention either from his admirers or his critics. It will provide the starting point for the present discussion of the debate on postmodernism.

Once the debate on postmodernism could have been entered with the following questions: which of the opposing positions more closely approximates the object defined in the debate? Or further: to what extent does the object in question correspond to the real object to which it is said to refer? One might have asked: what is postmodernism? (a question of essence) or when did it begin? (a question of periodization).

But these are the questions the debate poses to itself, questions that have been cleared in advance and which all the participants have been authorized to answer. Following Althusser, let us pose a very different kind of question, the kind Nietzsche called *hinterfrage*, insidious questions that the unwritten rules of civilized behavior tell us we must never ask because they are sure to embarrass and discompose.

Against which theories and philosophical positions do the utterances on postmodernism work in order to occupy the place they do? What theoretical statements have been evicted, forced out to make room for this debate? And finally, in what way does the debate allude to this exclusion which is its tactical objective and to which it therefore cannot help but allude?

It will perhaps seem strange to speak of an entire debate constituting an intervention, especially when the very relevance of Marxism seems to be in question. To speak of the debate as a unity is to risk idealism, something like a Hegelian reconciliation of opposites.

Hence a first thesis: the debate is a *de facto* alliance between irreducibly different theoretical forces. There is nothing given or natural about this alliance. In fact, it is nothing more than a temporary, unstable convergence of objectives. Moreover, it is an alliance in which some are unwitting or unconscious participants. By bringing to light its conditions and premises, we just may succeed in breaking apart this alliance.

One of the terms of agreement may be glimpsed in Jameson's argument that 'every possible position on postmodernism in culture, whether apologia or stigmatization, is an implicitly or explicitly political stance on the nature of multinational capitalism today'.[5] This brief statement speaks volumes about the dangers of the retreat into the theoretical fortress: (1) the reduction of 'every possible interpretation' to a 'for' or an 'against' and therefore also the reduction of criticism to judgment (but on the basis of what norms?); (2) the mechanistic identification of the mere 'appreciation' of a movement in art, architecture or literature not only with a specific analysis of world capitalism but even with a political attitude towards it (for or against). It is not accidental that in the same essay Jameson asks us to reconsider the virtues of a 'pedagogical and didactic' art (cleansed of course of all traces of Stalinism and Zhadanovism) that the left might offer as its own alternative to an imperialist postmodernism.

What is important here is the way that analysis slides into celebration or condemnation: do we mourn the loss of the authenticities and essences that alone permitted opposition to the established order, the truths that gave the lie to the falsity that guaranteed domination; or conversely, do we celebrate their passing as a liberation, the inauguration of an era of untrammeled free play, an era in which Nietzsche's 'innocence of becoming' realizes itself once and for all?

We may recall Hegel's analysis of the struggle between Faith and the Enlightenment. Both, he argued, saw an identical reality before them, a reality which they simply approached from different starting points.[6] A presence had passed away from the world: the Enlightenment celebrated this passing away as a liberation. Faith mourned it as a loss. Thus, the opposition of Faith and Enlightenment was not the contradiction of the epoch but rather the opposition through which a certain form of thought divided into itself to achieve identity. Hegel argued that the contradiction of the epoch could emerge only when Enlightenment separated itself from Faith to discover that the difference it had imputed to the other was in fact its own, a difference internal to itself. In a similar way, perhaps Marxism, by separating itself from postmodernism, will discover its own internal difference, the difference that divides it from what it fears about itself.

Let us then attempt to grasp the conflict internal to the field staked out in the debate, apart from the apparent opposition between sanctification and abomination. If I have spoken of a disavowed solidarity between the disparate positions that compose the debate, against which theoretical force or forces has this alliance been concluded?

One of the most theoretically decisive positions taken by the debate as a whole is not transparently a position at all. It appears at first to be rather a rule or convention of argument. Each intervention takes great care to speak of the widest possible range of subjects: art, architecture, music, film, philosophy, politics and science. As Lyotard put it: 'Not only can one speak of everything, one must.'[7] Of course, one of the major objectives of philosophical analysis over the last thirty years has been to track down and dismantle all ruses of a totalizing reason that gathered together the most diverse historical phenomena only to reduce them to a single essence. It is therefore hardly surprising that the return of totalization would not be heralded as such. It has reappeared unannounced and unrecognized in the guise of a mode of exposition. A sympathetic reviewer of Perry Anderson's *In the Tracks of Historical Materialism* called it 'assertion without argument'.[8] This method certainly has its advantages, the major one being brevity. Thus Lyotard can write the metanarrative of the end of metanarratives in politics, art, criticism, philosophy and science in a mere eighty pages. In the same way, Anderson asserts the rapid rise and fall of structuralism and post-structuralism in linguistics, psychoanalysis, philosophy and politics in a text of approximately the same length. Partisans of both works will undoubtedly point out that they provide us with an 'overview' or 'summary' of an admittedly complex and confusing epoch. Unfortunately, these overviews are situated at such a great distance from the diverse objects they seek to describe that real specificities resolve into one blurred, harmonious totality. As Hegel remarked of the totalizing formalisms of his day, they can conceive of the whole only as a 'dark night in which all cows are black'.[9]

But just as the return of (a repressed) totalizing reason is overdetermined, so are its effects manifold. First, the now growing rejection of the most important of the contemporary French thinkers is the too predictable outcome of the way they were initially received by the Anglo-American academy: the hero-worship, the vulgar imitation, the reduction of their work to a question of style or even tone. They were set up as idols to be worshipped and adored but never studied or worked on. Thus, thought continues to vacillate between exoticism and provincialism, between a merely 'clever' eclecticism and a plodding reaffirmation of commonsense. In fact, the Marxists who are so eager to embrace the certitudes of sense-experience, formal logic and human nature have forgotten why these doctrines were called into question in the first place. The generation that now rushes to analytic reason forgets that it once rejected Wittgenstein, Austin and Quine with the same carelessness that it now rejects Derrida, Deleuze and Foucault. Having been content to denounce analytic philosophy without grasping its internal conflicts, they are now in a position to return to what they never understood.[10]

A brief study such as Anderson's, even if it failed to provide an overview, might have simply designated a series of problems to be investigated. It might have served as a map (however rough) to guide us through an exceedingly complex theoretical epoch. Unfortunately, this is not the case.

Let us take as an example Anderson's treatment of Lacan. In a total of no more than five pages, the case on Lacan is opened and closed. The entire Lacanian corpus assumes such an extraordinary coherence and homogeneity that it stands or falls on the single statement, now familiar to every undergraduate in comparative literature, that 'the unconscious is structured like a language'. From a Marxist scholar of Anderson's stature we would have expected a rigorous discussion that would at least touch on the following issues; (1) against which doctrines or concepts did Lacan intervene with this slogan (which, after all, dates back to the early fifties)?; (2) did Lacan modify this statement in any way between 1953 and 1977?; (3) does the concept of language function in an identical way in 'The Rome Discourse' (1953), *The Four Fundamental Concepts of Psychoanalysis* (1964), and *Encore* (1973)? Instead, we are given a 'conclusive objection': because the Freudian conception of the unconscious is incompatible with generative transformational grammar, Lacan is simply wrong. Case closed.[11]

Whether this judgement is true or false is not the point (in fact the assertion is too vague to permit validation). It functions in a very determinate manner to block a serious examination of the uneven and contradictory unfolding of Lacan's thought. The same may be said for Anderson's treatment of Derrida, Foucault and Deleuze. Such treatment does not open problems, it buries them. It does not analyze and intervene, it denounces and retreats. Whoever says that we have done with Lacan (much of whose work has yet to be published) must first educe a body of arguments and demonstrations. Let us admit not only that such work is unfinished but that it has not yet even begun.

In a precisely symmetrical way, Lyotard reduces every tendency in Marxism to the metanarrative of the emancipation of alienated labor, as if history for Marxism is simply the progressive interiorization of an expropriated human essence. Since 'there are no more metanarratives', Marxism, which according to Lyotard is logically confined to this narrative form (so much for infinite openness!), must be jettisoned, and with it outmoded concepts like 'class struggle' and 'revolution'.[12] It is not hard to see the implicit teleology operating here (which seems to be reserved primarily for marxism). Marxism is granted a beginning, middle and an end only to be spirited away in a progression that leads thought beyond progress. To divert attention from this already hackneyed theoretical sleight of hand, we are told that 'it is known' that the struggles of the working class in late capitalism can do no more than regulate the system, just as 'it is known' that Marxism is the totalizing and totalitarian model for the bureaucratic state apparatus in the East.[13] Marxism is the exception in a world without finality; it has no future. The conflicts and antagonisms that traverse the entire history of Marxism disappear into the dark night of the metanarrative to end all metanarratives.

Finally, the most extreme example: Jameson's 'Postmodernism or the Cultural Logic of Late Capitalism'. In this long essay, Jameson describes postmodernism as a 'radical break' or something like a Kuhnian paradigm shift that encompasses the entire set of theoretical and cultural practices. Further, it is a 'cultural dominant' whose domination is constantly enforced by the logic of capital. Thus, 'aesthetic production today has become integrated into commodity production generally'.[14] Art is ruled by the same commodity logic that impels fashion: innovation for innovation's sake. Such art (Jameson cites the example of Andy Warhol) escapes meaning. In direct opposition to the work of Van Gogh which exhibits a plenitude of effect, postmodernist art is superficial and anaesthetic. Controlled by the same logic, 'the poststructuralist critique of the hermeneutic ... is useful to us as a very significant symptom of the very postmodernist culture which is our subject here'.[15]

At this point we may begin to wonder in what sense the cultural dominant is merely dominant, that is, where are the resistances underneath its domination? Is it not more properly speaking an essence that permeates every instance of the social totality? And what sense does it make to speak of 'instances' at all when art, literature and film (aesthetic production *in toto*) have been integrated into commodity production? The 'cultural logic' in question here is in fact the law of a totality whose essence is equally expressed in Althusser, Edie Sedgewick and the Clash. For Jameson, the only alternative to this specific conception of the cultural dominant (which is exactly what Althusser described as the essence of an expressive totality), would be to 'fall back into a view of present history as sheer heterogeneity, random difference, a coexistence of a host of distinct forces whose effectivity is undecidable'.[16]

In fact, the domination of the 'systematic cultural norm' Jameson describes is absolute. Being a Marxist, he is thus presented with one small but highly symptomatic problem: as an oppostional voice there is no room for him in the homogeneous plenitude of this totality. It is here that he shows us his hand: there is no opposition because 'criticism and resistance depend on the possibility of the positioning of the cultural act outside the massive Being of Capital, which then serves as an archimedean point from which to assault this last'.[17] Unfortunately, Jameson's analysis of the postmodernist totality has led him to conclude

> that distance in general including critical distance in particular has very precisely been abolished in the new space of postmodernism. We are submerged in its henceforth filled and suffused volumes to the point where our now postmodern bodies are bereft of spatial coordinates and practically (let alone theoretically) incapable of distanciation; meanwhile, it has already been observed how the prodigious new expansion of capital ends up penetrating those very pre-capitalist enclaves (Nature and the Unconscious) which offered extraterritorial and archimedian footholds for critical effectivity.[18]

There are a number of points to take note of here. Revolutionary Marxists have always tried to conduct their interventions according to the example set by Marx (*The Eighteenth Brumaire*), Lenin (the writings from 1917) and Trotsky (*The History of the Russian Revolution* and various writings on Germany, France, Spain, etc.). The lesson to be learned from these writings is the opposite of any dogmatism: they show us that a given conjuncture can be grasped only on the basis of the antagonisms internal to it. In fact, a conjuncture is no more than an accumulation of contradictory and conflicting forces of different origins and which produce different effects.[19] In Jameson's account of the present, the irreducible and overdetermined conflict is eclipsed by a pure systematicity. The historical present becomes an undifferentiated totality of contemporaneous moments in which instances lose their relative autonomy and art, architecture, literature, philosophy – even the Marxist philosophy of Althusser – are no more than unmediated expressions of 'the Being of Capital'. The classical thesis that 'class struggle is the motor of history', i.e., that as capitalism establishes its domination it simultaneously constructs and organizes the force which opposes that domination (the industrial proletariat) begins to sound positively postmodern! In his desire to escape theories of random difference and disorder, Jameson embraces a theory of domination without resistance or revolt and a theory of capitalist development devoid of unevenness or contradictions.

But most remarkable here is the fundamental theoretical complicity between Jameson and Lyotard. Both agree that Marxism is in fact a metanarrative, a narrative of all narratives that by its very nature requires a superior, transcendental space outside of the totality that it describes. Both Jameson and Lyotard seem to agree that such transcendental instances once existed but have now vanished into the purely present. Jameson cites two examples of what he calls 'pre-capitalist enclaves' which by virtue of their 'extraterritoriality', that is, their exteriority to a given conjuncture, permit 'critical effectivity'.[20] Faced with the puzzling assertion that one of these 'enclaves' is the unconscious, we can only ask in what sense it is possible to speak of the unconscious as an 'enclave' (let alone 'pre-capitalist'). Such an assertion belongs more properly to Jungian psychology than to psychoanalysis as understood by Freud and Lacan. In fact, the claim to transcendentality brings to mind the Hegelian Beautiful Soul of which Lacan spoke so many times. The Beautiful Soul denounces the disorder of a world from which it has withdrawn precisely to avoid having to recognize the extent of its own participation in that disorder: 'It lives in dread of besmirching the radiance of its inner being through action and existence. In order to preserve the purity of its heart, it flees from contact with actuality and persists in a state of self-willed impotence.'[21]

Thus, according to Jameson, Marxism is faced with an impossible situation insofar as it can conduct its theory and practice only from the very metaposition that postmodernism has abolished. But let us be very clear: an unbridgeable gulf separates the idea common to both Lyotard and Jameson that 'there are no more metanarratives' from Lacan's statement 'there is no metalanguage' or Althusser's assertion that 'there is no metaphilosophy'.[22] For the fact that many philosophies (including tendencies in Marxism) have imagined themselves to be metanarratives does not make the fantasy true. As Marx once quipped, 'One does not judge an individual by what he thinks about himself.' There is not now nor has there ever been a metanarrative or a transcendental space.

Theory exists everywhere in a practical state. Marxism, whatever the conceptualizations it has offered of its own practice, has never functioned as a metanarrative. In its practical existence, it speaks of nothing other than a struggle for which there is no outside and which is never structured according to the order of a logic or a law. Political practice acts within a conjuncture in order to act upon it, caught or 'entangled' (Lenin) in the very relationship of forces it attempts to modify.

In the totality described by Jameson there is no relationship of forces because there exist no opposing forces. We are thus treated to the tragi-comic spectacle of Marxists not only painting themselves into a corner but out of the picture entirely, leaving us with the dubious hope of an impotent and irrelevant transcendence (the 'splendid isolation' of the fortress). We should not confuse the grand totalities that are constructed throughout this debate with Hegelian philosophy. For Hegel at least portrayed a reason that actualized itself only by means of its contradictions and a truth that was always immanent in the movement of thought. In a famous phrase, he wrote that 'the true is the bacchanalian revel in which not one member remains sober'.[23] Perhaps not even Lyotard or Jameson.

In the postmodernist totality that functions as a given throughout the debate, art, literature and culture in general have lost their relative autonomy. Culture has not disappeared; quite the opposite. It has expanded to the point of explosion throughout the social whole. Culture has been overcome, generalized and preserved, in a word, *Aufgehoben* in the most classical sense of the term. According to Jameson, the *Aufhebung* of culture has resulted in a society of the simulacrum in which the real has become 'so many pseudo-events'.[24] Once again, the analysis of the Marxist Jameson coincides to a striking degree with that of an outspoken anti-Marxist and defender of classical liberalism – here, Jean Baudrillard. One more time, we are confronted with a disjunctive dilemma, this time organized around the theme of representation. How wrong we were to think that the interrogation of the concept of representation characteristic of high poststructuralism constituted in any sense an irreversible displacement. In fact, the debate acts to restore the old antinomies and thereby to exclude what was new. For Jameson is only the latest in a long line of Marxists who have proven utterly incapable of conceiving of a form of determination proper to literature or art outside of representation. Accordingly, a work is either anchored to and controlled by a reality which is the guarantee of the meaning of the work to the extent that it is external and therefore foreign to the work, or the work has no relation to reality and is thus simply false, illusory. From within the order that constructs this dilemma, any questioning of the ideas of representation or referentiality, even from a materialist position, can only be felt as an attack on the very notion of the determination of the work of art. Of course, this is not to deny what objectively happened as a result of the partial dismantling of the immense conceptual armature that constitutes representation as it organizes our thinking about works of art, literature and culture in general: the immaterialists (Baudrillard, Lyotard and the Yale School among others) rushed in to claim 'indeterminacy', 'freeplay' and even 'the end of representation'. Althusser has shown that the theoretical forces of the established order always exploit such 'openings', i.e., crises, breaks, mutations in knowledge (scientific or otherwise) for apologetic ends, for the sanctification of what exists.[25] The more important a mutation in knowledge, the more it permits and invites an intervention by the forces of the dominant conceptual regime whose objective is to annul and neutralize the effects of the mutation.

If Marxists argue that culture cannot be grasped as a true or false representation of reality, it is not to argue as Baudrillard does that 'the real is no longer real', that there exists no reality but only illusion.[26] In fact, Baudrillard moves pre-emptively to occupy the place that might otherwise be open to Macherey's directly counterposed statement: 'Art and reality are not two independent domains, external to one another, between which we can only find mechanical relationships. On the contrary, we must understand that art is something completely real, completely material.'[27] What is at stake in this conflict is precisely the *knowability* of the diverse practices that we sum up as 'culture'. To declare them free and immaterial is to render them *unknowable*, to place them beyond the grasp of a knowledge that is in turn caught up in the struggle between opposing social forces. But at the same time, we must be very clear that to retreat to the notion of art as representation as a defense against the immaterialists can only intensify the force of their intervention by paradoxically conserving an external reality at the expense of the reality of the work of art itself. It is a strange materialism indeed that insists on the illusory nature of the social products it confronts and converts them into shadowy simulacra in order the more readily to denounce their falsity. On this point, the two otherwise opposing camps agree, and the effects of this disavowed unity multiply throughout Marxist thought, closing off paths that had barely been opened.

The cost of this theoretical retreat is clear. Beyond denunciation, Jameson has very little to say about 'the art of the simulacrum'. He fears, for example, that Andy Warhol's *Diamond Dust Shoes* 'does not really speak to us at all'.[28] A mere surface without depth, the work as part of postmodern culture is paradoxically both a pure 'superstructural expression of a whole new wave of American military and economic domination throughout the world' (would not this constitute a meaning?), and an unanalyzable artifact which, insofar as it questions mimesis, possesses 'the contingency of some inexplicable natural object'.[29]

Thus, an absolute determination (culture as expression) simplified to the greatest degree converges with a dubious knowledge that consists solely in the despairing recognition that the postmodern work of art is in fact unknowable. Jameson seems unable to grasp that this unknowability reflects the inadequate character of the theoretical constructions through which the object is known, rather than the nature of the object itself. The result: the apocalyptic fantasies so common in this discussion. The work of art once full of meaning and affect and possessed of a depth that seemed infinite has now become empty, alien and cold, no longer a representation of reality but a simulacrum of the simulacrum, a false representation of what is itself false.

The simulacrum: is this what the great poststructuralist readings of Plato uncovered? Hardly. The current description of art and culture as simulacra are quite simply Platonic in the most traditional sense of the term. Moreover, they restore to Plato the meaning that was properly his before Derrida and Deleuze called that meaning into question. In the *Republic*, as is well known, Plato argued that the particular is a representation of the form and that art is a representation of the particular and thus a representation of a representation. Art is that which has wandered too far from the gravitational pull of the form. His denunciation of art as mere appearance is not based on the hypothesis of its immateriality but precisely the opposite: its irreducible materiality. Plato fears that the effects produced by the work of art will escape the control of the determining form, scattering like seeds to sprout wherever they land. Similarly, the work is never indeterminate or *causa sui* but is 'illegitimately begotten'.

Art and writing torment the Platonic system because they are unthinkable within its terms. They constitute a reality that must be denied because it cannot be grasped. But in every charge levelled against art, it is its materiality that is described. Aristotle in his own way recognized this dilemma only to dismiss it at the beginning of the *Poetics* as a non-problem that could only be an obstacle to the correct posing of the problem of the specific nature of art. Aristotle thus took several giant steps away from the notion of art as representation and towards an exploration of its material existence.

One final word on the subject of art. I have noted the striking absence of the concept of contradiction from Jameson's considerations of culture in general. This absence extends to his treatment of literature and art. He expresses his concern that 'our recent criticism from Macherey on, has been concerned to stress the heterogeneity and profound discontintuities of the work of art, no longer unified or organic but now a virtual grab bag or lumber room of disjoined subsystems and random raw materials and impulses of all kinds.'[30] Here again, thought lurches between a nostalgia for the organic unity of the work of art and a fear of the randomness of its heterogeneous parts. Let us do Macherey the simple justice of reading him. This is what he says:

> It is not a question of positing ... the indefinably open character of works, their radical disorder, etc. Disorder, non-order – that is to say, the totality of real contradictions through which we must explain literary products – is not an absence of order, a primitive and indeterminate power of the negative within it, which would dissolve works by restoring them to a sort of primal violence, that of their transgression. The incomplete, unfinished character of the works, their internal decomposition must be treated as the form of their material determination.[31]

It is neither an accident nor a failure of scholarship that Jameson has attributed to Macherey ideas opposed to Macherey's own. For the very notion which is the *starting point* for any serious examination of art from a materialist position, the notion of overdetermination, is utterly foreign to the entire debate. I say starting point because it is obvious that serious work in this domain has not yet begun – the debate itself is the most powerful confirmation of this fact. In the absence of a concept of the overdetermined material existence of the work of art, Marxism, faced with an art and literature that question the very foundations of traditional philosophical reflection (and which are thus objectively an aid to the rectification of Marxist theory) can do no better than cry 'Apocalypse Now!', taking for the end of art what is in reality a crisis of its own theory.

We may now see how the concept of history as a succession of expressive totalities separated by radical breaks combines with a series of quite distinct theoretical mutations and torsions within Marxism to produce what Derrida has called 'the apocalyptic tone adopted in recent philosophy'.[32] By positing the waning of affect, the loss of meaning and authenticity, these Marxists have opened the way to Lyotard and Baudrillard, who simply add Marxism to the list of radical losses. Even more instructive is the way in which an intransigent critique of teleological reason imperceptibly permitted (with the help of dominant thought) the rise of the improbable idea of the *end of teleology* (which has a more paradoxical character than the related and equally incorrect theories of the end of the subject and the end of representation). For the idea that teleological thought has come to an end could never be totally

disengaged from the idea that this end was its end, its telos, its fulfillment. Now it seems as if all the theoretical forces of the established
order gather together for one 'final offensive'. In an extremely amusing
essay, Derrida captures the element of the ridiculous in the current
proliferation of apocalyptic fantasies:

> It is not only the end of this here but also and first of that there, the end of
> history, the end of the class struggle, the end of philosophy, the death of God,
> the end of religions, the end of Christianity and morals ... the end of the
> subject, the end of man, the end of the West, the end of Oedipus, the end of
> the earth, Apocalypse Now, I tell you, in the catacylsm, the fire, the blood, the
> fundamental earthquake, the napalm descending from the skies by helicopter,
> like prostitutes and also the end of literature, the end of painting, art as a thing
> of the past, the end of the past, the end of psychoanalysis, the end of the
> university, the end of phallocentrism and phallogocentrism and I don't know
> what else.[33]

In his mock-obituary of thought, Derrida alludes to one of the key
objectives of his own work, an objective he shares with Althusser and
Deleuze, among others. He has shown that, from the very origins of
philosophy, the concept of representation, for example, has been the site
of conflicting descriptions and interpretations, some of which at any
given time have escaped the logic of what could conceivably be called
representation to oppose it. Similarly, by borrowing the title of his essay
from Kant, Derrida shows that the question of 'the end' is perennial in
philosophy, the symptom of an internal conflict to be analyzed. But
beyond the fact that philosophy has already died a thousand deaths, that
is, beyond its never-ending preoccupation with an end which never
comes because it has occurred from the very beginning, there arises a
more pertinent question: what are the objectives or ends of those who
declare the end of this or that?

Let us briefly take the example of that veritable coroner of contemporary thought, Baudrillard. Not content in the mid-seventies to
announce the death of Marxism and psychoanalysis (both of which he
has since periodically exhumed in order to declare them dead once
again), he has announced the death of something called 'the social' in his
In the Shadow of the Silent Majorities. Once it seemed that the masses
made history. But this was merely a simulacrum, perhaps the simulacrum of our epoch. Here, Baudrillard simply inverts the traditional
notion of alienation to return us, despite his praises of indeterminacy,
chaos and flux, to a world so perfectly ordered that it easily tolerates
contingencies and accidents. In the state of revolt, the masses lose themselves and thus cease to be what they well and truly are. Accordingly,
the 'withdrawal of the masses into their domestic sphere, their refuge

from history, politics and the universal and their absorption into an idiotic humdrum existence of consumption' is precisely a *return* of the masses to the state proper to them, a state which is their end (*telos*) and their essence (*ousia*).[34] At rest, they have abandoned their previously alienated, simulacral state to become 'the only referent which still functions ... that of the silent majority'.[35] Baudrillard celebrates a silent world, a world that has rid itself of every hint of conflict or contradiction. And since no conflict disturbs the homogeneity of this world, to speak of revolt is to condemn the masses as they truly are in the name of some outdated ideal. Once again, as throughout the debate on postmodernism, transcendence is held up as the condition of revolt (in the very determinate absence of contradiction). He exploits the questioning of transcendence to the advantage of the established order to proclaim a 'perceptual peace' based on the silence, passivity and depoliticization of the masses. Baudrillard pronounces the final ritual exclusion of the masses: 'the mass is dumb like beasts, and its silence is equal to the silence of beasts ... it is without truth and without reason. It has been attributed with every arbitrary remark. It is without consciousness and without unconscious.'[36]

The entire work is an incantation that seeks to fix the masses once and for all as they are in a period of defeat demobilization. It repeats with a symptomatic frequency: there was revolt but there is no longer any. The incantation in fact resembles an obsessive ritual designed to ward off a dreaded eventuality. Thus, although Baudrillard assures us that revolt is no longer possible, he cannot help but warn us of the consequences of the 'impossible' event: 'the true artlessness is that of socialists and humanists of every shade who want all wealth to be redistributed.... It is the *wrong use of wealth* which saves a society. Nothing has changed since Mandeville and his *Fable of the Bees.* And socialism can do nothing to prevent it.'[37] So Baudrillard fervently hopes.

'Without memory of morning or hope of night' (Beckett), without lost paradises or imminent apocalypses, antagonistic classes go on fighting a most disorderly and unpredictable struggle. Now we see what Marxism so fears in postmodernism and poststructuralism and why in its fear it has been unable to distinguish between its friends and its adversaries. It fears itself, or rather its own practice, whose image it cannot bear to contemplate. Marxist theory has confronted its inadequacy to its own practice and thus its own unequal development, its own contradictions. Just when we thought we had escaped our destiny, we ran right into its arms.

Perhaps all of us in one way or another have been duped by the subjectless cunning of the struggle in theory. A rationalist fantasy of order, a dream of logical guarantees that would guide our practice and validate our theory, disarmed and prevented us from grasping the conflict of forces internal to the field that remains inescapably ours. For there is no metanarrative, no transcendentality. We act within a specific conjuncture only to see that conjuncture transformed beneath our feet, perhaps by our intervention itself, but always in ways that ultimately escape our intention or control, thereby requiring new interventions *ad infinitum*. On a field of conflicting forces whose balance of power shifts endlessly, we have no fixed reference points, nothing to guide us but the knowledge of our own errors. One such error, the knowledge of which ought by now to have emerged clearly enough, is the very concept of postmodernism itself. In its totalizing, transcendental pretensions, this concept precisely forecloses progress in thought by denying the possibility that the fissures, disjunctions, breaks in contemporary social reality are symptoms of an impending crisis. For the signal feature of postmodernism most inimical to historical materialism is its claim to be the end of all crises, the end of all narratives, the end of resistance and revolutionary transformation. The debate on postmodernism will prove to have been productive to the extent that it awakens in us the consciousness of its own limits, which are not the limits of history itself (as the partisans of postmodernism claim), but rather the boundaries of that territory where Marxist theory has always intervened most effectively: the present conjuncture. The only truly irremediable error would be to believe that this present will endure forever.

Notes

1. Fredric Jameson, 'Postmodernism, or the Cultural Logic of Late Capitalism', *New Left Review* 146 (July–August 1984); Terry Eagleton, 'Capitalism, Modernism and Postmodernism', *New Left Review* 152 (July–August 1985); Jürgen Habermas, 'Modernity – An Incomplete Project', in Hal Foster, ed., *The Anti-Aesthetic*, (Port Townsend, WA: The Bay Press, 1983).

2. In addition to *The Republic*, see *The Phaedrus* and *The Sophist*. See also, Jacques Derrida's 'Plato's Pharmacy', in *Dissemination*, trans. Barbara Johnson (Chicago: University Press, 1981); and Gilles Deleuze, *Logique du sens* (Paris: Editions de Minuit, 1969).

3. Louis Althusser, *Essays in Self-Criticism*, trans. Grahame Lock (London: NLB; Atlantic Highlands [N.J.]: Humanities Press, 1976), p. 72.

4. Louis Althusser, *Philosophie et la philosophie spontanée des savants* (Paris: F. Maspero, 1974), p. 116.

5. Jameson, 'Postmodernism', p. 55.

6. G.W.F. Hegel, *The Phenomenology of Mind*, trans. A.V. Miller (Oxford: Oxford University Press, 1977), pp. 341–55.

7. Jean-François Lyotard, 'Presentations', in *Philosophy in France Today*, ed. Alan Montefiore (Cambridge: Cambridge University Press, 1983), p. 133.

8. Ronald Aronson, 'Historical Materialism as Answer to Marxism's Crisis', *New Left Review* 152 (July–August 1985), p. 77.

9. Hegel, *Phenomenology*, p. 9.

10. Without doubt, the most interesting and engaging work to emerge from this debate is Jacques Bouveresse's defense of reason in general and philosophical reason in particular; see

Rationalité et cynisme (Paris: Minuit, 1984). Put somewhat vulgarly, this work is a social democratic defense of progress against the right-wing populist anti-intellectualism characteristic of a growing sector of the French intelligentsia.

11. Perry Anderson, *In the Tracks of Historical Materialism* (London: Verso, 1983), p. 43.

12. Jean-François Lyotard, *La condition postmoderne* (Paris: Minuit, 1979), pp. 27–8.

13. Ibid.

14. Jameson, p. 56.

15. Ibid., p. 61.

16. Ibid., p. 72.

17. Ibid., p. 87.

18. Ibid., pp. 76–7.

19. See Louis Althusser, *For Marx*, trans. Ben Brewster (New York: Random House, 1970); in particular the essay, 'Contradiction and Overdetermination'.

20. Ibid., p. 87.

21. Hegel, *Phenomenology*, p. 400.

22. Jacques Lacan, 'La Science et la verité', in *Ecrits* (Paris: Editions du Seuil, 1966), p. 867; Althusser, *Philosophie spontanée*, p. 56.

23. Hegel, *Phenomenology*, p. 27.

24. Jameson, p. 87.

25. Althusser, *Philosophie spontanée.*

26. Jean Baudrillard, *Simulations*, trans. Paul Foss, Paul Patton and Philip Beitchman (New York: Semiotext(e), 1983), p. 25.

27. Pierre Macherey, 'The Problem of Reflection', *Sub-Stance* 15 (1976), p. 19.

28. Jameson, p. 59.

29. Ibid.

30. Ibid., p. 75.

31. Macherey, 'The Problem of Reflection', p. 18.

32. Jacques Derrida, 'Of an Apocalyptic Tone Adopted in Recent Philosophy', *Oxford Literary Review* 6, 2 (1984).

33. Ibid., pp. 20–1.

34. Jean Baudrillard, *In the Shadow of the Silent Majorities*, trans. Paul Foss, Paul Patton and John Johnstone (New York: Semiotext(e), 1983), p. 39.

35. Ibid., p. 19.

36. Ibid., pp. 28–9.

37. Ibid., pp. 80–1.

PART TWO

◆

Postmodernism, Feminism and Popular Culture Theory

7

A Jury of their Peers: Marlene Gorris's *A Question of Silence*

Linda Williams

In a now classic article of feminist criticism, Elaine Showalter argues for a theory of women's writing based on a model of the specific and 'self-defined nature of female cultural experience'. Borrowing from feminist historian Gerda Lerner and anthropologists Shirley and Edwin Ardener, Showalter points out that women's culture is not so much a subculture as a dual perspective of living and participating in a dominant male culture with boundaries that overlap, but do not entirely contain, the non-dominant, 'muted' culture of women. She thus views male and female experience as two overlapping circles with much of the woman's muted circle falling within the boundaries of the dominant circle but with a small crescent of experience that she dubs, following Edwin Ardener, a 'wild zone' or 'no-man's land' of woman's culture that is entirely off limits to men. Where women know the male crescent, if not through personal experience, at least through myth and legend, men have no experience or knowledge of the female crescent precisely because there is so little women's art known to men.[1]

The explicitly feminist artist thus faces a dilemma: whenever she attempts to speak and validate the mysterious 'wild' zone of woman's experience she runs the risk of making a leap to a mythic level of female identity conceived outside the limits of all existing language, all 'known' reality. Yet not to run this risk is to remain trapped within the limits of patriarchy's definition of what it knows: man as subject, woman as other. My purpose is not to bemoan the limitations of this dilemma – which are inescapable – but to see how an exemplary work of feminist film art negotiates its difficulties.[2]

The problem, as I see it, is that once an explicit work of feminist art begins to press the 'muted' 'wild zone' of woman-specific consciousness to speak, it may speak too clearly in facile parables rather than in aesthetically rich language. In this case, the tension inherent in the feminist revision of patriarchal language becomes mere reversal: black becomes white, passive women become Amazonian guerillas; and the gorgon Medusa grows beautiful and laughs. But if, as Showalter and others have noted, women's culture must inevitably envelop the social, literary and cultural heritages of both the muted female and the dominant male groups, if women really have a 'double-voiced discourse', 'inside two traditions at once', or if, as Ruby Rich puts it in a slightly different context, women are the 'ultimate dialecticians',[3] then we need feminist texts that can reveal this duality, this tension in the often unspoken contradictions between the dominant and the mute.

More than any other feminist film of the last decade, Marlene Gorris's 1984 Dutch film, *A Question of Silence*, seems to me to avoid the pitfalls of a facile or utopian feminist revision while speaking eloquently from within the still 'muted' experiences of its three women protagonists. The film is about the spontaneous and unmotivated murder–mutilation of a male boutique owner by three women shoppers. They commit the crime after one of them – a near catatonic housewife – is caught shoplifting a dress. Instead of meekly returning the garment as the smug male owner seems to expect, Christine stubbornly shoves it back in her bag. Two other women watch with interest this spectacle of an obviously guilty woman refusing to act guilty. They come to her defense and then, slowly, deliberately, join in her offense, taking garments themselves.

What follows is a gradual escalation of an initial crime against property into the ritual mutilation and murder of a male scapegoat. We see almost none of the actual violence of this scene – just enough to know that hangers, clothes racks and ashtrays serve as weapons. The bulk of the film is the investigation into this crime by a court-appointed woman psychiatrist. The investigation culminates in a hearing on the sanity of the defendants in which the psychiatrist, much to the annoyance of the court, declares the women sane.

The three women cannot or will not explain why they commited the crime. During the investigation, the psychiatrist earnestly attempts to find the psycho-social explanations for their acts. But each woman resists the imposition of a clinico-juridical discourse that would explain her crime by judging her mad, then leave her to grow truly insane in the clean, brightly lit panopticon that is the Dutch penal system. The psychiatrist must finally agree that they are three 'very ordinary women'. The only way to 'read' this crime, she learns, is to see it as proceeding from that portion of women's culture and experience which is truly not known to men. Her investigation thus leads her directly into Showalter's wild zone.

Showalter's first method of understanding the wild zone of female culture is to visualize it as a place – a 'no-man's land' where women congregate. There are few such places outside the home, but a woman's dress shop is certainly one of them. Although the psychiatrist could never argue the point in a court of law, it is clear that the crime could not have taken place in a more male-defined space; nor could it have taken place in that space if the shop-owner had been a woman. Neither fact can be used to excuse the crime, but both are important to its women readers. For only in this space could the women let out the rage and defiance they did not even know was in them, only in this space could Christine channel her rage into action, and only in this space could Annie and Andrea identify with this rage, own it, and finally share in its expression as well.

Showalter's second method of understanding the wild zone is through the experiences women share. In the film three scenes stand out from the jigsaw puzzle of flashbacks elicited by the psychiatrist's interviews. Each contains a relatively insignificant detail that takes on meaning only in relation to its similarity to the other women's common experiences. These details could never be mentioned in a court of law or even among the women themselves should they find a way to talk to one another. Nor does the psychiatrist ever speak of them. Yet they are there in the full visual rendering of experience by which cinematic flashback can sometimes belie the specific memories of its reminiscers.

Each has to do with coffee or tea. Coffee first appears innocuously enough in an early scene depicting a bit of banter between Annie, the overweight and jolly waitress, and a male customer in the cafe where she works. The customer calls out for a refill and jokingly adds the insult that a few more steps couldn't hurt Annie's ample figure. She laughs heartily and serves the coffee, even as the police enter to pick her up for the crime that has not yet been revealed to us. The incident is unremarkable except in retrospect, in relation to the accumulated rendering of the experiences of all three women, each of whom is insulted and put in her place through some aspect of her conventional role as server, but not customer. In retrospect Annie's laughter will come back to haunt both the audience and Janine, the psychiatrist.

A second, more pointed, scene shows Andrea, the efficient executive secretary, at work at a board meeting with her boss and several male advisors. When asked about a detail of their overseas investments, Andrea answers with slightly more command of the facts than befits a mere secretary. The advice is not taken kindly by her boss. But he takes his revenge indirectly, first, by growing irritated at the sound her spoon makes stirring her coffee – one of his advisors even stays her hand – and second, by taking the advice of this same male advisor, who recommends the opposite of Andrea's plan. It is clear that the issue is not her ability to give sound advice, but the fact that a mere secretary has stepped out of her role as discreet notetaker and coffee-server to do so.

In this prolonged scene built upon the noise of a coffee cup and spoon, we begin to read the small indignities of women's lives. These indignities could never be offered in a court of law as justification for the rage unleashed in the boutique, but they nevertheless clearly present humiliations other women can understand. But it is finally through Christine's eerie silence that we come to experience the ultimate indignity of women's lives. Christine stands in her kitchen amid the chaos of three children and a hurried husband who is about to leave her holding just the saucer, as if she were a table. Through the social determination of a life that has asked her only to serve, Christine has become an inanimate thing. 'It is no wonder she has stopped talking', explains Andrea, in one of the film's few moments of direct explanation, 'no one was listening'.

Each of these humiliating incidents is experienced by a woman alone, in a space that does not seem to belong to her even if, as in the case of Christine's kitchen, it should. There is no other woman to recognize or name the experience. As it occurs, the woman does not appear able to name it herself. The shared aspects of women's experience represented by the film are thus entirely forms of negative alienation, while the only instances of shared experience occur at the scene of the crime and later in the courtroom. Although the film certainly could have contrived to make the spatial and experiential aspects of women's wild zone coincide in an easy parable of feminist solidarity, I think it is important that it does not. A comparison to a work that does just that is instructive.

Susan Keating Glaspell's 1917 short story, 'A Jury of Her Peers', has recently entered the canon of feminist literature.[4] Like Gorris's film, the story concerns a female murderer and a male victim. A farmer's wife, Minnie Foster, is arrested for the strangulation murder of her husband. Minnie's story is never told directly, but it is pieced together by two groups of male and female investigators. While the sheriff and county attorney vainly search her house and barn for clues to the motive, their wives, relegated to the space of kitchen and parlor, do some unofficial investigating of their own. They discover ample motive for Minnie's crime in her husband's systematic destruction of all life and beauty in her world. They decode the poverty of the house, the stove that doesn't draw, the patchwork of her wardrobe, the broken neck of her canary and her presumed reaction to this cruelty in sewing that goes awry, chores that are left undone and finally her revenge, the strangulation of her sleeping husband.

As the female jury of peers comprehends the significance of each piece of evidence, they systematically destroy it, erasing clues to Minnie Foster's guilt. As Annette Kolodny has noted in an article on the story, their reading thus amounts to a complete reordering of 'who, in fact, has been murdered ... what has constituted the real crime in the story'.[5] Even more revealing than their ability to read the deeper nature of the crime is their immediate sense of their own participation in it: 'Oh, I *wish* I'd come over here once in a while! ... That was a crime! Who's going to punish that?'[6]

Kolodny's major point about the story is that the women readers of the crime expand the literal male reading into a larger, figurative, under-standing of its modus operandi: strangulation. The male reading sees only that a man is strangled, that his wife is the likely suspect and that they themselves are the expert readers of the evidence; the female (figurative) reading sees the many ways in which a woman's life has been strangled, that the husband is the likely suspect, and that they them-selves are the true investigators into the crime. Their very expertise lies in their ability not to judge from on high but to act, as Carol Gilligan has shown with respect to the 'moral development' of women in general, as an empathic jury of peers sensitive to extenuating circumstances.[7]

Thus in Kolodny's terms, women are the better readers of other women's literal and figurative truths because of their shared experiences. The two women in Glaspell's story are able to make Minnie Foster's kitchen and house 'speak' in her defense when she herself cannot or will not speak. The story even implies that they help her to beat the rap as well. For Kolodny, 'A Jury of Her Peers' is a parable of female reading and solidarity that speaks its parable of the unique ability of women to read the supposed 'insignificance of kitchen things'. But I am concerned that the elevation of such parables to the status of key texts within the emerging canon of feminist art may have a simplistically utopian influ-ence on the sort of work we begin looking for from feminist artists. Much as the tale satisfies as an example of table turning, I think it would be a mistake to take it as the sort of feminist revision most called for now. What interests me instead are not the remarkable similarities between Glaspell's story and Gorris's film, but their illuminating differ-ences.

In 'A Jury of Her Peers', the feminist moral has been facilitated by the congruence of Showalter's first two categories of the unique cultural experience of women: the spatial and experiential. The isolated experi-ences of each housewife are able to emerge when two of them get together in the kitchen and parlor of a third woman. Only in this no-man's land are these first two women able to reorder the significance of the third woman's experience.

In Gorris's film, however, the separation between the spatial and experiential aspects of the wild zone of women's cultural experience emphasizes the very real difficulty women have in finding the places where they can speak their experience to one another. Thus, where Glaspell's reversal of the initial patriarchal terms of judgment is facilitated by the convergence of the spatial and experiential realms, Gorris's film separates these realms and thus separates the women from one another. There is no positive way for them to articulate what they nevertheless begin to know that they share. The violence of the crime and the negative disruption of laughter in the courtroom are their only forms of speech.

The viewer of the film, like the internal reader–investigator within the film, cannot base her reading on a simple reversal of an initial male judgement. Instead, she must engage in a deeper and more complicit process of identification with mute and wild zones of experience that are not yet known and that certainly may not help her to beat the rap of male judgement. What is missing from Glaspell's story and Kolodny's criticism, then, is the third aspect of Showalter's wild zone: its 'metaphysical' or 'imaginary' side. Showalter writes,

> If we think of the wild zone metaphysically, or in terms of consciousness, it has no corresponding male space since all of male consciousness is within the circle of the dominant structure and thus accessible to or structured by language.... In terms of cultural anthropology, women know what the male crescent is like, even if they have never seen it, because it becomes the subject of legend (like the wilderness). But men do not know what is in the wild.[8]

The genuine sense of excitement and danger generated by the two screenings of Gorris's film I have attended might be partly explained by the film's demonstration that women do not necessarily know what is in 'the wild' either. For the film suggests that the most genuinely heroic moment of feminist consciousness consists in a woman's decision to cast her lot with an identity that has not yet been spoken and that cannot as yet speak itself. Unlike Glaspell's story, there is no neat parable, no pat reversal of judgement that can metaphorically explain the crime. There is only a radical silence erupting into violence when the women first get together, and erupting into laughter when they meet again.

This laughter occurs when the male court begs Janine the psychiatrist for at least a 'tentative provisional diagnosis' that would make the job of categorizing the crime as simple insanity easier. Janine refuses to declare the women insane; she even goes on to insist that the sex of the victim

and his position as owner of the boutique are important factors precipi-
tating the crime. To counter this, the prosecutor argues a ridiculous
parallel: the crime could just as well have been perpetrated by three
male shoppers on a female shop-owner. Annie the waitress is the first to
laugh. Soon Christine and Andrea join in, as do various female spectators, including a chorus of four silent women whom we recognize as also
having been present at the scene of the crime. Finally, Janine laughs too.

Raucous, disruptive laughter achieves the recognition and solidarity
among women that Janine's earnest attempts at communication had
failed to achieve. When the laughing women are ordered to leave the
court so that the trial might proceed in their absence, a pregnant
moment ensues as the significant female actors – Janine, the three
defendants, and the four silent witnesses – all converge at the center of
the courtroom, a low railing and a pit between them. They repeat looks
of recognition that had occurred the first time the defendants had been
led into the pit. But that first look of recognition served merely to reveal
Janine's awareness of a silent bond between the defendants and the
chorus of women spectators. By the time of this second look, Janine's
laughter has spoken her solidarity with these silent women. She has
joined the 'high heeled army of Furies' referred to by the prosecution at
the very moment they are led, like the Furies of Aeschylus, out of the
light, down into the bowels of the earth.

But the film does not end on this note of solidarity. It ends, rather, on
a moment of suspension between the known world of patriarchal light
and the unknown world of matriarchal shadow. In the parking lot
outside the courtroom, as Janine's husband angrily honks his car horn
for Janine to come, she once again encounters the chorus of silent
witnesses to the crime. Janine turns to look at them, and on this look the
frame freezes. The spatial, experiential and metaphysical realms of
female difference are recognized in her look, though they still have not
been spoken.

A Question of Silence offers no near parables, no pat reversals, no
clear motives and, most importantly, no clear language that states
women's truths. It offers a silence that questions all language, a laughter
that subverts authority, a judgement that never gets pronounced. In all
of this it does not so much work to *revise* its underlying patriarchal myth
of the irrationality of women as it reopens all the questions supposedly
solved by such a myth. In the final play of Aeschylus's *Oresteia*, a
female chorus of 'Furies' is sold out in the first court of law by a male-
identified goddess who is always for the male.[9] Sweet-talked by Athena,
the Furies go quietly to their new home beneath the earth, making way
for the progress of the city state and its new codes of justice. Repressed
and renamed, the 'Eumenides' now mask the ancient war between the

sexes symbolized by Clytemnestra and Agamemnon's cycle of revenge.

Gorris's film returns to this war and to the original matriarchal power repressed by this myth. Where the male myth gets rid of the unsightly, raucous Furies by stage-managing a quiet exit, Gorris restages this descent into the bowels of the earth in a feminist revision that transforms her Furies's original rage into subversive laughter. These Furies exit convulsed by the absurdity of a male reason that cannot understand women. Like Cixous's Medusa – who was also part of a monstrous sisterly trio – they have been revised. But although they are laughing, Gorris has not simply changed the monstrous into the beautiful, the negatives into positives, the repressive ending into a liberatory one. In fact, the film does not so much revise the *Oresteia* with a female-defined happy ending as it reopens all the questions supposedly solved by Athena's original judgement against women. Like 'A Jury of Her Peers' it asks what real judgement of women by women might be. But unlike Glaspell's story, it does not proceed to perform that judgement itself. The language of such judgement, it suggests, does not yet exist.

The power of *A Question of Silence* as feminist art thus lies in its resistance of all the male paradigms by which female deviance has been understood, in its insistence on the wildness of women's cultural experience and, finally, in its refusal to narrate the positive, utopian identity of women.

Notes

I would like to offer my usual thanks to my friend and colleague Judy Gardiner for her thoughtful advice on this article.

1. Showalter, 'Feminist Criticism in the Wilderness', *Critical Inquiry*, 8 (winter 1981), pp. 179–205.

2. The fundamental dilemma addressed by Showalter's essay is that of all feminist attempts to define the difference of women without falling into ahistorical models of the biological, linguistic or psychic nature of that difference. Her solution is to move beyond these first three models to a fourth: a cultural model of women's difference that has the advantage both of being more general and of taking the social context as primary to the others. But in naming the 'y' crescent of female experience a 'wild zone' that has no parallel to the male crescent 'x', Showalter herself runs the risk of re-essentializing woman's experience in the social. She argues, for example, that this wild zone is unique to women and unknown to men. Although I realize there are inevitable problems in seeking a solution to essentialist qualities in feminist art by invoking a theory that itself has recourse to an essentialist position, I also recognize that the most important question about this art may not be whether it makes some sort of leap beyond the constraints of patriarchal language and thought, but how it goes about doing so.

3. See Michelle Citron, Julia Lesage, Judith Mayne, B. Ruby Rich and Anna Marie Taylor, 'Women and Film: A Discussion of Feminist Aesthetics', in *New German Critique*, 13 (winter 1978).

4. Glaspell, in Lee Edwards and Arlyn Diamond (eds.), *American Voices, American Women*, (New York: Avon Books, 1973) pp. 359–81.

5. Kolodny, 'A Map for Re-Reading: Or Gender and the Interpretation of Literary Texts', *New Literary History*, 11 (spring 1980), p. 462.

6. Glaspell, p. 378.

7. Carol Gilligan, *In A Different Voice: Psychological Theory and Women's Development* (Cambridge: Harvard University Press, 1982).

8. Showalter, p. 200.

8

Mikhail Bakhtin and Left Cultural Critique

Robert Stam

In the last few years, the Russian social and literary theorist Mikhail Bakhtin (1895–1973) has become one of the most influential and controversial thinkers on the contemporary scene. Called by his biographers one of the 'leading thinkers of the twentieth century', Bakhtin published, under his own name or in collaboration, books and essays on subjects ranging from linguistics (*Marxism and the Philosophy of Language*, 1929), to psychoanalysis (*Freudianism: A Marxist Critique*, 1927) to literary criticism (*The Formal Method in Literary Scholarship*, 1928; *Problems of Dostoevsky's Poetics*, 1929; and *Rabelais and His World*, 1965). Recently, Bakhtin's influence has spread to many parts of the world, crucial Bakhtinian terms have gained wide dissemination, and the exegetical application of Bakhtin's ideas is proceeding apace. My purpose here will be to explore the specific relevance of Bakhtin's thought for left cultural critique. How might Bakhtin help us transcend some of the widely sensed inadequacies of traditional left cultural analysis? How can Bakhtin help us forge a left critical method which goes beyond dogmatism, beyond puritanism, beyond economism, and beyond cultural defeatism? How might such celebrated Bakhtinian categories as 'dialogism', 'heteroglossia', 'tact', and 'carnival' shed light on popular culture and the mass media? How might Bakhtinian conceptualizations help us analyze, teach and perhaps even generate mass-mediated culture?[1]

There are, it should be pointed out, many Bakhtins; there is Bakhtin the revolutionary, Bakhtin the Marxist, Bakhtin the anti-Stalinist, Bakhtin the populist, and Bakhtin the crypto-Christian. There is a left reading of Bakhtin (Fredric Jameson, Terry Eagleton, Tony Bennett, Ken

Hirschkop), and a liberal reading (Wayne Booth, Michael Holquist, Katerina Clark, Gary Saul Morson).[2] The last few years have witnessed, in fact, a kind of posthumous wrestle over the political soul of Bakhtin. As an extraordinarily complex, contradictory and at times enigmatic figure, Bakhtin has been open to appropriation by the most diverse ideological currents. I will see him here, however, as a kind of radical populist or 'para-Marxist' working 'alongside' Marxism – and certainly not against it as some of his commentators would have it – and a 'trans-Marxist' in a sense that he corrects some of the oversights and blindspots of Marxist theory. My reading here will be quite partial, interested less in arguing a definitive interpretation of what Bakhtin 'really thought' or in ironing out the manifest contradictions of his work than in proposing a partial appropriation of certain features of his thought for the strategic purposes of a radical hermeneutics of the mass media.

The left has often displayed a schizophrenic attitude toward mass-mediated culture. As the 'children of Marx and Coca Cola', as Godard put it in *Masculine, Feminine*, leftists participate in a mass culture they often theoretically condemn. But even apart from this split between personal habits and political stance, the left has shown theoretical ambivalence about the *political* role of the mass media. On the one hand, a certain left (Herbert Schiller, Armand Mattelart, and in a different way, Theodor Adorno and Max Horkheimer) excoriates the mass media as the voice of bourgeois hegemony, the instrument of capitalist reification, an overwhelming apparatus or 'influencing machine' allowing little resistance. In this more pessimistic phase, the left laments the media's 'total manipulation' of 'false needs' and 'false desires', and practices, as a didactic corollary, a kind of pedagogy of displeasure, thus ceding a crucial area to the enemy. Another left, in contrast, salutes the revolutionizing impact of modern reproduction techniques (Benjamin), or the mass-mediated subversion of the traditional class privileges of the literary elite (Enzensberger), detecting progressive potential in mass-mediated cultural products, finding inklings of empowerment in the working-class anger of a Bruce Springsteen or evidence of emancipatory desire in the collective enthusiasm for superstar concert-telethons for Farm Aid and Amnesty International.

Thus the left has oscillated between melancholia and euphoria, alternately playing the nudnik and the polyanna. Any number of analysts, fortunately, have sought to go beyond this ideological manic-depression by stressing the gaps, fissures and contradictions lurking just below the apparently unperturbed surface of the mass media. In 'Constituents of a Theory of the Media', Hans Magnus Enzensberger spoke of television as a 'leaky medium', corporately controlled but pressured by popular desire and dependent on 'politically unreliable' creative talent to satisfy its inexhaustible appetite for programming.[3] More important, Enzensberger took exception to the manipulation theory of the media as mass deception, emphasizing instead their address to 'real needs' and 'real desires'. Picking up this utopian strain, writers such as Fredric Jameson, Richard Dyer and Dick Hebdige have highlighted the mass-culture response to what Jameson has called the 'elemental power of deep social needs'. Two excellent recent collections, Tania Modleski's *Studies in Entertainment* and Colin MacCabe's *High Theory/Low Culture*, continue this tradition by proposing a dialectical synthesis which eschews both the elitist pessimism of manipulation theory and the naive affirmative celebrations of the uncritical apologists for mass-mediated culture.[4] Neither collection, however, takes advantage of a theorist who might further buttress and animate this more dialectical view – Mikhail Bakhtin.

Bakhtin offers cultural analysis, as Todorov points out, a unitary, transdisciplinary view of the human sciences and of cultural life based on the common textual nature of their materials.[5] Bakhtin's broad view of 'text' as referring to all cultural production rooted in language – and for Bakhtin no cultural production exists *outside* of language – has the salutary effect of breaking down the walls not only between popular and elite culture, but also between text and context. The barrier between text and context, between 'inside' and 'outside', for Bakhtin, is an artificial one, for in fact there is an easy flow of permeability between the two. The context is already textualized, informed by what Bakhtin calls 'prior speakings' and the 'already said', while the text, as Bakhtin and Medvedev argue in their polemic with the Russian Formalists, is 'redolent with contexts', at every point inflected by history and shaped by events. Thus Bakhtin's 'historical poetics' avoids the twin traps of a vacuous apolitical formalism and of deterministic versions of Marxism in which artistic superstructure simply 'reflects' an economic base, proposing instead a kind of mobile 'juxtastructure' of mutual and in some ways reciprocal determinations.

The Critique of Formalism

This, then, is the first advantage Bakhtin offers left analysis: a thoroughgoing critique of all structuralisms and formalisms which at the same time avoids the trap of vulgar Marxism. Writing in the twenties, Bakhtin managed to criticize a moribund formalism and a nascent structuralism, while forging his own brand of Marxist-inflected trans-structuralism. In *The Formal Method in Literary Scholarship*, co-authored with Pavel Medvedev, Bakhtin shows that he, like the formalists, is sensitive to the specificity of textual mechanisms – literature as literature – but unlike them, he refuses to dissociate these mechanisms from the ensemble of discourses – including those of everyday life – or from larger social and historical processes. With uncanny prescience, Bakhtin thus simultaneously anticipated and superseded the linguistic-structuralist turn, and his interlinked critiques of both Saussurean linguistics and formalist poetics point the way to the possible transcendence of the aporias generated by those movements.

The foundational text, in this regard, is *Marxism and the Philosophy of Language,* which first appeared under Voloshinov's name in 1929, and which constitutes Bakhtin's first direct intervention within the contemporary tradition of reflection on language. While Bakhtin agrees with Saussure that a discipline should be created to study the 'life of signs within society', he differs in his view both of the nature of signs and of their role within social life. Rejecting what he sees as Saussure's mentalistic individualism, which locates language and ideology within the individual consciousness, Bakhtin's 'translinguistics' sees both consciousness and ideology as semiotic, as existing only insofar as they are realized within some kind of semiotic material, whether in the form of 'inner speech' or in the process of verbal interaction with others, or in mediated forms like writing and art. Linguistics for Bakhtin forms part of the broader study of ideologies, for the 'domain of ideology coincides with the domain of signs'. The individual consciousness is decentered, for 'signs can only arise on inter-individual territory'. Debunking the cherished myth of the monadic ego, Bakhtin posits consciousness as a socio-ideological fact rather than as the product of an autonomous self-generating cogito.

Whereas the Saussurean tradition regards speech as individual and the language system as social, and therefore as antinomies, Bakhtin sees the two as constantly imbricated. Speech produces utterances, which are social by definition, since they are inter-individual, requiring a socially constituted speaker and addressee. The Saussurean *langue/parole* dichotomy implicitly reproduces the venerable bourgeois individual-versus-society trope that Bakhtin is at great pains to reject. For Bakhtin, the individual, even in his/her dreams, is permeated by the social; indeed, one develops individuality not against but through the social. The process of constructing the self, for Bakhtin, involves the hearing and assimilating of the words and discourses of others (mother, father, relatives, friends, representatives of religious, educational and political institutions, the mass media and so forth), all processed dialogically so that the words in a sense become half 'one's own words'. With maturity, these words transform themselves into what Bakhtin, in 'Discourse in the Novel', calls 'internally persuasive discourse':

Such discourse is of decisive significance in the evolution of an individual consciousness: consciousness awakens to independent ideological life precisely in the world of alien discourses surrounding it, and from which it cannot initially separate itself. The process of distinguishing between one's own and another's discourse, between one's own and another's thought, is activated rather late in development. When thought begins to work in an independent, experimenting and discriminating way, what first occurs is a separation between internally persuasive discourse and authoritarian enforced discourse, along with a rejection of those congeries of discourses that do not matter to us, that do not touch us.[6]

A self is constituted by acquiring the ambient languages and discourses of its world. The self, in this sense, is a kind of hybrid sum of institutional and discursive practices bearing on family, class, gender, race, generation and locale. Ideological development is generated by an intense and open struggle within us for hegemony among the various available verbal and ideological points of view, directions and values.

Although *Marxism and the Philosophy of Language* offers a quasi-Marxist critique of psychologism, it is no less critical of a vulgar, mechanistic Marxism that relegates the world of signs and ideology to a 'superstructural roof' on an economic foundation. Bakhtin shares with Marxism the premise that cultural processes are intimately connected to social relations, that culture, as the site of social difference and contradiction, is deeply involved with power. But for Bakhtin every ideological sign is more than 'a reflection, a shadow, of reality'; it 'is also itself a material segment of that reality'. Even consciousness is linguistic, and therefore social, and thus an objective fact and a social force. The semiotic form of consciousness is 'inner speech', which when translated into outer, public speech has the capacity to act on the world. Entering into the discursive systems of science, art, law and ethics, it becomes a powerful force, capable even of exerting an influence on the economic strata. The Bakhtinian conception of language, then, constitutes a vehicle for avoiding the trap of mechanistic economism: 'The category of mechanical causality can most easily be surmounted on the grounds of the philosophy of language.'[7] As complex networks of ideological signs, literature, the cinema and the mass media generally must be conceptualized as much more than mere reflection. Bakhtin sees literary study (and we can easily extend his terms to mass-media analysis) as situated within three interconnected environments: the generating literary environment, the generating ideological environment, and the generating socio-economic environment.[8] Rather than a hierarchical base/superstructure model, Bakhtin presents the mediation between the two as a series of concentric circles, constantly rippling in and out, each with its own dynamism and specificity.

The Limits of Semiotics

Bakhtin's location of meaning not in linguistic form but rather in the use of language in action and communication – the utterance – his insistence that these meanings are generated and heard as social voices anticipating and answering one another – dialogism – and his recognition that these voices represent distinct socio-ideological positionings whose conflictual relation exists at the very heart of language change – heteroglossia – have immense importance for the theory, analysis and even the praxis of mass-mediated culture. While the semioticians were highly successful in calling attention to the 'specifically literary' and the 'specifically cinematic', they were less successful in linking the specific and the non-specific, the social and the cinematic, the textual and the contextual. The abstract, objectivist presuppositions of semioticians in the Saussurean tradition obliged them to speak of 'codes', while for Bakhtin all utterances, including artistic utterances, are determined not by the systematicity of codes but by the ever-changing circumstances of the communication. The semioticians as a rule recognize only textual contradiction and displacement, failing to make the crucial link between textual and social contradiction. As Graham Pechey points out, the formalists, despite their generally apolitical stance, ironically described textual contradiction in terms redolent of social struggle, but in ways which left the realm of literary contradiction entirely cut off in a hermetically sealed world of pure textuality. Pechey goes on to point out that Bakhtin and Medvedev have the courage to take the formalist metaphors seriously – especially those terms, such as 'revolt', 'conflict', 'struggle', 'destruction' and even 'the dominant', which easily resonate with class and social struggle – applying them back, as it were, to the social itself.[9]

Both semiotics and formalism require the Bakhtinian concept of 'heteroglossia', i.e. a notion of competing languages and discourses which would apply equally to 'text' and '*hors-texte*'. Heteroglossia refers to the dialogically-interrelated speech practices operative in a given society at a given moment, wherein the idioms of different classes, races, genders, generations and locales compete for ascendancy. It refers, further, to the shifting stratifications of language into professional jargons (lawyers, doctors, academics), generic discourses (melodrama, comedy), bureaucratic lingos, popular slangs, along with the specific languages of cultural praxis.

The languages composing heteroglossia represent 'bounded verbal–ideological belief systems', points of view on the world, forms for conceptualizing social experience, each marked by its own tonalities, meanings and values. A given linguistic community shares a common language, but different segments 'live' that common language diversely. Each group or class deploys the linguistic–semiotic system in order to shape its own characteristic meanings. Individualistic language, Bakhtin writes evocatively, is the 'special ideological form of the "we experience" of the bourgeois class'.[10] The role of the artistic text is not to represent real life 'existents', but rather to stage the conflicts inherent in heteroglossia, i.e. the coincidences and competitions of languages and discourses. A 'translinguistic' analysis of the mass media would retain the formalist semiotic notion of textual contradiction, but rethink it as heteroglossia.

Language and Power

Like the semiologists, Bakhtin discerns language everywhere. 'Manifestations of ideological creativity,' he writes in *Marxism and the Philosophy of Language*, 'cannot be entirely segregated or divorced from the element of speech.' But unlike most semióticians, he also sees language as necessarily imbricated with power. The sign, for Bakhtin, is material, multi-accentual and historical; it is densely overlaid with the traces of its historical usages and lives in dialogical interrelation with other material signs. Less interested in the arbitrary sign than in the 'situated utterance', Bakhtin's 'social semiotic' avoids the prudish scientism of a certain 'value-free' structuralism, enabling us to reintroduce both politics and culture into the abstract model constructed by the semioticians. Marxists have often been understandably hostile to structuralism and semiotics on the grounds that the structuralist privileging of the synchronic is inherently ahistorical and undialectical. Bakhtin's emphasis on the historically situated utterance, however, reconciles what is best in Marxism with what is best in semiotics by opening up language to the diachronic and to history.

Bakhtin shares with Marxism the assumption that cultural processes are intimately linked to social relations and that culture is the site of social struggle. His specific contribution, however, is to highlight what might be called the linguistic dimension of class struggle. Human beings are not simply born into language as a master code; they grow into it, and help shape it, as woman or man, worker or boss, peasant or landowner. Every apparently unified linguistic or social community is characterized by heteroglossia, whereby language becomes the space of confrontation of differently oriented social accents, as diverse 'sociolinguistic consciousness' fight it out on the terrain of language. While the dominant class strives to make the sign 'uni-accentual' and endowed with an eternal, supra-class character, the oppressed, especially when they are conscious of their oppression, strive to deploy language for their own liberation. The Bakhtinian formulation has the advantage of not constricting liberatory struggle to purely economic or political battles, extending it to the shared territory of the utterance. Bakhtin locates ideological struggle at the pulsating heart of all discourse, whether in the form of political rhetoric, artistic practice or everyday language exchange. Bakhtin's language-oriented view of social practice brings a discursive dimension to the leftist axiom that 'everything is political'.

There is no political struggle that does not also pass through 'the word'. Language and power intersect wherever the question of language becomes involved with asymmetrical power arrangements. As a potent symbol of collective identity, natural languages, for example, form the focus of deep loyalties existing at the very razor's edge of national differ-ence. In South Africa, blacks protest the imposition of Afrikaans as the official language of education; in the United States, Latinos struggle for bilingual education and examination. But even monolingual societies are characterized by heteroglossia; they englobe multiple 'languages' or 'dialects' which both reveal and produce social position, each existing in a distinct relation to the hegemonic language. Patriarchal oppression, as feminist socio-linguists point out, passes through language, as does feminist resistance to oppression. Issues of race also intersect questions of language, power and social stratification. Black English in the United States was often called 'bad English', because linguists failed to take into account the specific African historical roots and the immanent logical structure of black speech. Indeed, a good deal of quotidian politics operates in the microcosmic form of everyday language exchange. Oppression often 'passes' not only in the form of the billy club or the pink slip but also in the more subtle forms of face-to-face discursive interaction: the cop's subtly or not-so-subtly discriminating language; the male doctor's condescending tone and language toward his 'hysteri-cal' woman patient; the welfare bureaucrat's patronizing of the welfare recipient; the boss's complimenting 'the girls' in the office; the bourgeois matron's speaking baby-talk to the maid. Resistance, similarly, takes the discursive forms of whispered words of solidarity or loud collective proclamations of protest. Language, for Bakhtin, is collective instrument, not a prison-house but an arena for struggle.

Political combat also takes place on what Bakhtin would call the 'terrain of language'. The struggle over events in Central America, for example, is permeated by ideological conflicts manifested in a kind of 'war of nomenclatures' fought in Congress, the media and the streets. Political power consists partly in the capacity to place one's terms and phrases and tropes into wide circulation. The Reagan Administration, at least before the Iran–Contra scandal, had largely succeeded in imposing not only its images but also its terminology. The so-called opposition, which claimed to 'share the president's goals but not his methods', largely acquiesced in the Orwellian distortions perpetrated by the White House. Thus the Democrats, and the media, were prodded into referring to 'Nicaragua', the internationally recognized name of a sovereign state, as the 'Sandinista–Marxist government' or the 'Communist government of Nicaragua', phrases which in the North American context clearly have a delegitimizing function. The Contras, the real terrorists, were dubbed 'freedom fighters', or the 'democratic resistance'. The wholesale slaughter of Nicaraguans was euphemistically rendered, even by liberal pundits, as 'pressure' on the Sandinistas, a word more likely to evoke shiatsu than assassination, while mass-murder by death squads in El Salvador was sanitized as 'human rights violations'. A political opposition so completely trapped in the language of its enemy, I would suggest, has already lost half the battle.

The Nuances of Tact

In the social life of the utterance, each 'word' is subject to rival pronunciations and 'social accents'. Bakhtin and his collaborators invented an entire cluster of terms to evoke the complex social and linguistic codes which govern these rival pronunciations and accents (most of the terms have simultaneous verbal and musical connotations): 'social accent', 'social evaluation', 'tact' and 'intonation'. In a brief but suggestive passage from *The Formal Method in Literary Scholarship*, Bakhtin speaks of 'taktichnost' or 'speech tact' as referring to a 'formative and organizing force' which regulates everyday language exchange.[11] The term 'tact' strikes us as somewhat improbable because we associate it with questions of etiquette and diplomacy, whereas Bakhtin uses 'tact' in its musical sense of 'that which sets down the basic meter'. 'Tact' refers to the 'ensemble of codes governing discursive interaction', i.e., to the social laws which govern these rival pronunciations and accents. 'Tact' is determined by the 'aggregate of all the social relationships of the speakers, their ideological horizons and the concrete situation involved in the interlocution'. 'Tact' gives form to everyday utterances, 'determining the genre and style of speech performances'.[12] In this sense its meaning is not so far removed from the Webster's dictionary definition as 'the delicate perception of the right things to say and do without offending'. But here the right to offend is socially regulated, distributed inequitably along class, race and gender lines.

The cinema is superbly equipped to present the extra-verbal aspects of linguistic discourse, precisely those subtle contextualizing factors evoked by 'tact'. The sound film especially can be seen as the *mise-en-scène* of actual speech situations, the visual and aural contextualization of speech. In the sound film we not only hear the words with their accent and intonation, but witness the facial or corporeal expression which accompanies the words – the posture of arrogance or resignation, the raised eyebrow, the intimidating look, the ironic glance which modifies the ostensible meaning of an utterance, in short, all those elements discourse analysts have taught us to see as vital to social communication. While written language can evoke such discursive phenomena, the cinema presents them, as it were, 'in tact'. As a powerful condensor of unspoken social evaluations, film has the power to represent the complexities of verbal behavior, the ways that words are always 'saturated', as Bakhtin puts it, with 'accents' and 'intonations'. With its capacity for contexting words not only through *mise-en-scène* but also through its other tracks (music, noise, written materials), film is ideally suited for conveying what Bakhtin calls 'contextual overtones'. Film dramaturgy, meanwhile, has its special tact, its ways of suggesting, through camera placement, framing and acting, such phenomena as intimacy or distance, camaraderie or domination, in short all the social and personal dynamics operating between interlocutors.

The suggestive notion of 'tact' points to the possibility of a politically informed discourse analysis of concrete social exchanges. The discursive rules of 'tact' operate not only in the fiction film – think for example of the evolving relations between master and servant in Losey's *The Servant* – but also in non-fiction films and television programs. In countless documentaries (including 'progressive' ones) about oppressed or colonized people, the off-screen voice of a narrator takes on intonations of domination and omniscience. Studio-protected, this voice speaks in regular and homogeneous rhythms, while the human subjects of the film speak haltingly, in direct sound. The voice speaks of them confidently in the third person, while they speak of themselves hesitantly in the first person. The narrator becomes the voice of knowledge and mastery, while the narratees are the voice of undiscriminating experience. The voice translates their 'alien words' into the impersonal discourse of objective truth.

'Tact' also metaphorically evokes the power relations between film and audience. Does the film establish distance or a kind of intimacy? Does the film lord it over the audience as do many Hollywood 'blockbusters' and 'superspectacles' (the terms themselves imply the arrogance and aggression of technological and financial exhibitionism), or is it obsequious and insecure? Is it confident of the sympathies of its audience, or, as is the case with many left–liberal films like *Missing* or *Latino*, does it constantly seek to reassure a mainstream audience? Does a film assume an interlocutor of a specific gender or class or nation? Does a film ignore the possible reactions of women or take them into account? Does it assume a lily-white audience or make room for black identification? A film like *Adventures in Babysitting,* for example, seems to assume an audience of well-off white suburbanites for whom blacks, Latinos, and the working class represent a menacing world of difference and otherness. Hollywood films like *Black Sunday* or *Ishtar* similarly take it as read that the cinematic scapegoating of Arabs or Moslems will offend no one. These films, like all films, make specific assumptions about the audience's ideology and cultural preparation; they take a specific attitude toward what Bakhtin would call their 'projected interlocutor'.

The television talk show constitutes a comparably refractory social microcosm whose 'tact' might easily be analyzed as a product of the relations between all the interlocutors (on and off-screen), the concrete situation of the conversation, and the aggregate of social relationships and the ideological horizons informing the discourse. At the center of such shows we find the key Bakhtinian trope of the dialogical interplay of speaking subjects, of persons in literal or metaphorical dialogue. In the wings, meanwhile, there are the unheard participants in the dialogue: the network managers and the corporate sponsors who 'speak' only through the commercial messages. Facing the celebrities in the literal space of the studio is the in-the-flesh surrogate audience, an ideally participatory version of the invisible audience at home with whom host and guest also speak, an audience that is itself a cross-section of a populace traversed by contradictions involving class, gender, race, age and politics.

What might emerge from such an analysis would be a profoundly mixed situation, mingling the crassest manipulation with subliminally utopian appeals and modestly progressive gestures. Take, for example, *The Oprah Winfrey Show.* Its star, considered purely as an image, is at once an updated Mammy figure and the very model of an articulate and expressive facilitator presiding over an important network program who does, on some level, challenge the patriarchal and ethnic hegemonies of the Phil Donahues and Johnny Carsons. The programs themselves tend to foreground female discontent with male attitudes and behavior, issues discussed in an atmosphere of spontaneity, identification and communitarian solidarity. At the same time, as a 'situated utterance', we can view Oprah's immense capacity for what Bakhtin would call 'responsive understanding' as a marketable commodity that attracts viewers and sponsors. The ultimate **telos** of this dialogue, we are reminded, at least in the eyes of its corporate managers, is to attract an audience to be sold to sponsors.

In the world of the talk show, the corporate sponsors wield the ultimate discursive power; they have the right to suspend or even terminate the conversation. A cold cash nexus, in other words, severely compromises what appears to be the warm exchange of an 'ideal speech situation' (Habermas) based on 'free and familiar contact' (Bakhtin). (The 'joke' in Martin Scorsese's *The King of Comedy* consists in having its protagonist try to 'collect' on the implicit promise of television's 'warmth'; Rupert Pupkin literally believes that talk-show host Jerry Langford, modeled on Johnny Carson, is his 'friend'.) The communicative utopia is compromised, furthermore, not only by corporate getting and spending but also by the obsession with ratings, by the search for ever more sensational victims (Oprah, Donahue) or events (Arsenio Hall) or absurdities (David Letterman), by the peripheralization of any truly alternative discourse, and by the insistent success trope underlying the shows and fostering vicarious identification with the ephemeral triumphs of 'stars'. The discourse is further marred by other hidden and not so hidden agendas having to do with the promotion of books, films and shows. The conversation, in sum, is neither free nor disinterested; the discourse is bound by the innumerable restraints of corporate and social 'tact'.

Television news programs also display their peculiar 'tact'. The ideologically informed presentation of the news pits discursively competent adults – the newscasters, the politicians, the managers – against a stammering infantilized populace. Those at the top of the discursive hierarchy – from the anchorperson at the apex to the correspondents and reporters as supporting players – patronize the 'extras', the people on the street. The suave articulateness of the newscasters is underwritten by scripted texts, rehearsals and editing, and their well-nigh infallible fluency contrasted with the equally constructed inarticulateness of those at the bottom of the hierarchy.[13] To take another example, think of Ted Koppel's *Nightline*. Since Koppel, thanks to television, repeatedly meets in an electronic *tête-à-tête* with heads of state, and since he is framed in an identical manner, we subliminally begin to see him as a head of state. He has the power to cut off his interlocutors or cage them within a rectangle, or reduce them to the size of a postage stamp. We are not surprised, therefore, when Koppel interrupts or rhetorically badgers renowned Third World leaders – 'Will you renounce violence, Mr Tambo?' – it seems entirely within his rights.

Local 'Eyewitness News', meanwhile, adopts a more integrative 'tact'. Here, chummy guys and affable gals impersonate ideal good-time neighbors, collectively forming the image of a lively and caring 'news family'. 'From Our Family to Yours' is a typical eyewitness news slogan. One is struck by the almost surreal discontinuity between the morbidity of most of the news items – the daily harvest of rapes and murders, abandoned babies, child molestation – and the cheerful familial atmosphere surrounding the newscasters. The impression is that the world 'out there' is nasty and brutish, but that life 'in here' – i.e., in the mirrored domains of the television studio and the homes – is comfortable and permeated by trust. This contrast of cold world and warm home constitutes an electronic updating of an old, ideologically determined Victorian dichotomy. (The television set, we know, is often metaphorized as the 'electronic hearth'.) In the studio, a contrived atmosphere of self-conscious informality fosters the impression that we all belong to a harmonious community sufficiently at ease to kid and joke. Here too, however, many icy calculations form part of the fabrication of 'warmth', since we know that the happiness of the news team is a construct favored by news consultants preoccupied with improving ratings.

Eyewitness news exemplifies the insight developed by Hans Magnus Enzensberger, Richard Dyer, and Fredric Jameson that to explain the public's attraction to a medium, one must look not only for ideological manipulation but also for the kernel of utopian fantasy from which the medium constitutes itself as a projected fulfillment of what is desired and absent within the status quo. Eyewitness news takes the dystopian realities of contemporary urban life under late capitalism, and through an artistic 'change of signs' turns them into the simulacrum of a playful and egalitarian *communitas*, a world characterized by communicative transparency and 'free and familiar contact'. For what could be more utopian than this newsroom world of ludic productivity, where professionals seem to be having the time of their lives, where work, as in a musical comedy, is incessantly transformed into play? Within this electronic representation, benign father figures preside over a multi-ethnic symbolic family whose synecdochic figures 'represent' the community at large. Whereas ethnic groups might be at each others' throats in the streets, and even on the filmed reports shown on the news, the newscasters themselves live in a racial utopia that suggests an ideal image of the community itself.

Cultural and Political Polyphony

Bakhtin's music-derived trope of 'polyphony', originally formulated in reference to the complex play of ideological voices in the work of Dostoevsky, refers, although from a distinct angle, to the same phenomenon designated by 'dialogism' and 'heteroglossia'. The concept of 'polyphony' calls attention to the coexistence, in any textual or extra-textual situation, of a plurality of voices which do not fuse into a single consciousness but rather exist on different registers, generating dia-

logical dynamism among themselves. Neither heteroglossia nor polyphony points to mere heterogeneity as such, but to the dialogical angle
at which voices are juxtaposed and counterposed so as to generate
something beyond themselves. I would like to speak here of one dimension of polyphony – and of its political consequences. While all cultures
are polyphonic in that they include distinct genders, professions and age
groups, some cultures are striking in being ethnically polyphonic. Bakhtin's multi-ethnic source culture, existing at the crossroads of Europe
and Asia, provided innumerable exemplars of cultural polyphony. The
New World countries of the Americas, similarly, deploy myriad cultural
voices – that of the indigenous peoples (no matter how oppressed and
muffled that voice may be), that of the Afro-American (however
distorted or suppressed), that of the Jewish, Italian, Hispanic and Asiatic
communities – each of which condenses, in its turn, a multiplicity of
social accents having to do with gender, class and locale. Much of the
potential force and audacity of the national cinemas of the Americas
derives from their capacity to stage the conflicts and complementarities
of heteroglot culture. The people of Brazil, for example, products of
ethnic and cultural *mesticaje*, represent a multitude of exiles and dia-
sporas – indigenous people made alien in their own land, blacks brought
by force from Africa, immigrants from Europe, Asia and the Middle
East. The force and originality of much of Brazilian art comes from its
polyphonic orchestration of cultural figures and references. Mario de
Andrade's modernist novel, *Macunaima* (1928), noisily incorporates all
the cultural voices of Brazil. Nor is it an insignificant coincidence that de
Andrade was consciously elaborating, in the twenties, a concept of artistic 'polyphony' entirely consistent with Bakhtin's. The protagonist of the
novel, like that of Joaquim Pedro de Andrade's filmic adaptation four
decades later, embodies this polyphony by being at once native American Indian, Black African and Brazilian Portuguese. A composite
character, Macunaima epitomizes the ethnic roots of Brazil itself. The
very language of the novel, moreover, orchestrates words of indigenous,
African and European origin, thus providing the linguistic equivalent of
Brazil's cultural syncretism. In a country where Indians have been the
victims of genocide, and where blacks are oppressed in subtle and not so
subtle ways, the positing of a multi-racial national hero inevitably makes
a political statement as well.

North American culture, and North American cinema, also have
immense polyphonic potential. In films like Alan Parker's *Fame* and
Mazursky's *Moscow on the Hudson*, or Woody Allen's *Zelig*, a New
York setting, a city which is itself a paradigm of heteroglossia, helps
generate a rich weave of ethnic voices. A Bakhtinian analysis of such
films would point both to their polyphonic potential and to the political

myopia which undermines that potential. In *Fame*, youthful representatives of diverse communities – black, Puerto Rican, Jewish, gay –
collaborate within a kind of utopia of artistic expression. In *Moscow on
the Hudson*, the Robin Williams character enters into dialogic interaction with a similar gallery of synecdochic ethnic figures – black,
Italian, Puerto Rican, Jewish. Each dialogue is inflected by the specific
accents of a culturally defined interlocutor. Zelig's capacity to take on
the accent and ethnicity of those with whom he interacts finally makes
him an ambulatory polyphony of cultural voices. His chameleonism
merely renders visible and physical what is usually invisible – i.e., the
process of synchretizing which occurs when ethnicities brush against and
rub off on one another. The self in a context of polyphony is necessarily
syncretic, especially when that polyphony is amplified by the media.
Zelig demonstrates this syncretism by giving us an allegorical figure who
dwells in what Bakhtin calls the 'in-between of social interaction', who is
at once white and Jewish and black, Indian, Mexican, Chinese.

While these films evoke the play of ethnic and cultural polyphony,
they fail to reveal the political obstacles to true polyphony and equality.
Rather than subvert the existing power relations between the diverse
communities, they tend to orchestrate superficially defined ethnic types.
Fame ultimately subordinates polyphony to a 'making it' ethos less
dedicated to transpersonal community than to individual 'Fame!'
Moscow on the Hudson begins as critical both of political repression in
the Soviet Union and of laissez-faire cruelty in the United States, but
finally degenerates into just another sentimental immigrant saga. And
Zelig ultimately retreats from the utopian implications of its cross-
cultural chameleonism by having its protagonist rediscover his 'true self',
acquiesce in middle-class values and speak in the clichés of fifties liberalism and pop psychology. Zelig becomes a bland all-American, an
uncritical parrot of the reigning ideology, while the film offers precious
little indication of the limitations of its protagonist's vision. A Bakhtinian approach to such films, in any case, would tease out, in an 'anticipatory' reading, the latent utopias stirring within such texts, while
unmasking the ways in which they repress their utopian potential and
fail to signal the real social and political impediments to community.

Each cultural voice, for Bakhtin, exists in dialogue with other voices:
'Utterances are not indifferent to one another, and are not self-
sufficient; they are aware of and mutually reflect one another.'[14] Social
diversity is fundamental to every utterance, even to that utterance which
on the surface ignores or excludes the groups with which it is in relation.
All utterances take place against the background of the possible
responding utterances of other social points of view. To the 'No Blacks
Allowed' of Howard Beach racists comes the responding chant:

'Howard Beach, Haven't You Heard? This is not Johannesburg!' Even the most devout believer and practitioner of apartheid cannot ultimately separate himself from the echoing black response to white supremacism.

This profoundly relational vision differentiates Bakhtin's thought from an innocuous liberal pluralism, and does so in several senses. First, Bakhtin sees all utterance and discourse in relation to the deforming effects of power. Second, Bakhtin does not preach a pseudo-equality of viewpoints; his sympathies, rather, are clearly with the non-official viewpoint, with the marginalized, the oppressed, the peripheralized. Third, where pluralism is accretive and 'tolerant' – it 'allows' another voice to add itself to the mainstream – Bakhtin's view is polyphonic and celebratory. Any act of verbal or cultural exchange, for Bakhtin, leaves both interlocutors changed. The historical dialogue between blacks and whites in North America, for example, has profoundly changed both parties. Even white racists are not untouched by black culture; their speech, their music, even their body language bears the traces of black influence. Official America seems reluctant to recognize the extent to which it has been Africanized, although Africanization is everywhere evident. In the eighties, the majority of white popular singers work within a black-inflected musical idiom. Virtually all of the participants, black and white, in the music video 'We Are the World' sing in a melismatic, soulful, improvisational gospel style, in homage to black musicality which was at the same time concretely linked to a project of relief for Africa. A phenomenon such as break dance, similarly, with its syncretic melange of African reminiscences, mime, mass-media allusions and modern dance, is only possible in a polyphonic culture.

A Bakhtinian analysis would also be aware of the dangers of 'pseudo-polyphonic' discourse. The notion of polyphony, with its overtones of harmonious simultaneity, must be supplemented by the notion of heteroglossia, with its undertones of social conflict rooted not in the random individual dissonances but in the deep structural cleavages of social life. The film or television commercial in which every eighth face is black, for example, has more to do with the demographics of market research or the bad conscience of liberalism than with authentic polyphony, since the black voice in such instances is usually shorn of its soul, deprived of its color and intonation. Polyphony does not consist in the mere appearance of a representative of a given group, but in the fostering of a textual setting where that group's voice can be heard with its full force and resonance.

Emilio de Antonio's satirical documentary about Richard Nixon, *Milhouse: A White Comedy*, offers a striking instance of this kind of relational polyphony. A sound–image montage plays off Nixon's innocuous 'I See a Day' speech against Martin Luther King's stirring 'I Have a Dream' oration – whose rhetoric and syntax the Nixon speech clearly imitates – showing transparent sympathy for the emotional force and political commitment of the latter while mocking the petit-bourgeois mediocrity of the former. Nixon's voice, promulgating the myth of 'equal opportunity', gradually gives way to the resonant authority of the voice of King, who denounces the barriers to equality while articulating a distant yet imaginable promised land of racial harmony, all in the powerful accents of the black southern preacher. In Bakhtinian terminology, the two voices have been counterposed at a 'dialogical' angle, generating a social message far transcending the individual content of the two discourses.

Dialogism

Bakhtin is one of the source thinkers of the contemporary discussion of 'intertextuality'. The term was introduced into critical discourse as Julia Kristeva's translation of Bakhtin's conception of the 'dialogic'. In the broadest sense, intertextuality or dialogism refers to the open-ended possibilities generated by all the discursive practices of a culture, the entire matrix of communicative utterances within which the artistic text is situated, and which reach the text not only through recognizable influences but also through a subtle process of dissemination. Dialogism is central not only to the canonical texts of the literary and philosophical tradition of the West, it is equally central to non-canonical texts. It is just as relevant to those cultural utterances not conventionally thought of as 'texts'. The idea of 'intertextuality' is in one sense a truism, known at least since Montaigne: that 'more books have been written about other books than about any other subject.' In this century, T.S. Eliot's essay on the relation between the 'tradition' and the 'individual talent' can be seen as a conservatively formulated prolepsis of intertextuality, one which assumes the 'integrity' of both the 'tradition' and the 'individual talent'. Bakhtinian dialogism, however, is far more radical, in that it applies simultaneously to everyday speech, to popular culture, and to the literary and artistic tradition. It is concerned with all the 'series' that enter into a text, be that text verbal or non-verbal, erudite or popular. The popular, moreover, constantly converses with the erudite, and vice versa. The most consecrated figures of the high cultural tradition dialogue with 'low' culture and popular language. The 'semantic treasures Shakespeare embedded in his works', Bakhtin writes:

> were created and collected through the centuries and even millennia: they lay
> hidden in the language, and not only in the literary language, but also in those

strata of the popular language that before Shakespeare's time had not entered literature, in the diverse genres and forms of speech communication, in the forms of a mighty national culture (primarily carnival forms) that were shaped through millennia, in theater-spectacle genres (mystery plays, farces, and so forth) in plots whose roots go back to prehistoric antiquity, and, finally, in forms of thinking.[15]

The Bakhtinian reformulation of the problem of intertextuality must be seen as an 'answer' to formalist and structuralist paradigms of linguistic theory and literary criticism, as well as to vulgar Marxist paradigms interested only in class-biographical and extrinsic ideological determinations. Bakhtin attacks the literary scholar–critic's exclusive focus on the 'literary series'. Bakhtin is interested in a more diffuse dissemination of ideas as they penetrate and interanimate all the 'series', literary and non-literary, and in what he calls the 'powerful deep currents of culture'. Literary scholarship, he argues, should establish closer links with the history of culture: 'Literature is an inseparable part of culture and it cannot be understood outside the total context of the entire culture of a given epoch.'[16]

The artistic text, then, must be understood within what Bakhtin calls the 'differentiated unity of the epoch's entire culture'. Dialogism operates within all cultural production whether it be literate or non-literate, verbal or non-verbal, highbrow or lowbrow. The films of a Godard or a Ruiz orchestrate the ambient messages thrown up by all the series – literary, musical, cinematic, journalistic, and so forth. But the same process operates within what is known as 'popular culture'.

In a marvelous article entitled 'Why is it Fresh? Rap Music and Bakhtin', Elizabeth Wheeler applies Bakhtinian categories to the world of 'hip-hop', i.e. the inter-related cultural universes of rapping, graffiti and breakdance.[17] The practice of rap, the form of popular music that combines turntable acrobatics with aggressive talking – the very word 'rap' means 'dialogue' – she argues, can be seen as embodying Bakhtin's theories of dialogism. Largely the creation of black and Hispanic working-class teenagers, rap is intensely, exuberantly dialogic. Like gospel, it is ultimately based on African call-and-response patters, and on a kind of interanimation of performer and listener clearly reminiscent of Bakhtin's interactive, performance-centered theory of language. The hip-hop musician, Wheeler argues, dialogizes ready-made materials as a function of inner-city expediency, since records are cheaper than instruments and music lessons. Found texts drawn from other songs, advertisements or political speeches are then juxtaposed ironically for the purposes of social comment. 'Rap, on a quite literal level, emerges from a dialogical process, from the conversations of members of a crew who trade rhymes, homages, and generally feed on each other's intensity'.

Performing close textual analyses of specific rap songs such as 'The Message' and 'La-Di-Da-Di', Wheeler finds numerous instances of specific Bakhtinian conceptions: 'polyphonic discourse', 'parodic carnivalization', 'hidden internal polemic', 'polemically colored autobiography', 'discourse with a sideward glance', and 'sarcastic rejoinder'.

The Carnival, Parody and the Carnivalesque

The most widely disseminated of Bakhtin's concepts is surely the notion of 'carnival', defined as the transposition into art of the spirit of popular festivities which offer the people brief entry into a symbolic sphere of utopian freedom. Bakhtin first sketched out his ideas on carnival in *Problems of Dostoevsky's Poetics*, but it was in *Rabelais and His World* that the notion received its fullest and richest formulation. The point of departure for the latter book was Bakhtin's conviction that Rabelais's work had not been understood because scholars failed to discern Rabelais's profound link to popular culture, or to appreciate the literary modes associated with carnival: e.g., parody and grotesque realism. As an artistic mode rooted in extra-artistic sources, carnival represents an attitude toward the world that has belonged to folk communities for millennia and has been transmitted to erudite culture by such writers as Rabelais, Shakespeare, Cervantes and Diderot. Carnival, for Bakhtin, expresses the people's 'second life', and it shatters, at least on a symbolic plane, all oppressive hierarchies, redistributing social roles according to the logic of the 'world upside down'. Carnival promotes a ludic and critical relation to all official discourses, whether political, literary or ecclesiastical.

After Rabelais, carnival in Europe was driven underground. Its elimination as a real social practice led to the development of salon carnivals, compensatory bohemias offering what Allon White calls 'liminoid positions' on the margins of polite society. Outside Europe, however, carnival, even in its literal denotation, remains very much alive. While most European carnivals have degenerated into the ossified repetition of perennial rituals, in Brazil and the Caribbean it remains a dynamic cultural expression crystallizing profoundly polyphonic cultures. Anthropologist Roberto da Matta describes Brazilian carnival in terms strikingly similar to those of Bakhtin. It is a collective celebration, at once sacred and profane, in which the socially marginalized – the poor, blacks, homosexuals – take over the symbolic center of social life. Carnival, at least in the liberatory thrust of its symbolic system (no one is suggesting that a few days of carnival literally overturn class and gender oppressions reinforced throughout the year) is subversive of hierarchy and alienation, a moment of collective catharsis offering a trans-individual taste of freedom.

It is important to remember that the Bakhtinian notion of carnival embraces a number of inter-related ideas, not all of them of equal use to left criticism: (1) a valorization of Eros and the life force (appealing to a Reichean left) as an actualization of the ancient myths of Orpheus and Dionysius; (2) the idea, more relevant to the left generally, of social inversion and the counter-hegemonic subversion of established power; (3) the idea, attractive to poststructuralists, of 'gay relativity' and Janus-faced ambivalence and ambiguity; (4) the notion of carnival as trans-individual and oceanic (appealing ambiguously to left and right alike); and (5) the concept of carnival as the 'space of the sacred' and 'time in parentheses' (appealing to the religiously-inclined).

Carnival is admittedly the Bakhtinian category most susceptible to co-optation, at times becoming the pretext for a vacuous ludism that discerns redeeming elements even in the most degraded cultural productions and activities. It would be wrong, for example, to see the beer-fueled carousing of fraternity boys in *Animal House* as a Bakhtinian celebration of people's culture, since fraternity boys and their macho rituals form an integral part of the power structure which authentic carnival symbolically overturns. Carnival in our sense is more than a party or a festival; it is the oppositional culture of the oppressed, the official world as seen from below; not the mere disruption of etiquette but the symbolic, anticipatory overthrow of oppressive social structures. On the positive side, it is ecstatic collectivity, the joyful affirmation of change, a dress rehearsal for utopia. On the negative, critical side, it is a demystifying instrument for everything in the social formation that renders collectivity impossible: class hierarchy, sexual repression, patriarchy, dogmatism and paranoia.

Real-life carnivals are, of course, politically ambiguous affairs which can be egalitarian and emancipatory or oppressive and hierarchical. They can constitute a symbolic rebellion by the weak or their festive scapegoating – on occasion both at the same time. As Peter Stallybrass and Allon White point out, it would be a mistake to see carnival in an essentialist manner as intrinsically radical.[18] Actual carnivals form shifting configurations of symbolic practices whose political valence changes with each context and situation. All carnivals must be seen as complex criss-crossings of ideological manipulation and utopian desire. As 'situated utterances', carnivals are inevitably inflected by the hierarchical arrangements of everyday social life. Da Matta's analysis of Brazilian carnival, for example, treats it as a unitary language, failing to take into account the extent to which black and white, rich and poor, men and women, gay and straight, live different carnivals. The slum-dweller who cannot afford to celebrate with rum, the mulatta maid who is mistreated all year and then erotically exalted during carnival, the transvestite who comes into ephemeral glory, all these come to carnival from a different and more marginal position than those who enjoy power all year long and who therefore have less need to overturn it symbolically.

Actual carnivals do not generally turn into revolutions, although oppositional movements can at times take on a carnivalesque atmosphere. In the United States the sixties were the privileged era of carnivalized politics, when demonstrations incorporated colorful elements of music, dance, costume and guerilla theatre, and where the line between performer and spectator was often blurred. In a symptomatic statement, Spiro Agnew dismissed anti-war demonstrations as 'just a carnival', an insult that masked a compliment. What interests us, in any case, is less actual carnivals than the genre's perennial repertoire of gestures, symbols and metaphors, which can be deployed to give voice to a desire for social and political justice. Countless Brazilian popular songs, for example, not only celebrate carnival but also associate it metaphorically with progressive change. During the decades of military dictatorship after 1964, leftist singer-composer Chico Buarque de Holanda composed a number of allegorical sambas in which carnival came to symbolize, if not revolution, at least the end of dictatorship. In his 'Apesar de Voce' (Despite You), which became popularly known as 'Letter to the Dictator', the singer portrayed a situation in which an unnamed repressive figure would be unable to prevent the 'immense euphoria' of a carnival-style liberation. In such an instance, carnivalesque strategies serve to crystallize popular irreverence and demystify the powerful.

The notion of carnival is also useful to the left in accounting for the popular appeal of mass spectacle. American popular culture often reverberates ambiguously with textual echoes of carnival. The Hollywood musical comedy, for example, can be seen as a two-dimensional spectacle in which the oppressive structures of everyday life are not so much overturned as stylized, choreographed and mythically transcended. Richard Dyer's analysis, in 'Entertainment and Utopia', of the Hollywood musical comedy as performing an artistic 'change of signs' whereby the negatives of social existence are turned into the positives of artistic transmutation, strikingly parallels Bakhtin's account of carnival.[19] For Dyer, the musical offers a utopian world characterized by energy (in carnival, gestural freedom and the effervescence of dance and movement), abundance (in carnival, omnipresent feasting, the fat of mardi gras), intensity (in carnival, the heightened theatricality of an alternative second life), transparency (Bakhtin's 'free and familiar contact'), and community (carnival as loss of self, collective *jouissance*).

This type of analysis can easily be extended to account for the appeal of contemporary music video. Donna Summer's 'She Works Hard for the Money' choreographs diverse kinds of women's drudge work into a joyous celebration of feminine solidarity in the streets. Eddie Grant's 'Dance Party' (not to mention Dr Pepper and Pepsi commercials), draws on the old carnival trope of people dancing in the streets. Literal echoes of Caribbean carnival sound in Lionel Ritchie's 'All Night Long', a music video whose music, lyrics and visuals celebrate a multi-ethnic and multi-styled utopia in which day changes place with night and even policemen forsake authority to twirl their batons and breakdance in a choreographed takeover of public space.

It is useful to distinguish between true carnival as communitarian festivity on the one hand, and 'ersatz' or 'degraded' carnivals on the other. In this sense, we can account for the appeal of many mass-mediated products as relaying, in a somewhat compromised manner, the distant cultural memory and imagery of authentic carnival. (A Nazi rally, as a dystopian ritual based on the annihilation of difference, a liturgical insertion into hierarchy rather than a liberation from it, might be seen as the ultimate degraded carnival.) The American mass media are fond of weak or truncated forms of carnival that capitalize on the frustrated desire for a truly egalitarian society by serving up distorted versions of carnival's utopian promise: Fourth of July commercial pageantry, jingoistic singalongs, authoritarian rock concerts, festive soft-drink commercials. What was once three months of the year spent revelling in the people's 'second life', is now reduced to yearly holidays that more and more resemble the work period from which they are supposed to offer relief. Carnival becomes reduced to a weekly 'Thank God It's Friday' ritual, by which the body is renewed for resumption of work on Monday. Bakhtin's boisterously vulgar marketplace becomes the muzak-filled consumerist utopia of the shopping mall. The effervescent play of carnival becomes the aerobics workout – dance as grim duty – and even parties become laborious forms of 'networking'.

In *Rabelais and His World*, Bakhtin described late medieval carnival as a utopian festival favoring 'free and familiar contact' and the 'intermingling of bodies'. It is useful to regard contemporary pornography, I think, as 'ersatz' or 'degraded' carnival. The commercial porn film, for example, can be envisaged as a torn shred of carnival, the detritus of a once robust and irreverent tradition. Pornography offers the simulacrum of a pan-erotic world where sex is always available, where women are infinitely pliable and always desirous, where sex, without amorous prelude and gloriously free of consequence and responsibility, lurks in every office, street and home. Some contemporary pornography remarkably fits Bakhtin's description in 'Forms of Time and Chronotope in the Novel' of an ancient literary genre, which he calls 'the adventure novel of everyday life'. Citing Apuleius's *Golden Ass*, Bakhtin offers the following account: 'At its center is obscenity, that is, the seamier side of sexual love, love alienated from reproduction, from a progression of generations, from the structures of the family and the clan. Here everyday life is obscenity.'[20]

In the contemporary period, the priapic nature of pornography serves an important social and ideological function. As real life becomes more repressed and puritanical, the sexual imagery, paradoxically, becomes more debauched, as if in compensation for a lost sexual playfulness. In the postmodern context, we are given what Arthur Kroker calls the 'theatrics of sado-masochism in the simulacrum ... [the postmodern body] doubled in an endless labyrinth of media images ...'.[21] In the age of what Karen Jaehne calls 'Great Detumescence', the on-screen display of sexual abundance plays a role analogous to that of the gilt and glitter musicals of the Great Depression. Pornography, in this sense, is a diversionary gratification, an attempt to recoup in the domain of sexual fantasy what has been lost in real festivity. While carnival is collective, participatory, and public, pornography is passive and usually monadic, whether consumed by an aggregation of vaguely guilty solitaries in the porn theaters or in the privatized space of the self-entertaining monad. While carnival comes for free, porn is paid for in cash, check, or money order. Rather than carnival's 'free and familiar contact', establishment pornography offers the anxious commerce of bodies performing ritualized exertions. On the actresses' faces we often read the simulation of desire, and on the man's, grim duty, physical stamina, the solitude of the long-distance comer.[22]

Television for its part constantly throws out the simulacra of carnival-style festivity. Celebrity roasts are updated versions of Bakhtin's 'festive symposia' where revellers play the game of 'excessive praise and blame'. Canned laughter is the substitute for the real laughter that is only possible in an ambience of community. Programs like *Fantasy Island* and *Love Boat*, as Horace Newcomb and Paul Hirsch point out, offer 'liminal' utopias, happy social microcosms set offshore.[23] Television also implicitly offers the possibility of universal Andy Warhol-style stardom, an updating of carnival's erasure of the line between the spectator and the spectacle. This participation takes countless forms. The spectator might get a call from a talk-show host, be thanked on the telephone, get interviewed by Eyewitness News, ask a question on the Phil Donahue Show, be mocked by a superimposed title on *Saturday Night Live*, sing a song on the Johnny Carson Show, appear on 'Dating Game' or 'People's Court', or even, and here we approach real stardom, perform on 'Star Search'. In all these instances, as Elayne Rapping puts it, the people literally 'make a spectacle of themselves', thus abolishing the barrier between performer and audience.

Bakhtin's Contribution to the Left

Bakhtin's contribution to left cultural and political analysis is potentially immense. The category of carnival not only accounts for mass media channeling of utopian desires, but also has relevance to the political strategies of the left. Bakhtin portrays parodic 'carnivalization' as the privileged arm of the weak and dispossessed. By appropriating an existing discourse for its own ends, parody is especially well suited to the needs of the powerless, precisely because it *assumes* the force of the dominant discourse only to deploy that force, through a kind of artistic jujitsu, *against* domination. Since the North American left has been historically placed in a disadvantageous and defensive position, it must try to deploy the dominant discourse in the material arts against itself.

Think, for example, of the electoral campaign that pitted Ronald Reagan against Walter Mondale. The Republican candidate spoke simplistically of 'morning in America', exploiting the discourse of 'fraudulent hope' (Ernst Bloch). Reagan clearly appealed to a kind of nostalgic utopianism, couched in the language of community, religion and spirituality. In this way, he commanded the attention of many people who on social and economic grounds should have been repulsed by him. Reagan and his public relations managers shrewdly exploited the desire for community while promoting policies that ultimately shatter community. They deployed, moreover, precise narrative and imagistic strategies: clear scenarios, Manichean characterizations, fast-paced action, and minimal thought – in short, the conventional array of devices of the Hollywood fiction film with which Reagan had been associated in the forties. (Grenada, for example, was cast as the damsel in distress, the Cubans as villains, and the US as hero, in an imperialist rescue fantasy whose happy ending was as meaningless as the traditional Hollywood clincher.) In generic terms, Reagan drew on the technological utopianism of science fiction ('Star Wars'), on the Manichean moralism of melodrama (the 'evil empire', the saintly fight against drugs and terrorism), and the gaiety of the musical comedy (Liberty Weekend, the Inaugural Ball), all as a cover for the gangster-style cynicism of film noir.

The Democrats, meanwhile, produced an earnest documentary to counter Reagan's slick fiction film. They lamented the fate of the country in sanctimonious voiceovers superimposed on images of deprivation and despair, thus playing into the hands of Reagan, who predictably portrayed them as 'prophets of gloom'. While the 'good news' President restricted himself to cheery platitudes, the Democrats brought the bad news of domestic deficits and foreign debacles. To the charms of fiction and entertainment, they counterposed the reality principle and the politics of guilt. By an associational boomerang, it was they who were bound to what they were denouncing. I am not suggesting that correct strategy would have imitated the mendacity of the Reagan campaign, but I am suggesting that the Democrats, at least up until Irangate, were paralyzed by an excess of 'respect'. They were intimidated by Reagan's popularity, as if that popularity were an insurmountable essence rather than a mediated construct. Rather than pit their enfeebled charisma against that of the Great Communicator, the Democrats should have confronted Reagan on the very terrain he had managed to dominate: mass-mediated language and symbol manipulation. Deploying audio-visual messages in conjunction with the voice and image of the President, they might have forged a link between image and reality, policy and consequence. Such a strategy, relying largely on the President himself, would have constituted a self-indictment more powerful than any verbal attack by a Democratic candidate. In a double operation, they should have proposed their own counter-utopia while 'carnivalizing' Reagan. Just as carnival revellers used grotesque realism to deprive the king of the symbols of his power in order to reveal him as a ridiculous figure, so the Democrats could have comically exposed the vacuity of Reagan's ideas and the puppet-like quality of his pronouncements, stripping him of his cue-cards and teleprompters and tearing the mask off his cruelty. In short, the opposition ought to have been doing to Reagan what he ultimately did to himself: auto-demystification.[24]

Bakhtinian categories display an intrinsic identification with difference and alterity, a built-in affinity for the oppressed and the marginal, a feature making them especially appropriate for the analysis of oppositional and marginal practices, be they Third World, feminist or avant-garde. Although Bakhtin does not speak directly to Third World concerns, his categories are eminently well suited to them. In this sense, his thought offers a corrective to certain Eurocentric prejudices within Marxism itself.[25] Marxism's ambiguous endorsement of the destruction of indigenous new world cultures in the name of the forward movement of productive forces entails an unconscionable disregard for the integrity and humanity of other cultures. In cultural terms, similarly, Marxists have sometimes been indirectly complicitous in the stigmatization of difference. One thinks, for example, of the Frankfurt School's analyses of popular culture, of Adorno's notorious remarks about jazz, and even of Ernst Bloch's claim that there is 'nothing coarser, nastier, more stupid' than jazz dances since the thirties, which are nothing more than 'imbecility gone wild'.[26] These remarks reflect deeply rooted ethnocentric prejudices against African-derived music and dance. Bakhtin, by contrast, speaks in *The Formal Method in Literary Scholarship* of non-European cultures as the catalysts for European modernism's surpassing of a retrograde, culture-bound verism. And Bakhtin's oxymoronic carnival aesthetic, in which everything is pregnant with its opposite, implies an alternative logic of non-exclusive opposites and permanent contradiction that transgresses the monologic true-or-false thinking typical of Western rationalism.

Bakhtin speaks little of the specific oppression of women, yet his work can be seen as intrinsically open to feminist inflection. It is certainly no accident that Bakhtin's positive-connoted words – polyglossia, dialogism, polyphony – so frequently feature prefixes that designate plurality or alterity. Rather than finding difference and multiplicity threatening, Bakhtin finds them exhilarating, and in this sense his thought opens to what Luce Irigaray calls feminine 'plurality' and 'multiplicity'. Bakhtin's theory of parody as the privileged mode of carnivalization and as the favored weapon of the weak accords perfectly with what Ruby Rich calls 'Medusan' feminist films. Rich takes the term from Hélène Cixous's 'The Laugh of the Medusa', in which the French theorist celebrates the potential of feminist texts to 'blow up the law, to break up the "truth" with laughter'.[27] Lizzie Borden's *Born in Flames*, Nelly Kaplan's *La Fiancée du pirate*, and Ana Carolina's *Sea of Roses* can all be seen as Medusan films that direct satirical laughter against what Irigaray called 'l'esprit de sérieux', or phallocentrism.

Unlike many theoretical grids, Bakhtinian method does not have to be 'stretched' to make room for the marginalized and the excluded; it is perfectly suited to them. Rather than 'tolerate' difference in the condescending spirit of liberal pluralism, the Bakhtinian approach celebrates difference; rather than expand the center to include the margins, it interrogates and shifts the center from the margins. Bakhtin's thought, properly deployed, does not retreat from radicalism; rather, it calls attention to all oppressive hierarchies of power, not only those derived from class but also those of gender, race and age. A Bakhtinian textual politics favors a more open reciprocal, decentered negotiation of specificity and difference; it does not advise feminist, black or gay struggles to 'wait their turn' while the class struggle achieves its ends. Bakhtin did not specifically address himself to all oppressions, but he staked out a conceptual space for them, as it were, in advance.

Bakhtin's broad view, embracing many cultures and millennia of artistic production, also has the potentiality of deprovincializing a critical discourse that remains too rigidly tied to nineteenth-century conventions of verisimilitude. In its fondness for intertextual parody and formal aggressions, the Bakhtinian aesthetic can be easily reconciled with modernist reflexivity and even with a certain avant-garde, but it is not compatible with an empty formalism. Bakhtin retains a certain allegiance to realism, not in the sense of mimetic reproduction of the real but rather in a quasi-Brechtian sense of revealing the 'causal network' of events, of communicating the profound sociality and historicity of human behavior. Bakhtin speaks of 'grotesque realism', i.e. an anti-illusionistic style that remains physical, carnal, material, that tells social truths but in stylized, parodic and hyperbolic rather than naturalistic form. His thought shares with the avant-garde a common impulse toward social, formal and libidinal rebellion, but the rebellion is here allied with, rather than hostile to, popular culture; or, better, it forges links with the adversary culture of the oppressed.

Bakhtin points the way to transcending some of the felt insufficiencies of other theoretical grids. His concept of dialogism, of language and discourse as 'shared territory', inoculates us against the individualist assumptions undergirding romantic theories of art, while still allowing us to be attuned to the specific ways in which artists orchestrate diverse social voices. His emphasis on a boundless context that constantly interacts with and modifies the text, helps us avoid formalist fetishization of the autonomous art object. His emphasis on the 'situated utterance' and the 'interpersonal generation of meaning' avoids the static ahistoricism of an apolitical 'value-free' semiotics. The notion of heteroglossia, finally, proposes a fundamentally non-unitary, constantly shifting cultural field in which the most varied discourses exist in shifting, multi-valenced oppositional relationships. Heteroglossia can be seen as another name for the social and psychic contradictions that constitute the subject as the site of conflicting discourses and competing voices. Bakhtin rejects the idea of a unitary political subject: *the* bourgeois, *the* proletarian. One can hear the voice of the proletarian in the bourgeois and the voice of the bourgeois in the proletarian, without denying that social class is a meaningful, even indispensable, category. A Bakhtinian view deconstructs the rigidities of the Stalinist base/superstructure model (in Bakhtin's day) and the paranoid defeatism of the 'dominant ideology' school of Althusserian Marxism in our own.

The left, we began by saying, has often displayed a schizophrenic attitude toward mass-mediated culture, sometimes endorsing entertainment uncritically and sometimes lamenting the delight that mass audiences take in alienated spectacles. Too often a puritanical Marxism throws out the baby of pleasure with the bathwater of ideology. This refusal of pleasure has at times created an immense gap between left cultural criticism and the people it purports to serve. Indeed, the political consequences of left puritanism have been enormous. An austere super-egoist left that addresses its audience in moralistic terms, while advertising and mass culture speak to its deepest desires and fantasies, not only exhibits severe theoretical limitations but also handicaps its own chances for success in the world. The broad American hostility to socialism has as much to do with the widespread misconception that socialist societies are 'gray', 'dreary' and 'anti-erotic' as with any conviction that socialist economics is unsound or socialist analysis invalid. A Bakhtinian approach appreciates rather than deplores the fact of mass-mediated pleasure, embracing it as a potential friend while recognizing its conditions of alienation. The point, as Enzensberger and others have shown, is that the consciousness industry and capitalism cannot ultimately satisfy the real needs they exploit. Thus the left, deploying 'anticipatory' readings, must treat mass media as inadvertently predictive of possible future states of social life.

A Bakhtinian analysis of popular and mass culture would think through the social logic of our personal and collective desires, while demystifying the political and ideological structures that channel our desires in oppressive directions. It would appeal to deeply rooted but socially frustrated aspirations – for new pleasurable forms of work, for solidarity, for festivity, for community. It would restore the notion of collective pleasure, of which carnival is but one form, to its rightful place within left thought. It would remind us of the collective pleasure, for example, of acting in concert for a passionately shared social goal – and would restore parodic, dialogic, and carnivalesque strategies to their deserved place in left artistic and critical practice. Aware of the double play of ideology and utopia, it would propose a double movement of celebration and critique. Alive to the inert weight of system and power, it would also see openings for their subversion. In this sense, Bakhtin synthesizes what Ernst Bloch calls Marxism's 'cold current' – the disabused analysis of oppression and alienation – with its 'warm current' – its intoxicating glimpses of collective freedom. In dialogue with Marxism and feminism – both of which it needs for its own completion – Bakhtinian thought can point the way to the transcendence of sterile dichotomies and exhausted paradigms. Most important, Bakhtin's conceptualizations suggest the possibility of a radical cultural critique applicable to the mass media that might crystallize the thrust of collective desire while being aware of its degraded expression, a cultural critique precluding neither laughter nor the pleasure principle.

Notes

1. For the purposes of this essay, I will be using the name 'Bakhtin' somewhat synecdochically to refer to the author both of those works written singly by him and of those co-authored with others.

2. For left readings, see Fredric Jameson, *The Political Unconscious: Narrative as a Socially Symbolic Act* (Ithaca: Cornell University Press, 1981); Terry Eagleton, *Against the Grain* (London: Verso, 1986); Tony Bennett, *Formalism and Marxism* (London: Methuen, 1979); and Ken Hirschkop, 'A Response to the Forum on Mikhail Bakhtin', in Gary Saul Morson, *Bakhtin: Essays and Dialogues on His Work* (Chicago: University of Chicago, 1986) and Ken Hirschkop, 'Bakhtin and Democracy', *New Left Review*, No 160 (Nov–Dec 1986). For liberal readings, see Clark and Holquist, *Mikhail Bakhtin* (Cambridge, Mass: Harvard University Press, 1984); Garry Saul Morson, 'Who Speaks for Bakhtin?' in *Bakhtin: Essays and Dialogues on His Work* (Chicago: University of Chicago Press, 1986); and Wayne Booth's 'Introduction' to Mikhail Bakhtin, *Problems of Dostoevsky's Poetics* (Minneapolis: University of Minnesota Press, 1984).

3. See Hans Magnus Enzensberger, 'Constituents of a Theory of the Media', in *The Consciousness Industry* (New York: Seabury Press, 1974).

4. See Tania Modleski, *Studies in Entertainment: Critical Approaches to Mass Culture* (Bloomington: Indiana University Press, 1986); and Colin MacCabe, *High Theory/Low Culture: Analysing Popular Television and Film* (New York: St. Martin's, 1986).

5. See Tzvetan Todorov, *Mikhail Bakhtin: The Dialogical Principle* (Minneapolis: University of Minnesota Press, 1984).

6. Mikhail Bakhtin, 'Discourse in the Novel', in *The Dialogical Imagination* (Austin: University of Texas Press, 1981), p. 345.

7. V.N. Voloshinov, *Marxism and the Philosophy of Language* (Cambridge, Mass: Harvard University Press, 1973), p. 24.

8. See M.M. Bakhtin and P.M. Medvedev, *The Formal Method in Literary Scholarship: A Critical Introduction to Sociological Poetics* (Cambridge, Mass: Harvard University Press, 1985), p. 26.

9. See Graham Pechey, 'Bakhtin, Marxism and Post-structuralism', in *Literature, Politics and Theory* (London: Methuen, 1986).

10. *Marxism and the Philosophy of Language*, p. 89.

11. M.M. Bakhtin and P.M. Medvedev, *The Formal Method in Literary Scholarship*, pp. 95–6.

12. Ibid.

13. I develop this argument further in 'Television News and its Spectator', in E. Ann Kaplan ed., *Regarding Television* (Los Angeles: American Film Institute, 1983).

14. M.M. Bakhtin, 'The Problem of Speech Genres', in *Speech Genres and Other Late Essays* (Austin: University of Texas Press, 1986), p. 91.

15. M.M. Bakhtin, 'Response to a Question from *Novy Mir*', in *Speech Genres and Other Late Essays*, p. 5.

16. M.M. Bakhtin, *Speech Genres and Other Late Essays*, p. 2.

17. This as yet unpublished article will appear in a collective volume to be entitled *Bakhtin: Radical Perspectives*.

18. See Peter Stallybrass and Allon White, *The Politics and Poetics of Transgression* (Ithaca: Cornell University Press, 1986).

19. See Richard Dyer, 'Entertainment and Utopia', in Rick Altman, ed., *Genre: The Musical: A Reader* (London: RKP, 1981).

20. See 'Forms of Time and Chronotope in the Novel', in *The Dialogical Imagination* (Austin: University of Texas Press, 1981), p. 128.

21. See Arthur Kroker and Michael Dorland, 'Panic Cinema: Sex in the Age of the Hyperreal', *Cineaction* 10 (fall 1987).

22. These ideas are developed further in my 'Bakhtin, Eroticism, and the Cinema: Strategies for the Critique and Transvaluation of Pornography', *Cineaction* 10 (fall 1987).

23. See 'Television as a Cultural Forum: Implications for Research', *Quarterly Review of Film Studies* (summer 1983).

24. Some of these reflexions were formulated in a paper authored by William Boddy, Marty Lucas, Jonathon Buchsbaum and myself, entitled 'Charisma, Jujitsu and the Democrats', and sent to those in charge of the television spots for Mondale/Ferraro – to precious little effect.

25. In his writings on India, Marx applauded the 'annihilation of the Asiatic society, and the laying of the material foundations of Western society in Asia', while Engels supported the French conquest of Algeria as a progressive step for the advancement of culture. Karl Marx, *Surveys from Exile* (London: Pelican Books, 1973), p. 320.

26. Ernst Bloch, *The Principle of Hope*, 3 vols (Cambridge: MIT Press, 1986), I: 394.

27. Hélène Cixous, 'The Laugh of the Medusa', *Signs* 1, 4 (1976), p. 888. For the Ruby Rich article, see 'In the Name of Feminist Criticism', in Bill Nichols, ed., *Movies and Methods* II (Berkeley: University of California Press, 1985).

9

Sliding Off the Stereotype: Gender Difference in the Future of Television

William Galperin

It is by now a commonplace that certain kinds of television are gender specific: televised sports, for example, are directed at a predominantly male audience, while soap operas have attracted a largely female constituency. The effect of this division, it has been argued, is to suppress men and women even further by reconciling them to their respective roles in society. If sports television 'functions primarily as a substitute and compensation for lack of success and fortune in the work week',[1] soap operas accomplish a similar function of simulating the 'success' of 'women's work', requiring the viewer to be engaged in several things simultaneously for the larger 'good of the family'.[2]

I wish to explore here the reconciliations by which men's and women's spheres of television work their alleged suppression. For if sports television effects identification with the athletes through a narcissistic fetishization of the male body, as Margaret Morse argues, it is no less true that sports television attracts both men and women and can be said, moreover, to have reconciled each gender to roles that in recent years have become increasingly similar. So, too, if soap operas are pitched toward a predominantly female audience, not only is this appeal made to the audience's 'success' within the home, as Tania Modleski demonstrates; the appeal is made also to the audience's circumscription in that workplace, and – along with the increasing numbers of men who find themselves 'at home' watching soap operas – through a subversion of the very patriarchy that has also co-opted women and *made* them sports fans.

I

My concern then is, first, with two versions of television, one feminized and the other patriarchal. In addition I shall correlate these versions of television with two parallel developments in American culture: the co-optation of women within the professional–managerial class; and the marginalization of men in the industrial working class. In this way, the difference between male and female television, which assuredly exists, may be demonstrated as much by the fact that the two 'televisions' have as their audiences (and by virtue of their individual functions) men and women respectively, as by the fact that women and men are attracted to sports programs and soap operas, respectively, in increasing numbers. Further, with the advent of the so-called 'prime time soap', we can see more clearly the implications of these transformations for the future of television and, less hopefully, the direction that both television and culture will likely take.[3]

My recognition that there is something more to the two versions of television than simple complicity with the divisive, ultimately repressive tendencies of culture, comes from a statement of Barthes's in *Roland Barthes*. Speaking of stereotypes which, he cheerfully admits, are every-where, Barthes observes that 'sometimes the stereotype (*écrivance*) gives way and writing (*écriture*) appears'. Barthes's definition of the stereotype – 'that emplacement of discourse where the *body is missing*, where one is sure the body is not' – is particularly crucial here, for it reflects a stance not always associated with him. As this definition of stereotypes suggests, Barthes holds forth the possibility of some ideal or perhaps natural state – where the 'body' is effectively released from culture – to which literature or even life can 'sometimes' provide access. In short, there is something in the text, according to Barthes, what he terms 'writing', that recalls some other state, some natural or perhaps transcendental condition, that stereotypes have in general displaced.[4]

This alignment of 'writing' with a privileged or otherwise unstereo-typed condition has special bearing on the question of gender differen-tiation in television. As I will show, it is in their various 'nostalgias', so to speak – in the intermittent slippage from *écrivance* to *écriture* – that men's and women's television are most clearly distinguishable. In men's TV, here exemplified by televised baseball, this slippage is essentially mysti-fying, moving from the predictable to the heroic – or to the relatively 'divine'. Such slippage, moreover, can be distinguished from those aspects of the heroic that *are* stereotypes and sufficiently a part of tele-vision to make these departures from stereotype quite unique.

In women's TV, by contrast – here soap operas – the slippage is in the opposite direction and pitched toward the identification of a natural (or what Kristeva would term a 'maternal') state free from the restraining hand of culture and the very hegemony that sports television mystifies. What transpires in the movement from *écrivance* to *écriture* is a writing *about* stereotype that is deconstructive and subversive of the governing (if arbitrary) assumptions behind the primary narrative.

In soap operas, typically, the so-called 'good' character is both conventionally good – that is to say, a virtuous and thus assailable patriarch (or a character supportive of the virtuous patriarch) – and unconventionally 'bad' by virtue of this assailability: it is in the assaults to which these characters are forever subject that the *desire* for their subjugation (and for the ideal state following it) is continually articulated. The good character is rendered unattractive, not by a subversion in the text *per se* (where he or she is forever wronged by a 'bad' person or twist of fate), but rather by a slippage in the text, where 'good' ultimately signifies the privilege of which 'the good' are possessed by fiat without ever realizing it. This would not only account for the popularity of the genuinely 'bad' characters on soap operas who, while sometimes a part of the dominant order, are at least the agents of subversion; it would explain as well the noticeable decline in popularity of those shows (I am thinking particularly here of ABC's *General Hospital*) that 'reward' the appeal of their subversive agents (in *General Hospital*, Luke Spencer) by recuperating them into good, patriarchal figures.

II

In her essay, 'Sports on Television: Replay and Display', Margaret Morse emphasizes the spectacular nature of televised football, which she contrasts to the experience of seeing a game live in the stadium or, for that matter, to the so-called 'game films', which are shot from atop the stadium for the purpose of analyzing a team's performance retrospectively. Unlike these 'quotidian' experiences, which exist roughly within the timescape of the game itself, televised sports are more spectacular and 'oneiric', thanks chiefly to the use and rapid editing of multiple camera angles, the deployment of the telephoto lense, the interposition of colorful graphics and, most important, the seemingly continuous recourse to replays in slow motion. In addition, the commentary, which, as Morse notes, alternates 'between "play-by-play" and "color" functions', enhances the 'liminality' of televised football in providing 'direct invitation to the scopophilia' already invited in the spectacular nature of the presentation.[5]

Based on a principle of narcissistic identification, whereby the 'electronic reshaping of the game' gives 'form to fantasies',[6] Morse's conception of televised sports remains one in which men in particular are given access to a power they otherwise lack. Moreover, as this view is in large measure a modification of Laura Mulvey's well-known pronouncements on the voyeuristic positioning of the female body in conventional cinema, it is not at all surprising that Morse regards the female spectator, or more properly the female gaze, as an outsider or third party in the hermeneutics of televised sports.[7]

But it is precisely on this highly exclusive notion of woman-as-outsider that Morse's argument requires supplementation. For if it is true that TV sports allow for an absorption of men by men, such acts of recognition are just as much acts of alienation, involving an emplacement of discourse where (as Barthes suggests) the body is necessarily missing. To the extent, in other words, that something is immediately accessible in sports television it is more in the way of second nature rather than in the way of that primary or psychological nature Morse describes: it is because sports television is more often than not stereotypical.

The live event, by contrast, is a much more spectacular one if only by virtue of the contingencies and distractions that attend the experience of seeing a game in person. These invariably include driving to the game, parking, the procurement of tickets and afterwards food and drink, and the often disconcerting experience of having to view a game in the company of other people who for one reason or another must themselves be objects of interest. Further, in the case of a sport like baseball, the spatial dimensions to which we are accustomed from television are so thoroughly altered that the business of attending to the proceedings at hand is in many instances a distraction from the game itself. Whether it is the flight of the ball, the positioning of a fielder, or the signs a coach is relaying to a man on base, the 'quotidian' experience of seeing a game live often gives too much of the 'quotidian', too much in the way of difficulty or contingency, to make that experience in any way predictable or stereotypical.

By comparison, what is made available through the medium of television is, if anything, singularly unspectacular. Indeed, even so ostensibly absorptive a device as the slow-motion replay has a strangely demystifying effect, particularly when – in the actual stadium – we are often unsettled by the disappearance of such an aid, and thus by an inability to possess and domesticate what has in fact *happened.* Nor is it the replay alone that renders the televised spectacle unspectacular. Explanatory graphics, highly coded interviews with the participants ('up close and personal') and, of course, the very rules of the game, which in television seem more rigidly enforced thanks to their enhancement by the rules and conventions of television – all contribute to a thoroughly predictable experience. This predictability goes so far as to encompass the unpredictable in sport. I cannot begin to enumerate the countless times when, in the final innings of a hopelessly one-sided game, a commentator in the hope of sustaining interest will remark, *à propos* an improbable comeback by the losing team, that 'stranger things have happened'. The commentary, with its predictable tropes and decorum, more than any other single aspect of televised sports, serves to normalize the spectacular, making the contingent always secondary to a prescribed discourse.

The outsider or third party in the hermeneutics of sports television is not necessarily a woman but anyone – male or female – who conceivably resists sports television as manifestly denatured, debased or otherwise stereotyped. This point can be illustrated by the following anecdote, which describes the conditions under which an outsider was provisionally made an insider. A noted art historian, who happens also to be a baseball fan, recounted how at a gathering of a group of highly respected scholars a number of the party were eventually distracted from the proceedings by the World Series, which they watched in an adjacent room. At a particularly key point in the game during which Bob Welch of the Los Angeles Dodgers was able after numerous attempts to strike out Reggie Jackson of the New York Yankees, another art historian, who was not a sports fan, entered the room and was immediately engrossed by what he saw on the screen. At the conclusion of the game, which ended with the strikeout, he turned to those around him and asked: 'Is it always like this?'

The answer, of course, is 'no'. What the art historian had seen, and undoubtedly had seen as art, does not happen very often. Granted, a World Series game does not happen every day and, in the majority of instances, is not decided in so dramatic a fashion. Yet having said this much, it must be granted too that Jackson was likely to strike out in any case, especially since he has more strikeouts than anybody in the history of baseball. My point is that even allowing for the excitement *written into* the Welch–Jackson encounter by the narrative of the game and of the preceding season (and, in some sense, the histories of both baseball and America), the art historian was responding to the 'representation' of the encounter as enhanced by the medium of television.

In particular, the art historian was admiring the work of NBC's Harry Coyle, who for over twenty-five years has directed the majority of the network's baseball telecasts. To be sure, Coyle's principal function is to transmit the game, whose appeal and excitement resided with the players' abilities and performances. Nevertheless, within the parameters of the game itself, there is much in the way of presentation that is left to the discretion of the director. The technology of sports television has progressed rapidly in the last fifteen years, so that in key contests like the World Series, a director may choose from as many as a dozen different camera angles in transmitting a game's proceedings. For the most part, these transmissions are determined by the action on the field, which in baseball almost always originates with a pitch to a batter and is usually recorded by a camera positioned in the stands behind the pitcher's mound. Still, Coyle's work is distinguished from that of his counterparts by his uncanny ability to 'edit' the game in progress – an instinct for which camera angle will most vividly record what must be recorded.

Coyle's accomplishments recall those of the famed German film-maker Leni Riefenstahl, particularly her *Olympische Spiele* (1936), which was perhaps the first film to employ a myriad of cameras in the narration of a sporting event. However, unlike Riefenstahl whose 'narration' was necessarily paramount and, in the time she was given to reconstruct the Munich Olympics, necessarily idealized, Coyle's work is only occasionally this way. Coyle's charge is not to propagandize sport, but to report it as it is being enacted. His purpose, first and foremost, is to describe the game – to transmit the action as it is taking place – rather than to narrate it, which only the events themselves will permit him to do. And yet, there are those moments in which description and narration effectively merge to create an experience like the Jackson–Welch confrontation in the 1978 World Series, where the game was clearly enhanced by a variety of representational devices, ranging from an amplification of crowd noise, to shots of the two opposing managers consumed by the activity before them, to the shot-counter-shot of the players themselves: the intensity of Welch's face in close-up as he repeatedly rejected his catcher's suggestions for pitches, and of Jackson's face as he stared at Welch, seeking to intimidate him.

These moments, which are unusual in sports television, yet sufficiently recurrent *in* televised sports to make them characteristic of what I am calling men's television, appeal by virtue of their defamiliarization, their mystification of the athlete so as to both mask and justify what is most familiar or stereotypical about him: namely, the primacy to which, in the discourse of Western culture, the male self is generally entitled. What is celebrated in these moments is almost always a triumph of the will or an exercise of individual power that transcends both the televised production and the *game itself*, whose rules often dictate such spectacular displays. The game-ending home run, like the game-ending strikeout, need not always appear heroic, and in most instances does not. This is even more true in football, whose most 'heroic' instances are virtually choreographed by the rules of the game. Accordingly, these moments in football, specifically those last-second passes whose completion gives victory to an otherwise losing team, are dubbed with names like the

'Hail Mary Pass' or the 'Immaculate Reception', which characteristically wrests authority from the players themselves. But in baseball, where individualism is more prevalent, the potential for the heroic, for a transcendent repositioning of the individual from *écrivance* (where he is merely a 'body' in a culturally prescribed text) to *écriture* (where he eludes the text in order to become our 'best self') is palpably in evidence.

The Jackson–Welch confrontation, while typical of Coyle's mystifying bent, is by no means his most notable achievement. That distinction undoubtedly belongs to the game-winning home run by Carlton Fisk in the sixth game of the 1975 World Series. The image of Fisk urging the ball to stay fair with both hands (and his jubilation upon succeeding) will be familiar to most baseball watchers, and is ordinarily replayed in the opening credits of NBC's *Game of the Week*. Still, Fisk's effort was not, in the game itself, the most devastating blow struck by the Red Sox, or even the most crucial. Bernie Carbo's three-run home run some innings earlier, against a more formidable pitcher, effectively rescued the Boston Red Sox from what at the time seemed certain defeat by the Cincinnati Reds. Yet we remember Fisk's home run; and we remember it, not because it ended the game, but because of Coyle's decision to interpose the shot of Fisk, willing the ball out, with the trajectory of the ball itself, making the batter, as it were, both player and providence. Several years later, when questioned about this directorial decision, Coyle responded rather modestly that the shot would have been impossible had the game been played elsewhere; for he had been able, thanks to the proximity of the left field wall in Boston's Fenway Park, and to the manually operated scoreboard there, to insert a camera in the scoreboard. As for the decision to utilize that particular angle, all Coyle could recall was his decision to 'go with it', which is altogether typical of his intuitive way with the game.[8] Yet I would argue, too, that if Coyle mainly presents stereotypes, his intuitions are no less informed by an intentional structure. The difference is that, whereas in most instances Coyle's is essentially the intentionality of the game (and of the rules by which the game is both played and represented), in the occasional divergences from stereotype, it follows a more heroic, more sublime trajectory from the familiar to the extraordinary.

III

The question of gender – whether it is only to men that the televised game appeals in its movement from *écrivance* to *écriture* – must now be pursued. For while it is clear that in the main televised baseball appeals to a male rather than a female audience, it can sometimes be no less attractive to the female gaze than, say, Homer or even Cecil B. DeMille. This may seem a melancholy fact to some feminists. But it remains true that these occasional slidings from stereotype are not only representative of the power and authority sufficiently valorized in our culture to attract an otherwise uninterested viewership, and that they mystify the bourgeois enfranchisement to which women are increasingly gaining access in their roles as managers and executives, thereby attracting an even broader constituency than before. Nor is this point lost on the networks, which customarily enlist moments such as Fisk's home run to attract more viewers, as ABC actually did in promoting *Monday Night Baseball* (for which they were obliged presumably to pay NBC). Nor is it lost on Coyle himself, who perhaps more than any other director actively incorporates the feminine gaze into his presentation.

The customary instance of this incorporation involves the spouse of a key participant, usually the batter, whose wife is observed between pitches cheering her husband on, frequently in a state of anxiety. However, one instance from the 1982 World Series shows that this incorporation can be more than simply a means for the audience – particularly its female members – to identify with the wife in her secondary, subordinate function. I am referring to an occasion when Gorman Thomas, the then touted slugger of the Milwaukee Brewers who had produced little up to that point in the Series, was finally in a position to drive in what proved to be a crucial run. During his time at bat, in which he was noticeably tentative (and not at all the hitter one had expected), Coyle's cameras shifted constantly to Mrs Thomas who, although anxious, actually appeared more composed, more self-possessed, than her husband. When Thomas produced his hit – a rather meagre one by his standards – the picture shifted once again to Thomas's wife who was observed letting out a sigh of relief.

What is interesting about this incorporation of the feminine gaze is its modification of the conventional myth of the man as hero and wife as suppliant. For it is the spouse, perhaps more than her husband, who is triumphant here, who actually complements and ennobles a performance that otherwise lacks distinction. One can only speculate on what Coyle would have done had Thomas struck out – but my guess is he would have returned to Mrs Thomas for a roughly similar effect: the composed resignation of which only the extraordinary or self-possessed are capable. Were it not for the narrative pressure exerted by Thomas's wife, a viewer whose expectations were themselves a kind of will or intentionality, the experience would not have satisfied in the way Fisk's home run or Welch's strikeout has also satisfied – or might have failed to satisfy had they been rendered in some other fashion. It is not that the wife's gaze feminizes the scene; if anything, the very opposite occurs: the female man, the abject Gorman Thomas, is masculinized and valorized by expectations that, for better or for worse, allow women equal access to the heroic. In contrast to the stereotypical scenario where the wife is passive and her husband active, passivity is here activated and activity rendered passive.

Women's access to the heroic is by no means new, nor is it unfamiliar to feminists today, who frequently view the problem in conflicting ways. Some feminists regard the achievement of power (and the establishment of a woman's tradition) a desirable end for women, while others view such an achievement as a repetition of the very hierarchy that women should forcefully resist.[9] Nor has the question been confined to women's power alone. In one of the more important feminist documents of this century, Simone Weil's *The Iliad or The Poem of Force*, the problem of a woman's response to power is broached with particular relevance to the subject at hand.[10]

Crediting the 'Greek genius' for its fascination with power, for fathoming the 'force' to which all (including Achilles) are eventually subject in *The Iliad*, Weil observes further that the Christian Gospels show a similar genius in the way 'that human suffering is laid bare, and we see in [them] a being who is at once divine and human'. In this way 'the accounts of the Passion show that a divine spirit, incarnate, is changed by misfortune, trembles before suffering and death, feels itself, in the depths of its agony, to be cut off from man and God.'[11]

Weil was sharply critical of human power, and it was undoubtedly this posture that led her to the company of workers rather than to more activist communist groups in the 1930s. All the same, even in her most wrenching descriptions of the effects of force in Homer, one finds a fascination with the powerful or, more properly, with the *authority* of power that does not escape its transmogrification in Christianity. Weil may argue that the Greek genius of Christianity entails more than 'the injunction to seek above all other things "the kingdom and justice of our Heavenly Father"'; yet it is clear, too, that the subservience to which Christ is reduced according to the Greek way is significant in that the subservient is actually 'divine' – making less, in Christ's example, the equivalent of more. Christ may believe he is 'cut off from God', but the fact that he is not – that God exists both 'incarnate' and elsewhere – is really the point of Weil's fascination.

I bring up Weil for two reasons: first, to show how a woman otherwise opposed to 'force' is nevertheless attracted to it; and second, to enlist this proclivity for authority as the very problem that soap operas have met head-on. That is, if televised sports can be said, on occasion, to render the divine incarnate – to mystify the human in the image of the

Father – soap operas tend rather to retrace this movement back to the very structure that requires that God be a *father*. Where the slippage in sports television tends merely to repeat the concession that Christianity has made to the human, granting humans transcendental access to divine force, the movement away from stereotype in women's television reveals how the Christian – including those aspects of the Christian that require us to imitate Christ in our subservience to authority – are ultimately part and parcel of a more immediate, patriarchal discourse. Indeed, in women's television the men invariably demand subservience, not because they are good men, but because their goodness is necessarily a condition of being men: the God who created us in his image needed us, particularly those whose glorification was already proven by social status, to attest to that fact.

More perhaps than even televised sports, soap operas are consumed by stereotypes. It is almost axiomatic, for instance, that newlyweds, particularly happy ones, will shortly encounter problems; that one act of infidelity will lead to pregnancy; that good women are necessarily long-suffering; and that good men are invariably successful. On the level of stereotype, soap operas adamantly defend both the dominant patriarchal culture and the ethic we call Protestant and, in conjunction with their defense, are invariably peopled with the highest achievers in American society: doctors, lawyers, and captains of industry. (That the word 'enterprises' frequently follows the proper name of the magnate who owns a company in a daytime drama reinforces the point.) On another level, however, soap opera tends to undo the Protestant ethic simply by defending it. Such tendencies may range from the merely extravagant – the assertion, for example, that this doctor or this lawyer is 'the best in his field' – to more subtle acts of subversion which require, as I have suggested, that conventionally 'good' characters – both men and women – be required to 'pay', as it were, for their moral and/or economic entitlement.

In CBS's Emmy award-winning *The Young and the Restless*, Mary Williams, a devout churchgoer who happens also to be the wife of a hard-working, incorruptible police officer, has been compelled in recent years to endure: her daughter's degradation by a playboy husband who continually cheats on her; her husband's disgrace when a prostitute (to whom he had given gifts in exchange for information) betrays him in a manner that suggests something more than a professional relationship; and, most recently, the appearance of her son in a nude magazine layout intended, as one churchgoer observes, to excite young women. On one level, the writers of *The Young and the Restless* simply follow the codes by which Mary may be seen as victim, as a meek person whose rightful inheritance of the earth has been forestalled by the more sinister, godless elements of society. But in the long run, it is impossible to sympathize with Mary or to derive solace from her victimization. This is not only because Mary is a stereotype (right down to her vintage housedresses and melancholy affect); it is because Mary, more importantly, is the victim of convention: of a daughter whose desire to rise in the world can only be facilitated by marriage to a wealthier man; by a husband whose sense of his own incorruptibility makes him vulnerable to those who shrewdly exploit his arrogant sense of self-worth; and by a son whose self-love (learned undoubtedly at Mary's hands) provoked him to pose nude in the first place. We cannot sympathize with Mary according to convention without deploring convention as a measure of our sympathy. In any single instance Mary may be sympathetic; however, the sheer number of these instances has an ultimately cloying effect. What gives way in *The Young and the Restless* is not the resistance to those conventions sympathy may occasionally support, but the convention of sympathy *itself*, which gradually founders on its own contradictions. So long as Mary continues to live in the manner to which she is accustomed, and to perform according to the customary codes, she is unavoidably her own worst enemy and one therefore to whom crises will continually fall.

I bring up the example of Mary Williams because her character shows the way that contradictions can be admitted to the text of a soap opera as opposed to allowing the primary narrative a power to mask or write over those contradictions. It has been observed, for example, how relatively liberal, so-called 'realist' films 'are unable to deal with the real in [their] contradictions', that the commitment of these works to a progressive rather than subversive function makes them blind to their idealizing tendencies.[12] In soap operas, by contrast, where the narratives are unfailingly conservative and stereotypical (abortion, for example, is never countenanced), contradictions have fewer places to hide and are always available as a subversive or 'revolutionary' device.

This is particularly noticeable in the amnesia of most soaps, where typically the injury one character may have done to another is conveniently forgotten following an unwarranted conversion of the injuring party from 'bad' to 'good'. A character can slide from one code so long as there is another stereotype on which to settle. Thus, a soap opera's conventions also expose the fellowship of the 'bad' and 'good', which the narrative only partly conceals. Soaps in this respect are not all that different from professional wrestling, save that wrestling is perhaps too self-reflexive, too inured to the dependency of the good upon the bad, to be as revolutionary. Where wrestling, like other postmodern spectacles, is determined to remember, recovering as detritus the various tropes of Western culture, soaps are sufficiently subversive to be able to forget, making amnesia not only necessary to the operation of their worlds, but a disease that quite literally afflicts one or another of the participants.

The most telling instance of the way amnesia functions in *The Young and the Restless* – of the way this too common of soap opera afflictions remains the signifier of a more pervasive ailment – involves the character of Victor Newman, a wealthy magnate whose authority and power have on numerous occasions saved him from becoming the villain he is always threatening to become. Newman's undecidability – based less on any real ambiguity in his character than on the entitlement that forever devolves upon the successful man, preventing him from ever becoming bad – reflects the safety-net that culture extends to those who least need it. If glorification is often measured by the success and power that come from hard work, so power and success continually warrant glorification. Newman can act very badly in ruthlessly terrorizing a photographer enamored of his model-wife, only to be recuperated when a woman employee terrorizes him in turn. In one sense, the latter act of terror remains a kind of feminine justice – a reversal that subjugates the authority figure to his own authority. Yet within the narrative of the show, which engenders sympathy for 'Victor', his 'victimization' proves a thoroughly unjustified revenge *against* women (the woman had, in fact, been the victim of sexual harassment) that is contested only in the narrative's failure to note this.

Such contradictions are altogether characteristic of the narrative surrounding Victor, but one contradiction in particular deserves further comment. Several years ago, in an utterly compulsive effort to command all of his wife's affections, Victor had a vasectomy without telling anyone. Nevertheless, within a year, after that marriage had dissolved, Victor was able to make the current object of his desire – a stripper – pregnant. At first, there was some attempt to resolve this contradiction as a physiological possibility. But in the intervening years Victor's vasectomy has been entirely forgotten, so much so that Victor is not only now capable of rendering a woman pregnant on one of the few occasions they have sex, but is also outraged when this same woman – with not a little provocation – has an abortion without telling him.

While the narrative has, following the conventions of soap opera, forgotten Victor's vasectomy (he remains a potent, powerful hero no matter what), the text virtually foregrounds this amnesia, making the triumph over physiology less a miracle than a commonplace or a metaphor for the triumph of culture over nature. So long as Victor is possessed of a penis, that penis will work. What returns with Victor's potency is not the repressed – that is to say, nature – but the repressor, whose dominion over nature is similarly reflected in the way that Victor excoriates his mistress for a similar action that, in light of her gender, is necessarily irreversible. In this strange passage where the literal is suddenly symbolic, abortions are always irreversible, and vasectomies only temporary.

Finally, in the narrative of the Abbott family, on whom the majority of the plots on *The Young and the Restless* center, the defense of patriarchy, specifically of the patriarch John Abbott, is relegated to a representational or purely fictive plane. At the level of narrative, John Abbott is a loving, responsible patriarch, enamored of his two daughters (the prettier of whom he has made president of his cosmetics empire), and deeply troubled by his prodigal son Jack (who is always embroiled in one power intrigue or another). The possibility that Jack remains his father's son, that his manipulation of people, especially women, inscribes in miniature his father's male dominance, never occurs to John Sr. Inscrutable at best, Jack is more often a disappointment. Yet the real disappointment in the show is not the son, whose opposition to his father periodically permits him a certain circumspection, but John himself, whose blindness to his own entitlement and to his own lapses as a powerful man continually makes him an object of subversion.

There is, for example, no single character in *The Young and the Restless* to whom more lies are told. The ostensible reason for this lying is the pristine disposition of the father, which cannot, it is assumed, bear the corruption the truth holds in store. But lies are told to John Abbott in his own image: just as John has succeeded in convincing himself of his purity and virtue (that he is literally and figuratively worth the millions he was destined to earn), so those nearest to John and dependent on him are obliged to follow his example. The point is not that these people are simply lying to John; it is that such lying uncovers a truth about the narrative of John Abbott – that it is *only* a *narrative* – of which neither John nor those lying to him are consciously aware. If John cannot possibly endure the truth, so those who would tell him the truth are too impressed with his lack of endurance, too co-opted by his mythology, to change things.

The text of *The Young and the Restless* is of course a different matter. For every concession to patriarchy that the primary narrative makes, for every lie it is disposed to tell, there is a rupture or movement against convention by which culture and its effects are made to appear arbitrary. Thus, the majority of crises in the Abbott family are not crises of behavior or action; they are crises of disclosure. What most threatens the society of *The Young and the Restless* are not the betrayals and infidelities, which do not alter the world a bit, but the 'truth' regarding those actions, which is altogether different from the knowledge of them. While it is almost always assumed that the knowledge of certain events will 'destroy' the lives of the patriarchs from whom these activities have been kept secret, only their knowledge accomplishes that devastation. Neither the events themselves, nor the viewer's knowledge, which can precede a character's discovery by as many as three years, exert a comparable influence. Thus, the effect of disclosure is largely mystifying in function: a protest against the fact that everything was normal *until* the discovery, which requires that the world subseqently wear the discoverer's face. It is not that the world is the least bit changed as a result of discovery; it is rather that the aggrieved discoverer is sufficiently powerful (and thus consumed by his own grief) to insist that the world be affected in kind, that the world be made his own imaginary creation.

The character in *The Young and the Restless* whose discoveries most consistently expose the arbitrariness of culturally sanctioned authority is John Abbott. Upon discovering long after the fact that his young (second) wife, Jill, had spent one night with Jack, John reacts in such a way that the world must share his injury. Forgetting apparently that he was instrumental in their liaison, that he had virtually forced Jill from the house on the day she was subsequently rescued by Jack in the middle of a blizzard, John does not express anger but instead suffers a stroke. Through his stroke, John not only communicates the personal injury he feels, he communicates it to a world otherwise unaffected. It is not enough for John simply to divorce Jill and banish Jack from both family and business – as he eventually will do. It is necessary that he first take revenge upon the world, which, thanks to his considerable influence in the lives of other characters, he temporarily refashions.

That John is able to change things so arbitrarily, that his knowledge has an ultimately greater effect on the world than our greater knowledge of his limitations, is typical of the way soap operas marshal the patriarchal world, and the conventional narratives that serve it, into an argument, a text, against patriarchy. While soaps undoubtedly derive their appeal from a variety of functions – not the least of which is their serial form – it is surely no coincidence that the majority of those who follow soaps have generally benefited less from the discourse of patriarchy than those who watch sports. This does not mean, of course, that those who are less entitled are necessarily opponents of patriarchy or that soap operas fail always to defend the dominant culture. Rather, the opposite is true: the discourse of patriarchy is so pervasive, so continuous in soap opera, as to become stereotypical. The more pervasive the stereotype, the more potential for stereotypes to turn on themselves (reflecting a nostalgia, again, for the 'body's' liberation) in the ways I have outlined.

In sports television something different takes place. Here, power and authority are so deeply entrenched, so thoroughly exploited in the very rules of the game, that they are in need of a more compelling defense. This defense, which also involves a movement from *écrivance* to *écriture*, has the different function of making what is too common to soap opera uncommonly interesting. Where human, specifically male, authority is a virtual convention of women's television, and vulnerable thanks to its stereotypicality, it is girded against demystification in sports television by occasionally rising above itself. Or, put another way: the plainly arbitrary rules of a televised sport, of which individual prowess is often a given, allow sports telecasts to inscribe in large what soap operas – in their movements from *écrivance* to *écriture* – accomplish only 'sometimes'. Hence, the two spheres of television are really moving in opposite directions: toward and away from exposing the arbitrariness of an essentially bourgeois, patriarchal hegemony.

IV

If this double movement were all that appeared on television, if the demystifying drift of soap operas could be seen as a corrective to the mystifying tendencies of sports television, there would be some cause for enthusiasm. But just as the stereotypes of sports television are merely tedious to those who do not follow sport, so the conventions of soap opera are more vulnerable on other occasions to patriarchal co-optation. I am referring specifically to the prime-time soap, whose emergence in the last decade reflects both the changing demographics of the viewing audience in general and that women in particular require a different kind of soap commensurate with jobs and careers that make it difficult and undesirable for them to follow daytime serials. The prospect, in other words, for a 'feminization' of prime time, for the introjection of the subversion of women's television into more standard television fare, remains unlikely. It is more likely that prime-time soaps such as *Dallas* and *Dynasty* actively mitigate the revolutionary currents of their daytime counterparts by eliminating precisely those features I have been discussing.

While almost all the night-time serials focus on a patriarch or figure of authority, the arbitrariness of his enfranchisement is played down by the various threats to him from more sinister forces. Compared, for example, to the character of Alexis (Joan Collins) on ABC's *Dynasty*, the patriarch, Blake Carrington (John Forsythe), is fundamentally a good person. There are, to be sure, a fair number of villainesses and schemers in *The Young and the Restless* as well. Yet these characters are also engaged in an effort to usurp authority from men because they otherwise lack power. This accounts not only for their inability to wage the kind of battles the Collins character fights at night, but also for the peculiar vulnerability by which these characters become objects of identification. The villainess, Jill Abbott, is a far more sympathetic character in *The Young and the Restless* than her ex-stepdaughter Ashley, who is both a good character and, as a measure of that goodness, president of her father's company. Similarly, more care is exerted in night-time soaps to avoid the kinds of amnesia that in daytime help point up the arbitrary discourse of patriarchy. Where actors are forever replacing one another in the same role on daytime television, night-time serials customarily attempt to explain the departure of an actor, usually by changing the plot to accommodate his or her disappearance. Not surprisingly, a comparable effort is made in prime time to avoid the flagrant lapses in memory that are a virtual staple of daytime serials.

In much the same way that sports television can be said to recuperate the stereotypes of power and authority, night-time serials are engaged in acts of rehabilitation. The difference is that where this recuperation is accomplished in sports television by the movement from *écrivance* to *écriture*, the recuperations of night-time serials issue chiefly from the modification of daytime stereotypes. The suffering of Mary Williams in *The Young and the Restless* is glamorized at night through characters such as *Dynasty*'s Crystle Carrington (Linda Evans), who is scarcely her own worst enemy.

So, too, for the rare night-time serial that boldly eschews convention, replacing the stereotypes of daytime television with the wisdom effectively gained from them, backsliding is the invariable fate. I am thinking specifically here of NBC's *St Elsewhere*, which began as *écriture* only to become *écrivance*. Initially, *St Elsewhere* managed to undo the male authority endemic to most 'doctor' shows by promoting a feminized man in the character of Donald Westphal, and by satirizing the impossibly anachronistic and sexist surgeon, Mark Craig. In recent years, Westphal has for all practical purposes given up parenting for womanizing, and Craig, a reprehensible instance of privileged authority, has become (thanks to the actor William Daniels) the engaging, if still exasperating, object of both sympathy and interest. Among those men and women (including critics like the *New York Times*'s John O'Connor) who found the early *St Elsewhere* a refreshing alternative to standard prime-time fare, these changes are roundly deplored. Nevertheless, for the majority of viewers, including many American women who are no longer so completely disenfranchised, night-time mystification is obviously preferable to a critique of America that only the truly disenfranchised are ever likely to appreciate.[13]

Notes

1. Margaret Morse, 'Sports on Television: Replay and Display', in E. Ann Kaplan, ed., *Regarding Television* (Los Angeles: American Film Institute, 1983), p. 62.

2. Tania Modleski, 'The Rhythms of Reception: Daytime Television and Women's Work', in *Regarding Television*, p. 69.

3. The last four years, for example, saw a rise in the percentage of men over eighteen who watch soap operas. Thus, although ratings for soap operas were generally lower in this period – thanks to the increase in women working outside of the home – a greater percentage of men were watching daytime serials. Correspondingly, there has been a dramatic increase over this same period in women watching sports on television, particularly on weekend afternoons. In 1984–85, for example, NBC's baseball *Game of the Week,* which airs on Saturday afternoons, registered a 23 per cent increase in the audience of women between the ages of 18 and 49. In other words, if men's 'daytime' television is fast becoming women's daytime television, so women's television is, to an admittedly lesser extent, becoming television for both sexes. Nor do the statistics involving men who watch soap operas take into account those recorded on VCRs for viewing at a later time, when the 'man' presumably is in the house. At all events, both transformations, particularly the dramatic shift in the numbers of women watching sports, would seem to support my overall conclusion that the more enfranchised the viewer, the more likely he or she is to watch a show that generally promotes the discourse of patriarchy. I would like to thank Grey Seamans of NBC and Dave Poltrack of CBS for making this information available.

4. *Roland Barthes,* trans. Richard Howard (New York: Hill and Wang, 1977), p. 90. Such claims for 'writing' as a potentially radical or liberating mode (with a strangely biological resonance) are also shared by followers of Barthes, notably Julia Kristeva. What Kristeva terms a 'revolution in poetic language' is pitched similarly to a recovery in art of a pre-symbolic, pre-subjective condition, whereby the child (and now the writing subject) remains attached to the semiotic *chora* of the mother's body. *Revolution in Poetic Language,* trans. Margaret Waller (New York: Columbia University Press, 1984).

5. Morse, pp. 47–54.

6. Ibid., p. 54.

7. Ibid., p. 58. See also Laura Mulvey, 'Visual Pleasure and Narrative Cinema', *Screen* 16 (autumn, 1975), pp. 6–18.

8. These comments were made during an interview with Coyle in a pre-game show during the 1982 *World Series.*

9. For the various points of view regarding women's authority today, see Elaine Showalter, ed., *The New Feminist Criticism: Essays on Women, Literature and Theory* (New York: Pantheon, 1985).

10. Simone Weil, *The Iliad or The Poem of Force,* trans. Mary McCarthy (Wallingford, PA: Pendle Hill, 1956). The essay was originally published pseudonymously in December 1940 and January 1941 issues of *Cahiers du Sud* (Marseilles).

11. Ibid., p. 34.

12. Colin MacCabe, 'Realism and the Cinema: Notes on Some Brechtian Theses', in *Tracking the Signifier* (Minneapolis: University of Minnesota Press, 1985), p. 44.

13. I wish to thank Christina Zwarg for her help in the preparation of this essay, particularly her suggestion that the question of stereotype and the divergence from it would help elucidate the differences in men's and women's television.

10

Poetry/Punk/Production: Some Recent Writing in LA[1]

David E. James

'I don't like Los Angeles,' Ruth Rae whimpered. 'I haven't been there in years. I *hate* LA.' She peered wildly around.

'So do I,' the pol said as he locked the rear compartment off from the cab and dropped the key through a slot to the pols outside. 'But we must learn to live with it: it's there.'

Philip K. Dick

'In our days everything seems pregnant with its contrary'

Anon

The photograph in Charles Bukowski's most recent collection of poetry, *Dangling in the Tournefortia*, shows him casual in a T-shirt, now late in middle age but still 'grizzled', belligerent and apparently unchanged by the international success which, more than that of any other single writer, made a place for Los Angeles on the map of contemporary poetry and in doing so identified him as its exemplary practitioner. The mutual ratification in his work of a determinedly vulgar diction, a refusal to construct the line as a metrical or conceptual unit, and a limited repertoire of banal activities (drinking, vomiting, betting, pissing) enacted in a similarly limited terrain of stucco apartments and streets from the track to the liquor store produced a fully articulated model of *poesis* that has been available for general use. It does no disservice to the vigor of Bukowski's originality and the importance of his example also to recognize that the primary stance of the mode he uses is so widespread that it can be properly thought of as a public production, a social inevitability that he seized upon and clarified; and so we can redefine his achievement as in part entrepreneurial, the negotiation of that mode into

163

a literary establishment which at the time of his intervention was constituted in quite different terms. And while that stance embodies the alienation that is so central to the modern experience as a whole, still the
contemplation of an alien and self-destructing environment by an
alienated and self-deprecating narrator has proven a particularly useful
and appropriate means of situating sensibility in Los Angeles, a city that
has typically had little occasion for poetry.

Though the notion of a school overstates the commonality of those
poets who write in Bukowski's mode, as well as being contradictory to
the resolutely isolated stance that is its basic premise, still it can be seen
everywhere. Wanda Coleman's change of key, to take a particularly
dramatic example, easily segues from the white male to the black female
version. 'Where I Live' features the same working-class streets and businesses, the same casual violence and sexuality, the same problems with
landlords and police and the sideswiping of the same cars that comprise
Bukowski's world and, apart from the inversion in color and gender,
celebrates them with the same wry machismo:

> the country is her pimp and she can turn a trick
> swifter than any bitch ever graced this earth
> she's the baddest piece of ass on the west coast
> named black los angeles
> (Coleman reads this on
> *Voices of the Angels*)

Given the peculiarly powerful identification between the place and the
persona, and the degree to which this composite '20 Century Fox' all but
totally occupies the poem, it is right that in her moments of self-
consciousness Coleman will reflect on the dependence of her voice upon
the world she creates, inevitably drawn to wonder whether she is 'poet
writing a poem / or a poem writing a poet' (p. 97). With a similar
concern, Bob Flanagan, finding himself telling his girlfriend in a bar that
her poems are no good, going to the icebox for a beer and then going to
the john, attempts to escape the codes that reach out from the genre to
strangle life; he fails and knows it when his girlfriend beats upon the
bathroom door, demanding to be let in to piss in what, inevitably,
announces itself as a 'Bukowski Poem'. The stance that began as a rejection of rhetoric and artifice, an attempt to affirm the sufficiency of plain
speech and the everyday situation, itself became conventionalized. The
anti-poem became the poem, the ordinary guy became a role. Appropriately then, in the photograph I mentioned, Bukowski's T-shirt is
adorned with a large, pop-star type photo – of Charles Bukowski.

The conjunction of identity and displacement, the *différance* manifested here, can of course be theorized in many ways: psychologically, as

a Goffmanian social self-presentation; semiologically, as the gap between signifier and signified that allows the play of the former celebrated by all kinds of postmodernists; or economically, as a marketing strategy, a prerequisite for product identification. And no doubt these theorizations do have a validity that correctly chastens any desire for the authentic or full image as naivety. To recognize such is, however, not to pre-empt a more comprehensive understanding of all of them, and of their place in the doubleness Bukowski and his image exemplify, as the sign of a particular historical condition. That evaporation of presence at exactly the point when it most insists upon itself may then be recognized as a chronology, as the destiny of all culture under capitalism in which the processes of consumption return upon the activity of production to displace it from itself and its intrinsic pleasure and redefine its telos as something other. While these conditions are general throughout the consumer society, they are felt in a peculiarly crucial way in Los Angeles, circumscribing and inhabiting all art, even and perhaps especially that which attempts to escape them.

The effects of the intense media-tion of experience associated with this city have historically been explored in a narrative tradition in which a love-hate (and typically more hate than love) relationship with Los Angeles has more or less closely converged upon an analysis of Hollywood as the tinsel front for a decadence variously diagnosed in moral, anti-communist and, most recently, left-semiological terms. The frequency with which such an ambivalence recurs within Hollywood – in, for example *Sullivan's Travels, Sunset Boulevard, Heat* – is such that it would seem to have been felt as fully inside the business as outside, taking the place in industrial production as a whole of that space of self-consciousness in individual films, that problematizing of representation which has now become a staple of avant-garde cinema. Nevertheless, the hegemony of the film industry over the city's social and intellectual life until very recently made it the measure of everything else, effectively devaluing or expelling any cultural production that could not be integrated within it. As a result writing, painting and certainly conversation here evidence a recognizable stylistic fertilization and determination from the silver screen, the finish-fetish of the painting and sculpture of the late 1960s being only the most luminous instance.

Poetry, however, of all the arts the least useful to the film industry and in its recent forms least compatible with its ethos, has, as if in recognition of the unavailability of its present forms to profitable marketing, constructed itself in antithesis to everything assumed by Hollywood. There have been crossovers: actors such as Richard Thomas and Suzanne Somers are published poets and some of the best known local poets, Harry Northup and Jack Grapes for instance, have worked in

Hollywood. In these cases at least the contradictions between the two spheres do not appear to be as great as I have presented them: for Northup, acting in *Alice Doesn't Live Here Any More* and *Taxi Driver*, is remembered in his poetry as a moment of psychic and artistic plenitude that occurs outside LA: 'When i finished working on "Alice ..." and they sent me back to the / city on a plane i felt like i was being taken back to prison' (p. 142). With a different order of self-consciousness, Michael Ford often uses recollections of old TV shows and movies as the lens to look at the world with and the vocabulary to make it over into the poem; the sky at 6 a.m. for example is 'gray the way it was / back in a black & white movie / *The Misfits*' (p. 38). But, to the extent that (as his title affirms) *The World is a Suburb of Los Angeles*, it is also true that the passage away from the metropolis which reveals only a world already known through the media is also a passage back in time. The nostalgia for B-movies is a nostalgia for childhood, as well as for a Hollywood that no longer exists.

The various crises suffered by the film industry in the fifties, the attempts at regrouping in the late sixties and the subsequent decision to deal exclusively in the pre-teen and redneck markets are only maguffins in the big story that describes the supplanting of cinema by music as the hegemonic cultural force in the post-war period.[2] This development – not unconnected of course with the marketing of stereo systems, the constantly renewable consumption of music in the commodity form of records produced by hit parade fashions, the ability of sound to penetrate all life processes from the supermarket to the bedroom by way of the car and thus to become a totally continuous commercial environment – was, until the late seventies, resisted more in Los Angeles than elsewhere. Though there had been a thriving jazz in the forties and fifties, after the sixties, despite the presence of a recording industry and so a plethora of musicians and apart from brief openings like the Doors, local music had been as bland as the lifestyle it publicized. But down from the *Ladies of the Canyon*, well beyond the *Hotel California*, other developments were brewing.

By the summer of 1977, the effects of the English punk explosion relayed by records of the Clash and the Sex Pistols and by the personal appearance of the Damned, was being felt in LA.[3] *Slash*, a magazine devoted to the new music that later pioneered recordings by local bands, was founded and a few clubs in Hollywood began to feature local music. But rather than being centralized in Hollywood, the significant music developed in a number of suburbs dispersed through the southland, especially in the beach cities of Orange County. Taking the anger, the negativity and the anti-professionalism of the Sex Pistols as a point of departure, hundreds of bands sprang up in garages in those endless, homogenized cinder-block tracts. Between 1979 and 1982 (when X, after placing second in the *Village Voice* Jop and Pazz poll with their second album, *Wild Gift*, left Slash records for a national label), the music was ignored by major record companies, rejected by mainstream critics, and repressed by local police (though Penelope Spheeris's documentary about it, *The Decline of Western Civilization*, did receive some attention). As a result of this ghettoization and shielded by its notoriety for violence, a local social and artistic underground developed, having the time and space to form itself relatively coherently before being co-opted. Called thrash or hardcore (the latter's reference to pornography being an indication of its transgressiveness), the music was the most advanced in the country, the only white musical production that was both populist and avant-garde.

The songs were short, very fast, essentially dance music for a very physical and aggressive dance style, primarily male though with women joining in; its characteristic innovation was for members of the audience to climb up on the stage and dive head first or upside down into the crowd below. Defined against the immediately prior disco and urban cowboy industrial fashions, clothes were deliberately ugly (motorcycle boots, torn T-shirts, with a mix of chains and bandanas), though in the artier fringes recycling of any pre-hippie clothing was legitimate. The lyrics were the vehicle of anger; where they were not undecipherable, they were typically anti-authoritarian, anti-humanist or nihilistic rants, detailing the grievances, the psychic hopelessness and rage of that group which was excluded from all the post-sixties social reform rhetoric: white, heterosexual, lower-middle-class males. All liberal shibboleths were rejected in lyrics that were indiscriminately anti-fascist, anti-communist, anti-boredom, anti-Reagan, anti-police, anti-everything.

The excess that is punk's stock-in-trade tends to polarize response to it into extremes of rejection or endorsement. Treating it as an aesthetic phenomenon, the former can point to its inversion of all standards of taste or meaning, or unravel its aporias in the manner of Enzensberger on the Beats, while the latter identifies punk's particular vocabularies as the only currently viable option. In social terms these polarizations produce punk as the final modernist capitulation to decadence, irrationality, and despair or as a completely recalcitrant stance against the bland conformity of mass society and the naturalization of consumption within it. Both positions – and it seems to me that each is in some sense right and that it is precisely this coincidence of 'everything ... with its contrary', of resistance and dissent with exploitation and collusion, that makes punk the exemplary postmodern cultural phenomenon – do however imply a degree of autonomy for cultural practice which a materialist approach may supplement and contain by attending to punk's historical determination and to the way in which it acts out the contradictions of both the society at large and its own role in it.[4] Thus it is possible to extend Dick Hebdige's reading of English punk's production of a coherent grammar of contradiction in the deliberately ungrammatical fragmentation and recombination of social codes[5] so as to see this disorderly order as itself in process, not just chronologically (in the continuing displacements that make fashion) but also logically: the contradictions are themselves perpetually in a contradictory relationship to the means of their production.

On the one hand, punk's self-definition on a series of mutually ratifying, homologous levels – the minimalism of the music against the overproduced self-indulgence of mid-seventies rock; the ideology against the hypocrisy of political discourse and the evaporation of dissidence into academic and other bourgeois forms; the rituals against the appropriation of social relations by the media industry – made its attempt to produce itself outside the entertainment business internally logical and indeed allowed its utopian aspiration, one form of which was the innovation of alternative modes of cultural production and of social relations attendant upon them. Thus, the increased audience participation in concerts with open passage through the stage and the flourishing of recording and record distribution outside corporate channels, as well as the constant formation and dissolution of bands and the do-it-yourself philosophy that allowed the typical producer/consumer proportions to be inverted – all were anithetical to capitalist social relations as they are typically reproduced around culture. It is not inappropriate therefore, following Benjamin's distinction, to stress punk's progressive position in the overall relations of production even if its attitude to them was often unclear, inconsistent or even occasionally reactionary.[6] Whether or not such political confusion is generalizable, to force a decision between punk as proto-fascist or punk as anarcho-syndicalist seems to me to be beside the point, since whatever political potential it might have had was very quickly absorbed and defused by the media industry; punk's moment of opposition could not be held consistently in place.

So, as the antagonism to the industry that largely defined the initial period of incubation eroded, punk became the site of a continuous process of engagement and disengagement, of hostility and desire. And as punk was drawn into the operations of commercial entertainment, it was drawn into enacting the primary contradiction of capitalism – the private ownership of socialized production – on two levels or in two stages. First, when a stable band was isolated and developed a career for itself, even within the subculture, then it began the process of merchandizing back to the group what it originally enacted for it. Playing a central role in subcultural identification, embodying and articulating the essential gestures and images as well as providing the aural energy that is punk's central ritual pleasure, the bands' original success was only the mark of the accuracy with which they spoke the popular voice: as they became 'professional', as authorship was isolated and as the art became a commodity, the original social function was lost. Second, this particularization of the artist and the simultaneous specification of the rest of the subculture as audience was re-enacted on a larger scale when the music entered society at large via its appropriation by the media industry, when the style that began as the articulation of popular energies became reified and available for commercial reproduction. (A particularly vivid analogue to this was the rapidity with which punk styles were appropriated, not only by the music industry, but also by the fashion industry and by various industrial movies such as *Road Warrior, Blade Runner* and *Liquid Sky*). The contradiction between cultural and commodity production instanced here is of course endemic in capitalism and is the basis by which the media industry functions within it; but the tensions and contradictions are particularly great in punk. As distinct for example from black popular music, which does not take an oppositional stance against the media and where the success of an individual artist is celebrated as a proxy success for the community at large, co-optation and absorption were particularly ironic for punk because its primary stance and central stylistic manoeuvre was, precisely, negation. Continuing that tradition of modernisms – dada, anti-art, *art brut* – as well as of those more decorous acts of renunciation catalogued by Susan Sontag as 'the aesthetics of silence', punk came onstage to play the role of Kali – the ecstatic destroyer – but, nonplussed, found its gesture short-circuited in a culture of Devourers.

The intrinsic sensual pleasure of its own vehemence and energy apart, punk was therefore inherently dependent on some other form, initially on the context in which it occurred and subsequently, once that antipathy had been established, on its own previous self, which it was continually forced to cannibalize and reject in order to maintain transgression. Having by definition no positive terms, and in the absence of any social movement that could supply them, punk was thus condemned not only to manifest itself purely as style, but condemned to manifest itself as a style that would always be in the process of pushing itself over into self-parody, to the point at which it would find itself able only to mimic its former gestures. Like Bukowski it would eventually wear its own image, an image that was in fact very much like Bukowski's:

> My house smells just like the zoo
> It's chock full of shit and puke
> Cockroaches on the walls

Crabs are crawlin on my balls
Oh – I'm so clean cut
I just want to fuck some slut

Chorus: I love livin' in the city
I love livin' in the city

('I Love Living In The City,' lyrics by Lee Ving,
copyright Toxic Tunes, quoted by permission)

On the other hand, as it assumed Bukowski's pose, supplanting
Hollywood as the dominant cultural point of reference in the city, punk
not only provided the space for a new and newly vigorous literary
production but also caught other writing in its drift. Direct cross-overs
and cross-fertilizations may be instanced by any number of local
versions of Allen Ginsberg recording with the Clash; the most remarkable is a double album compilation of verbal art, *The Voices of the
Angels*, eighty tracks featuring as many artists, a spectrum of poets
(including Bukowski and Coleman as well as others discussed below),
musicians and 'ordinary' people. The album is remarkable not for the
complexity of the verbal or aural effects (though there are plenty of
both) so much as for the continuity it makes plain between spontaneous,
popular language production (including a lot of play on the authentic
speech patterns of different parts of the city), poetry and music. The
parallel strip in the open field of cultural production that is writing may
be mapped.

At one end is the music itself, for present purposes considered as a
poetry (lyrics) but also as the point where subcultural energy is articulated and mediated into society at large. At the other end is modernist
poetry which, in either its academic version or in its post-Pound and
Olson version, continues the task of preserving the tradition of imaginative autonomy against the depredations of the media industry, but typically unable to make contact with popular energies, especially when they
appear as immediate social necessities. Between these is a whole spectrum of writing in the course of which the qualities we associate with
poetry (self-contained, highly formalized construction; self-conscious
appropriation of authorship; attention to intricate personal perception,
etc.) may be observed in the process of being distinguished from a mass
of 'non-literary' practices. The field is intersected by other social practices such as commercial writing or graphic arts, any of which could be
used in place of poetry as a means of focusing the totality of cultural
production (and indeed a parallel analysis could be made of music
production as a whole, charting the degrees of diffusion of punk into

MOR and supermarket music). It can be subdivided in any number of ways, but the following adequately clarifies the transitions engaged in the movement from spontaneous social production into the self-consciousness of art:

a)   Fanzines more or less unalloyed with self-consciously artistic writing, e.g., *Beyond The Pale; Destroy; Flipside Fanzine; Night Voices; Outcry;* and *We Got Power.*

b)   Periodicals clearly originating from punk subculture and retaining strong reference to the music, but whose emphasis is on independent art, either visual or verbal, e.g., *Contagion; Death to the Fascist Insect That Feeds Upon the People; Kusa-Zoshi; Lowest Common Denominator; No Mag; The Rattler;* and *Umezowea.*

c)   Poetry magazines whose context is clearly that of orthodox means of production of poetry, but showing clear punk influence, e.g., *Barney; Snap; Little Caesar.*

d)   Poetry magazines outside the orbit of punk aesthetics and alternative means of production, e.g., *Invisible City* and *Sulfur.*

As one moves down the list, the publications tend to manifest increased production values with low quality xerography giving way to better printing and more substantial quasi-book format, though this is not absolutely generalizable. Those fanzines with a relatively large circulation are able to support offset printing; *Flipside* goes as far as a glossy, two-color cover, but otherwise retains the newsprint and the bad typing that the overall aesthetic demands. *Invisible City,* on the other hand, which through the seventies did a yeoman job of maintaining a dialogue with international modernism and, especially in its early years, with a variety of Third World radical writing (and, predictably, manifested its relationship to music via an interest in avant-garde jazz), signals its discomfort with the state apparatus inside which it exists (government grants) by publishing in a tabloid format. The classification made here of periodicals can be supplemented with books, though their greater cost and commitment to permanence – their greater investment in the object as distinct from social processes – means that they occur at the end of the spectrum opposite to punk aesthetics. In general the correlation between ideological orientation and mode of literary production[7] is direct: publications that are independently produced and distributed and that negate the conventions of commercial publishing almost invariably reproduce punk ethics. Conversely, even people with strong connections to the subculture seem to abandon those ethics when they engage more orthodox forms of publication: Exene Cervenka is lyricist and vocalist for X, while Richard Meltzer, who DJ'd one of the best punk shows on non-commercial radio, writes a useful pseudo-gonzo column in a local free paper where he is wont to extol the virtues of pornographic films and death in boxing matches. But in their slim volumes of verse they exploit rather than produce alternative stances. Cervenka's assembly of reflections occasioned by one night stands with X in undeserving small towns is pretentious and posed, full of bogus religiosity and self-indulgence, and Meltzer, apeing punk's salacious nihilism, finally reveals himself as liberal and a philistine. In 'Belsen is no longer a gas' he exhorts punks to 'go for' revolutionary communism ('go for the hammer / go for the sickle / you'll be glad you did'), thereby reproducing exactly the media-speak that punk stands against, and then supports this somewhat oversimplified political vision on the grounds that 'Hitler was just a fairy who dug blue-eyed South Bay / surfer boys', or that Adam Ant wears an American flag on his belt. The present concern with the second and third categories as the place where the separate energies and limitations of the two extremes intersect, and where the positive rather than the negative influence of music becomes visible, may be approached via the establishment forms to see what the preconditions and costs of such an exchange may be.

A model of the spontaneous modernist attitude to punk and a measure of its challenge is supplied in the latest issue of *Sulfur*. Founded and edited by Clayton Eshleman at California Institute of Technology, *Sulfur* is committed to the modernist tradition, traced back through *Catterpillar* to its sources; among the contributions to the first five issues were previously unpublished work by Pound, Dahlberg, Olson, Hart Crane, and W.C. Williams. Exactly at the center of No. 5 is the forthrightly titled 'Punk Rock' by Carl Rakosi, one of the original objectivists. Assuming the persona of a punk Hamlet addressing Polonius, he proclaims his rejection of political interest ('Poland can go to hell!') and explains how, while he was 'amort', the voice of his spirit instructed him to absent himself 'from the real brimstones awhile' and 'Neither serious / nor lyrical be.' Subsequently:

> My cockatoo's gone mad.
> He's trying out a new
> art form: conniption
> to the power of X
> and genitals as actors,
> claiming Rimbaud's space
> and all its perquisites.
> It takes a demon now
> to hold Persephone.

Beyond the accuracy of its summarizations and the pertinence of its images (I am assuming the reference is to the band X), what is interesting about the extract and indeed the poem as a whole is that, despite the vehemence of its hostility to punk, on a structural level it is sufficiently similar to it to make clear the continuity of the modernist problematic from one to the other. The disparity between the poem's subject and its style – between punk's violent negativity and Rakosi's elegant line, his echoes of Pound, his classical references as well as his displacement of the confrontation into such an overworked persona in a linguistic routing so alien and inflated – is so great that the poem is finally swallowed by its own irony. One of the narrator's remarks – 'we have come too late / to be serious' – is of course entirely true of punk, but it is also true of Rakosi's poem, which indiscriminately mobilizes modernist gestures to produce a mix as macaronic and unstable as the most eclectic post-punk exercise in musical deconstruction. Like punk, it too is constructed upon an absence, upon a nostalgia for fullness; what punk is – neither serious nor lyrical – is clear, but what a positive alternative could be is not sayable, not even exemplified in the process of the poem itself, which can do no more than continue to ironize its own ironic situation. The historical blindness of Rakosi's protest becomes clear when, a few pages further on in the same issue, Jerome Rothenberg's 'Academy of Dada' gives a preview of what punk may look like with sixty years of academic patina on it. The movement that George Grosz described as 'neither mystical, communistic nor anarchistic ... ours was completely nihilistic. We spat on everything, including ourselves. Our symbol was nothingless, a vacuum, a void,' now appears to Rothenberg as an endeavor 'to free the forces of poesis from / the gods of power' – not bad summaries of punk, either of them.

Rakosi does not live in Los Angeles; the community *Sulfur* and *Invisible City* document is a community of consciousness in which social linkages follow from aesthetic careers rather than producing them. Indeed, the international modernism that is the project of both these journals is defined in part by a fear of a strong sense of place as a parochialism. Their commitment is to something that is destroyed by the media industry and especially in Los Angeles – history. Of those Los Angeles poets who share this commitment, two are exemplary: Dick Barnes who, writing in the penumbral dissolution of the city into the surrounding towns and deserts, is able to glimpse the traces of a past that is constantly being erased by the insistent metropolitan present, and Clayton Eshleman himself.

Lacking the immediate social and historical continuity that makes possible Barnes's classical combination of carefully honed yet still easily colloquial verse, Eshleman confronts the romantic need to connect the interior consciousness of the individual with its collective form. His initial commitment is then to the image-making faculty as an order of experience whose primary coherence is intrinsic and transhistorical, a position which makes present to him an ecumenical range of cultural references (from Lascaux to Hiroshima, from Bud Powell to Buchenwald) and also produces the process by which his poems typically generate themselves by an imaginative free flow over an initial verbal situation, often negotiating their development across puns and other purely linguistic events. But, and this seems to me to mark the importance of his work, Eshleman's archetypes are not isolated outside history; they are constructed in confrontation with it. *Hades in Manganese* derives primarily from the petroglyphs in the Dordogne caves, read as a crisis in the paleolithic imagination that produced the conceptual distinction of man from the other animals. But this event, the first fall, is not simply described in the poems, so much as it is engaged as a present situation, an ongoing geopolitical crisis that always faces one, either in a visit to Dachau or in the structure of the TV news. Thus in 'Equal Time', after noting how the juxtaposition of a champion cherry-pit spitter trivializes the one minute allotted to a story about Vietnam refugees, Eshleman questions whether or not their plight can satisfactorily be registered in language at all. He does come up with an answer that seems to imply the need for a sensual and perhaps animal knowledge; it is not one I find satisfactory, but he does recognize a moral imperative, one form of which is the need for 'a structure that includes an altered sense of language', an 'evolving net that writing poetry throws out' (p. 67) that will be able to hold both the refugees and the champion in some relation other than the meaningless juxtaposition of the media broadcast.

Whatever traumas such a perspective may encounter, the optimism about the race that it is able to sustain is typically located in a proper use of the language as the repository of humanist qualities, constructed against the corrupting uses of it as instanced by the TV news. The summary form of this distinction is art versus media industry, a distinction that has been regularly established through the history of modernism, most thoroughly by the Frankfurt School's theorization of the negativity of the former as a bulwark against the latter. As we have seen, such a negativity is the central gesture of punk, though punk clearly lacks the extreme self-consciousness, the critical distance from the mass media, that for Adorno constituted the mode of negation; there is no reason to suppose that Adorno would have been any more perceptive about punk than he was about jazz, though the idea of him wandering through *The Decline of Western Civilization* does have a certain melancholy rightness – talk about scrutinizing life in its estranged form! But if punk's resistance has been as easily reproduced and co-opted as that of any other modernism, still the rapidity with which its negativity was drained at least obliges us to notice again that the possibility of that radical, extra-systemic otherness upon which Adorno depended has now disappeared; that the young poet, and indeed the young artist, no longer have access to an image of liberation outside the media, can no longer find the means to unlock the past and bring it to bear upon the present in the way that Barnes and Eshleman can.

In the past three or four years a new thrust has appeared in local poetry in which the pose of moral earnestness, erected in the seventies as a means of valorizing individual sensibility against a shallow cultural environment saturated with media triviality, has been replaced by a cooler and entirely more self-aware classical stance assumed inside the discourse of the media industry. And where the older form tended to topple under the weight of its own ravaged and floundering confessionality, in this new poetry an internally constructed irony keeps in check the excesses of first person pretence. These poets – Dennis Cooper, Jack Skelley and David Trinidad are exemplary – have a shared sensibility, often appearing as a camp taste for fifties design and the detritus of pop culture and they tend to publish in the same magazines (*Barney, Snap, Little Caesar*), frequently dedicating poems and books to each other and, even if the plentitude and collective productivity of an actual subcultural formation is present only at the edges where it intersects with homosexual social rituals, still a strong communal feeling is insisted on. The outstanding characteristic of this poetry is its inability either to identify with a relatively autonomous subcultural energy or to maintain access to a frame of values outside the media industry upon which an oppositional stance could be constructed. Whereas for Michael Ford classic Hollywood movies were available as *lingua franca* by which natural experience could be communicated, for the new generation the media is a total environment, seamlessly hegemonic and allowing no autonomous place, no extramundial pivot upon which the lever of negation could be balanced. This, the local form of appearance of the totalizing hegemony of the *société de consommation*, precludes – or, in the absence of any social movement to assert the contrary, appears to preclude – any dissent other than that constructed from the inside by an ironic appropriation and transformation of its vocabularies. The situation now experienced is summarized in a poem, 'Revolving Show', by Eileen Myles in *Snap*; the narrator begins by noticing the 'sheer stupidity of teevee' (the triteness of the all but unsayable cliché not fully mitigated by the deliberate clumsiness of 'teevee') only to conclude with the realization that 'I hardly see a thing / that doesn't look like television, / cool and convincing' (no. 1, p. 41).

Looking like television is a condition rejected by both punks and modernist poets in the different ways their respective counter-cultural stances allow. When such an extra-systemic point of reference no longer exists, then TV's assimilation of the status quo has itself to be reappropriated, refurbished as the moment of subversion. At this point, 'cool and convincing', renegotiated now purely as style rather than as a presence, makes the place for itself as the occasion for a deadpan irony which, like a cancer, may work from within, feeding off the very energies which would otherwise contain it. Such an irony, from which any overtly critical pose is precluded, must absolutely refuse to engage in moral evaluation; indeed, its only possible moral point of reference will be that of linguistic intelligence, perceptible in its manipulations of a range of more or less artificial discourses: the sensibility it voices is a sybaritic asceticism, meditating on the mantras of the beast. Jack Skelley, for example, with a linguistic and cultural range of four or five octaves, and an ability to shift effortlessly from a spirited intellection like an airborne Ed Dorn down to colloquial dumbness, is best when he melds bursts of highly stylized, even romantic, abstractions into a thick plastic pop-cultural goop. In this fragment of an address to Marie Osmond he turns on a barren cultural screen, transforming it into a vision which, however regressive ecologically, redeems it with the sheer pleasure of thought; noting that Marie's TV series has flopped and that her nine lovers hinted at in *Star* turn out to be members of her family, he invites her:

> ...let *me* be your conquering
> consort and you'll be a far richer heiress, when
> the shadows of Utah's long winter are fled,
> and you stand alone on the Rockies, surveying
> an ancient city of soft buildings, which transubstantiate
> and interpenetrate in moon-aluminum evening, where warm
> headlighted insects dance in circles, and golden
> movie star men stand upright among beasts,
> holding tokens of serpents, sunglasses, electric guitars.

Without any recourse other than its own wit, Skelley's poetry and its luminous, energized mental landscapes provide a place for the art to survive, a holding zone where the imagination can be kept alive until some genuine social movement provides the funds for a proper clean-up.

Just as Skelley's strength derives from the closeness of his approach to the flotsam of mass culture, so Dennis Cooper's edge comes from the facility with which he stalks sexual violence. Populated by high school hustlers and the adults on whom they prey, his world where sex, drugs and rock'n'roll mutually ratify each other, is endorsed by a narrative mode that would find it neither cool nor convincing to construct a

sustained distance from it. All his poems may well be dramatic mono-
logues, but the exact mix of memory and desire that stands between
Cooper and either the narrator or the heroes is never clear, even when
such a figure is describing how to strangle a boy while raping him.

> Even when they sleep or space-out
> on drugs, rock music remains in their lives. A black
> flag of it rules the unconscious. It draws their
> ideas crudely around them. It is their power. They
> are animals.

Though the kids in Cooper's poems tend to prefer the art bands from
New York and England (perhaps the Talking Heads' 'Remain in Light'
is echoed in the above) to the local music, whose rhetoric has been
aggressively anti-homosexual, still Black Flag's retention of early Sex
Pistols' power as the base upon which more sophisticated transformations are worked is beyond question. Recognition of the music's crude-
ness is to be taken as a specific aesthetic description of its expressionist
energy and not the mark of a reservation. And though Cooper's own
power resides in the closeness he maintains to the subjects of his writing
– its voice is not elaborated through the syntax, the diction, or the functions of the language of the middle-class hegemony or the modernist
poet – even the self-consciousness with which the fragments of teentalk
are assembled in the high-school poems is not sufficient to displace them
from the restricted discourse of the group.[8] Though it is entirely
surrounded by rock music, that group is still distinguished from the punk
subculture by virtue of its pure consumerism and of its specifically
homosexual priorities and discriminations. For pure restricted language
we have to turn to the fanzines.

An integral part of the subcultural ideological self-reproduction and
its most substantial writing, fanzines are an international phenomenon.
Some idea of their extensiveness may be gained from *Flipside's* regular
listings of new ones; the current issue gives names and addresses for
over 150. With their spontaneous, decentralized and anarchic mode of
production and their constant state of flux, they closely parallel the
music production and also echo its various degrees of distance from
hegemonic forms, ranging from single issues of only a few pages (the
first issues of *Night Voices* had eleven) loosely stapled together (having
a clear relation to the xeroxed concert fliers – another populist art form,
with whose function they merge) to more regular and substantial
productions such as *Flipside* which currently has a press run of 5,500
(*the minnesota review*, by way of comparison, has a circulation of
1,000). Given this range, generalizations are hazardous; nevertheless, all

fanzines provide extensive music coverage, especially of local music, though also of visiting bands, usually in the form of interviews and descriptions of concerts. This may be supplemented by record reviews, again usually emphasizing local production, along with news about punk goings-on in other cities and other countries – especially information about police riots and the misrepresentations of punk in the hegemonic press. These assessments do not usually approach punk culture critically, except in complaints about transgressions of it. Record and concert reviews are mostly positive, generally avoiding the kind of comparison that encourages competitive ranking, though reader polls (of the best band or record of a given year, for example) are common. The interviews tend to be personal rather than analytic and are trivial or non-sensical, refusing to engage the solemnity or respectful stance that would allow social distance between interviewee and interviewer/reader and so promote star consumption. Photographs, of audiences as much as bands, are plentiful along with cartoons, song lyrics, advertisements from independent record companies and letters from readers. *Beyond the Pale* even has a reading list, recommending Foucault, Barthes and Kafka, though such overt intellectualism is unusual.

While fanzines obviously document and disseminate punk, both within the subculture and also through its edges to interested elements outside, they do not serve a publicity function in the manner of the popular magazine press's parasitic relationship to the media industry. Rather, re-enacting early punk's independent methods of production and recapitulating punk styles, their function as representation is subsumed inside the process of the production of punk ideology. Apart from the music, they are the main forum, not simply for communication about punk, but for its construction; they are the place where the nature of punk – the particular social vocabularies and ideological formulations that constitute it – may be socially constructed, argued and clarified, the means by which punk writes itself. Though each fanzine as an enterprise exists in an economy which obliges it to produce itself as a commodity and though there are publications that exploit this condition, by and large the great value of the fanzines is that they do not attempt to appropriate social production. Their authorship is distributed throughout the subculture at large; they derive from it, rather than being produced by professionals for mass consumption. This popular writing is of course most clearly evident in the letters pages (the 'Voice of the Reader' in *Flipside*, comprising up to an eighth of the magazine) but most of the other material is also produced by the culture itself – the interviews, the reports from other cities. This popular plurivocality contrasts not only with standard consumer magazines, but also with that other form of reader production, the orthodox poetry magazine. Whereas securing access to a poetry magazine is contingent upon one's displaying oneself as original, distinct from other voices, access to fanzines is almost completely open and group values are typically emphasized. Concerned to form and protect the group, the letters refer to a limited number of issues, especially complaints about police violence, violence at concerts, careless club owners and bands selling out, complaints that make sense only by virtue of an implied social idea:

Dear Flipside:
Attention all assholes! The more I read the letters section the more pissed off I get. All this talk against violence, police brutality and bouncers. If you don't want violence then DAMMIT DO SOMETHING!!! Keep out of fights, don't waste longhairs, you didn't have short hair all your life. I'll bet that you people even listened to Led Zeppelin before you got your hair cut. To go farther than that I'll bet that some of you were even into disco. If you're interested in being or looking punk – it's not punk to beat people up. There is a thought to think about when you think 'what can I do to be punk'. Anarchy sucks!!

Sincerely, The Vermin

PS: Don't listen to your jack off friends, the Valley doesn't suck, more punks come from the Valley than Hollywood.

PPS: Ivan, alias Bob O. from the Valley don't you think it's about time you give up on Ziggy, you've been after her too long!

The linguistic and social transgressiveness of this relatively unself-conscious speech can be intensified to the point where the style itself becomes a content and, in commercial instances, a commodity. The following fragment from *No Mag*, the most commercial of the fanzines and one which clearly is attempting to transcend the subcultural for the mass cultural market – it accurately advertises itself as 'Sex Music Death Garbage' – displays such a problematical usage (see over). The standard dada technique, fragmenting images and recombining them agrammatically but in such a way that the thematic clash between the sanitized house-wife and the motor-cycle harlots is echoed in the graphic design, makes use of punk's negation. Similarly, the poem simply juxtaposes a list of more or less salacious everyday phrases, asserting authorship over them only by standardizing them in typographical equivalence and defamiliar-izing them by suppressing lexigraphic divisions. But where dada collage was composed of images from life, *No Mag's* is composed of images from the media, entirely drained of reference. With the exception of the foetus, they are already so highly stylized that their juxtaposition can signify only the absence of meaning; the composition as a whole remains a pose, a scatter-logical gesture of reflexive abruptment and closure. Other magazines, such as Contagion and *Umezowea* and *Kusa-Zoshi*

organize collages in a more coherently satirical fashion, variously formu-
lating textures of the horrors of modern life, coherent political explanation and often using original poetry. Exemplary, however, is *Lowest
Common Denominator* which also has the greatest proportion of
writing.

Edited and almost entirely written by two women, Carrie White and
Zizi Q, it is more or less typed, cheaply xeroxed and stapled, with low
resolution photographs, mostly of other punks. It presents itself as part
of a communal enterprise, acknowledging its 'kinship with *We Got
Power*, a cool fanzine', and introducing itself as 'purely a PUBLICation
for voicing opinion, expressing ourselves and to help open of [sic] further
awareness in fellow human beings'; it invites contributions and expresses
willingness to 'print most anything free of charge, including ads for gigs
& band promo'. Almost all the writing, both verse and prose, is about
the immediate music scene, recording the ups and downs, the practical
and ideological double-binds of being a punk. Zizi Q excels in a mode
that is only just this side of documentary; even stories that present them-

selves as fiction, such as an extended 'Punk Soap', have a reportorial edge that cuts across the surrealist distortion, often in such a way as to enable a closely rendered naturalism sharply to undercut an imagined utopian world outside LA, even outside punk. One of the most amusing and the most plangent, 'After That Night', describes how 'the Carrot Woman', after a self-destructive night of slam dancing and suicide dives from the stage, decides to abandon punk.

> Not a tear was shed but guilt overcame her as she realized she was abandoning her followers, her leaders, and her peers in between. She had to do it. She knew that if she were to stay much longer, her stale and stagnant scene would drag her down to a slow, violent death. This Carrot wanted to live and Jah was calling.

Responding to Jah's call she becomes a Rastafarian Carrot Person.

Carrie White's stories substitute for Zizi Q's humor a reductionist narrative mode, allowing a tightly circumscribed event to begin to unfold but cutting it short before it can generate any pattern of emotional involvement or align moral sympathies. As a result, they end in suspension, without closure. She often uses a persona, Michelle; but the lack of precise distance between the narrator and Michelle prevents the resolution of the irony. 'Michelle Spit on Two Girls', for instance, describes how Michelle is disgusted by the sight of two fourteen-year-old girls dressed like prostitutes in spandex and 'trendy dark glasses'. She turns her bike around to pass by them again:

> She let the liquid well up in her mouth and as she glided past them, Michelle spit on the two girls.
> 'Punk bitch,' they said, and Michelle cracked up hoping that they would run into some kind of bad trouble with their thumbs stuck out, asking for it.

Especially interesting is an issue constructed entirely around a police riot during a concert at a theater called Bard's Apollo. The issue, seven pages double-sided xerography, includes a large photograph of the theater, a page from a William Saroyan novel where Dostoevsky and the dependence of great writing on a painful life are discussed; photographs of various kinds of street language, poster fragments, extended graffiti and spray painted band names; accounts of the incident from the LA *Times* and from non-establishment papers; fragments of a poster stained with blood; and stories and poems by White and Q. Zizi Q's story explains how 'what promised to be an excellent gig, wound up by falling at the feet of authority'; she describes how the 'human beings' were forced out of the theater and onto the streets and eventually dispersed into the Hollywood Hills, where they spent the night trying to evade authority. Carrie White has several pieces including a monologue composed before she went to the concert:

```
I am going to go to the place where some people are choosing
to go to the place that particular place because it is
there that that physical thing is and it is not always
comfortable for other people to be seeing other people
getting that kind of charge        if they are feeling pain
in that charge and it is not that kind of fun it is a
serious fun stupid definitely not to be noticed by those
who don't care to look.
```

```
It is not always fun to feel the charge, even if you are
wanting it bad. Some things have very little to do with
fun. Even if they say it is fucking fun and        no more
and it's only fucking agression and that's all it is or
it's only fucking phsical because you know deep down
inside that there is fun there and very little else.
```

The precarious balance in this piece between art and non-art writing reproduces the ambiguity of the whole issue; the discrepancies between the various journalistic reports of the concert reveal the fictionality of each and so undermine the possibility of a distinction between a factual (textually transparent) writing and a fictional (textually opaque) version of the same event. But even as in the entire issue the different levels of writing dissolve into textual production, in doing so they do not migrate to the autotelic solipsism of mainstream postmodernism. Just as the various Steinian routines in the above extract, circling the moment of violence, build up tensions around it and mobilize a literary energy in corroboration of the explosive social ritual, so in the issue as a whole the various postmodern motifs (polyvocality, distribution of authorship, maintenance of the individual separate elements in the total construct, refusal of closure) transcend the aesthetic function and become a means of negotiating a moment of social crisis, a means of retaining and articulating energies in which the aesthetic and the social reinforce each other, make each other possible.

Despite the absence of any explicit or systematic inscription of a materialist understanding of the situation of the subculture in the society at large or of the nature of its aesthetic production, in this instance the art work ratifies that image of the collectivity it proceeds from, by which, as Fredric Jameson has argued, it becomes 'a *figure* for the ultimate concrete collective life of an achieved utopian or classless society'.[9] The coherence of *LCD*, which is as much a function of the social possibilities of its moment as it is a social achievement, is present then, not only in its articulation of the activities of the social group, but also in the reciprocation of that group's values in the modes of its production and social insertion, both of which are entirely contingent upon its subcultural location. And it is here that its value becomes clear. The immediate subcultural context in which it is constructed allows it the marginality which is the condition of its absolute imperviousness to industrial blandishments. Like Blake's 'Laocoön' plate, Ken Jacobs's film *Blonde Cobra*, the music of Whitehouse and a handful of other exemplary refusals, its determining aspiration is to negate the commodity function. So its significance is inseparable from the fact that it is virtually unobtainable, that it hardly even exists.

In its diverse musical, poetic and journalistic forms, punk culture in Southern California realized what may well be the only aesthetic negation possible in the contemporary West. In an epoch when the most thoroughly transitory experience or marginal practice can not only be commodified but mass reproduced virtually overnight, no mode of aesthetic production can ever finally escape from the circuits of the culture industries or be proof against the assimilative powers of hegemonic media. With film projects like *Ordinary Madness* and *Barfly*, Charles Bukowski has lately been welcomed by Hollywood, just as the moment of British punk has been rendered safe for nostalgia in *Sid and Nancy* and *Something Wild.* Nor did the exemplary moments considered here sustain themselves for very long. Their very transience, however, offers some measure of protection. One of the symptoms of the pathology of late capitalist culture is that, among the few remaining options for non-industrialized aesthetic expression, it enforces this ultimate intransigent negation of its very mode of production. To mourn the passing of punk culture would thus deny its signal importance: its significance could only ever be conjectural.

Notes

This essay was originally published in *the minnesota review*, 23 (fall 1984).
    1. Rick Berg, Alan Golding and Martha Lifson, as well as the editors of *the minnesota review*, all gave valuable advice on an earlier draft of this paper. Though I make my arguments by discussing specific writers, my overall interest is not in assessing individual achievements so much as in describing a cultural field; I have tried therefore to be representative, if not comprehensive, in selecting materials, but inevitably there are omissions. With the single exception noted below, I have limited myself to publications that are current and available at the time of this writing (spring 1983). Unless otherwise indicated, all references are to the following:

Books

Barnes, Dick. *A Lake on the Earth* (Los Angeles: Momentum Press, 1982).
Bukowski, Charles. *Dangling in the Tournefortia* (Santa Barbara: Black Sparrow, 1981).
Coleman, Wanda. *Mad Dog Black Lady* (Santa Barbara: Black Sparrow, 1979).
Cooper, Dennis. *The Tenderness of Wolves* (Trumansburg: The Crossing Press, 1982).
Eshleman, Clayton. *Hades in Manganese* (Santa Barbara: Black Sparrow, 1981).

Flanagan, Bob. *The Kid is the Man* (Hermosa Beach, CA: The Bombshelter Press, 1978).
Ford, Michael C. *The World is a Suburb of Los Angeles* (Los Angeles: Momentum Press. 1981).
Lunch, Lydia and Cervenka, Exene. *Adulterers Anonymous* (New York: Grove Press, 1982).
Meltzer, Richard. *17 insects can die in your heart* (Los Angeles: Ouija Madness Press, 1983).
Northrup, Harry E. *Enough the Great Running Chapel* (Los Angeles: Momentum Press, 1982).
Skelley, Jack. *Monsters* (Los Angeles: Little Caesar Press, 1982).
Trinidad, David. *Payane* (Los Angeles: Sherwood Press, 1981).

Periodicals

Barney (1140 1/2 Nowita Place, Venice, Ca. 90291).
Beyond the Pale (P.O. Box 585, Walnut, Ca. 91789).
Contagion (P.O. Box 402, Hollywood, Ca. 90028).
Death To The Fascist Insect That Feeds Upon The People (6732 Selma Avenue, Los Angeles, Ca. 90028).
Destroy (14421 Sherman Way, Box 11, Van Nuys, Ca. 91405).
Flipside Fanzine (P.O. Box 363, Whittier, Ca. 90608).
Invisible City (The Red Mill Press, 6 San Gabriel Drive, Fairfax, Ca. 94390).
Kusa-Zoshi (Autocratic Industries, Inc. [No address]).
L.A. Weekly (5325 Sunset Boulevard, Los Angeles, Ca. 90027).
Lowest Common Denominator (2265 Westwood Boulevard, Suite B-307, Los Angeles, Ca. 90064).
Night Voices (5300 Laurel Canyon Boulevard, #111, North Hollywood, Ca. 91607).
No Mag: A Quarterly Magazine (P.O. Box 57041, Los Angeles, Ca. 90057).
Outcry (1001 Fremont, P.O. Box 1194, South Pasadena, Ca. 91030).
The Rattler (5752 Virginia Avenue, #104, Hollywood, Ca. 90038).
Snap: A Quarterly of Arts and Writing (530 South Barrington, #108, Los Angeles, Ca. 90049).
Sulfur (Box 228077, California Institute of Technology, Pasadena, Ca. 91125).
Umezowea (7505 Hampton Avenue, #14 Los Angeles, Ca. 90046).
We Got Power (3010 Santa Monica Boulevard, #310, Santa Monica, Ca. 90404).

Records

Angry Samoans. *Back from Samoa* (Bad Trip Records).
Assorted Artists. *Hell Comes to Your House* (Bemisbrain Records).
Assorted Artists. *The Decline of Western Civilization* (Slash Records).
Assorted Artists. *Voices of the Angels* (Freeway Records).
Black Flag. *Damaged.* (SST Records).
Fear. *The Record* (Slash Records).
X. *Wild Gift* (Slash Records).

2. A full justification of this proposition could begin empirically, with the fact that by 1974 rock music was a $2 billion a year industry, having overtaken the movies ($1.6 billion) as the most profitable branch of the entertainment business (Steve Chapple and Renee Garofalo, *Rock'n'Roll Is Here to Pay* [Chicago: Nelson-Hall, 1977], p. xi), or with a list of instances where popular music is a dominant influence or point of reference for other media. Such a list could include, for example, industrial movies from *Blackboard Jungle* (1955), the first to use rock and roll as a soundtrack, through the appropriation of sixties counter-culture in *Easy Rider*, *Woodstock*, or *Gimme Shelter*, to more recent block-busters like *Saturday Night Fever* and *Flashdance* (David Ehrenstein has suggested that

'today it seems as if every third film that comes along falls back on rock for some sense of support' [*Rock on Film* (New York: Putnam's, 1982)]); avant-garde/art film from Kenneth Anger's *Scorpio Rising* through recent film and video which contains intro-diegetic engagement with punk bands (e.g. James Benning's *Him and Me*) or flows directly from the new music scene (e.g. the films of Vivienne Dick or Eric Mitchell), eventually to sup-posedly avant-garde work which is either virtually indistinguishable from MTV (Erica Beckman) or is actually itself music promos (John Sanborn); performance art's increasing engagement with the theatricality of rock concerts and with the music business (e.g. Yoko Ono, Laurie Anderson); the success of MTV; the revival of expressionistic referentiality in painting which is analogous to either punk's semiological self-consciousness (David Salle) or to its gestural brutalism (Julian Schnabel) and in general in constant dialogue with graffiti and, via that, with the Bronx rap/break/scratch nexus (documented in Charles Ahearn's film *Wild Style*); the approach of avant-garde music to the rock world via the minimalism of Steve Reich and Philip Glass and art-punk bands from DNA to Glen Branca; and even developments in the academy by which poststructuralists can meet Marxists on the bridge of subcultural 'writing' (e.g. Dick Hebdige's *Subculture: The Mean-ing of Style* [London: Methuen, 1979]). For the centrality of music in this entire art/fash-ion/business gestalt to be understood rather than merely specified, a formalist model of the history of its foregrounding could be put on a materialist basis by bringing to bear upon the material nature of different media and the specific senses or functions they address a theory to their different modes of social insertion. Thus what is significant about music is not just that its appeal is aural and that for some arbitrary or transcendental reason hearing has become a fashionable sense, but rather that the fact of its aural functioning made it a uniquely pliable medium in a period of expanding leisure time and the penetration of all life processes by the media industries; in essence, the fact that you could be listening to music all the time allowed it to supplant film, which you could watch for only a few hours a week. The accelerating monadization of everyday life, in which social relations are ever more completely superseded by individual relations with a video monitor, may well reverse the trend and subordinate music to the various kinds of visual production of that monitor – computer games, pornography, word-processing, video telephone, etc.

3.   For a full account of the renaissance of music in Los Angeles, see Peter Belsito and Bob Davis, *Hardcore California: A History of Punk and New Wave* (San Francisco: Last Gasp, 1983); Charles Bukowski, 'A History of L.A. Punk Rock', in *No Mag*, 1982; and Bella Jones, 'Slash: A History of a Brief Scene', in *L.A. Weekly*, Jan. 9–15, 1981. Of the records cited above those by Black Flag and Fear represent the music as it was originally developed. These and other bands are anthologized in *The Decline of Western Civilization. Hell Comes to Your House* gives an overview of the music in mid-1981 that includes developments out of hard-core (such as Gothic), while the Angry Samoans are represent-ative hard-core holdouts.

4.   For a theory of subcultures as means of symbolically resolving class contradictions, see John Clarke et al., 'Subcultures, Cultures and Class' in Stuart Hall and Tony Jefferson, eds, *Resistance Through Ritual: Youth Subcultures in Post-War Britain* (London: Hutch-inson, 1976), pp. 9–74. Although derived from American sociology of the fifties, British theories of subculture and of punks in particular are not directly applicable to American groups organized around parallel or identical artistic activities. In fact, Southern California punk culture has structurally more in common with hippies and other essentially middle-class counter-cultures than with early British punk; that is, it is 'a diffuse counter-cultural milieu' rather than 'a tight subculture' (p. 60). This reflects not only the transient, hetero-geneous social flux of the area, its relative economic mobility, but also American punk's greater dependence on media determination. While Dick Hebdige does recognize various processes of co-optation, he underestimates the spectacular engagement of even English punk and his analysis of it essentially in terms of social contradiction has to be further 'mediated' in transferring it to the US.

5.   esp. pp. 90–127.

6.   Walter Benjamin, 'The Author As Producer' in *Reflections*, trans. Edmund Jephcott (New York: Harcourt Brace and Jovanovich, 1979), p. 222.

7.   The term is Terry Eagleton's; see his *Criticism and Ideology: A Study in Marxist*

Literary Theory (London: Verso, 1978), esp. pp. 44–101.

8. Bruce Boone has used the terms 'elaborated' and 'restricted' to differentiate between the language patterns of the hegemonic class or cultural group and of a subculture respectively. See his 'Gay Language as Political Praxis: The Poetry of Frank O'Hara', in *Social Text*, vol. 1, No. 1, pp. 59–63. The terms derive from the British sociologist, Basil Bernstein.

9. *The Political Unconscious: Narrative as a Socially Symbolic Act* (Ithaca: Cornell University Press, 1981), p. 291.

Notes on Contributors

MIKE DAVIS is on the editorial committee of the *New Left Review* and is the author of the widely acclaimed, *Prisoners of the American Dream: Politics and Economy in the History of the U.S. Working Class* (Verso, 1986). He is currently writing a history of California.

WILLIAM GALPERIN teaches English at Rutgers University. His book *Unmaking Wordsworth's Anti-Climax: The Interpretation of a Career* is forthcoming from the University of Pennsylvania Press. His essays on film and photography have appeared in *MLN*, *The Bennington Review* and *The Western Humanities Review*.

DAVID JAMES is associate professor and chair of the English department at Occidental College. His study of black film in the 1960s appeared in *The Year Left* II.

FREDRIC JAMESON is Distinguished Professor of Comparative Literature at Duke University, where he directs the Graduate Program in Literature. He has published widely on Marxism, literary theory, post-structuralism and postmodernism. His books include *The Prison House of Language* and *The Political Unconscious*, and most recently *The Ideologies of Theory: Essays 1971-1986*.

E. ANN KAPLAN directs the Humanities Institute at the State University of New York at Stony Brook. She has written widely on women in film, film noir, television and the director Fritz Lang. Her *Women in Film: Both Sides of the Camera* appeared in 1983, and her most recent book is *Rocking Around the Clock: Music Television, Postmodernism and Consumer Culture*. She is currently working on a book on *Motherhood and Representation*.

WARREN MONTAG is the author of essays on Marxism and psycho-analysis, literary theory, and philosophy. He is co-translator of the *Spontaneous Philosophy and the Spontaneous Philosophy of Scientists* by Louis Althusser, forthcoming from Verso in 1989.

FRED PFEIL is a fiction writer and cultural critic. His essays have appeared in the *Nation, New Statesman,* and *College English.* His novel, *Goodman 2020,* was published by Indiana University Press in 1986. He is completing a collection of essays on narrative and postmodernism to be published by Verso.

DANA POLAN is an Associate Professor of Film and English at the University of Pittsburgh. His *The Politics of Film and the Avant-Garde* appeared in 1983, and his most recent book is *Power and Paranoia: History, Narrative and the American Cinema 1940–50.*

ROBERT STAM teaches in the Cinema Studies Department at New York University. He is the author of *Reflexivity in Film and Literature: From Don Quixote to Jean-Luc Godard,* and the co-author (with Randall Johnson) of *Brazilian Cinema.* He is presently on a Guggenheim Fellowship.

LINDA WILLIAMS is Associate Professor of English at the University of Illinois at Chicago. She is the author of *Figures of Desire: A Theory and Analysis of Surrealist Film* and the forthcoming *Hard Core: Power, Pleasure and the Frenzy of the Visible.*